THE CURSE OF THE PHARAOHS

THE CURSE OF THE PHARAOHS

Philipp Vandenberg

Translated by
THOMAS WEYR

BARNES
&NOBLE
BOOKS
NEW YORK

This edition published by Marboro Books Corp.,
a division of Barnes & Noble, Inc.,
by arrangement with HarperCollins Publishers.

1992 Barnes & Noble Books

ISBN 1-56619-007-X

Printed and bound in the United States of America

M 9 8 7 6 5 4 3 2 1

Contents

DEATH WILL SLAY WITH HIS WINGS
WHOEVER DISTURBS THE
PEACE OF THE PHARAOH

*—Inscription on tablet
found in Tutankhamen's tomb*

THE
CURSE
OF THE
PHARAOHS

1   The Curse

"You know," mused Dr. Gamal Mehrez, a powerful, thick-set man with bushy eyebrows and thick lips, "there are strange coincidences in life."

We were sitting on the edge of the swimming pool of Cairo's Omar Khayyam Hotel, near the Bridge of the 26th of July that spans the Nile, drinking Campari and talking about the much-publicized curse of the pharaohs, said to strike anyone involved in the discovery of the tomb of the pharaoh Tutankhamen, and perhaps other tombs and mummies as well.

As Director-General of the Antiquities Department of the Egyptian Museum of Cairo, Mehrez was master of an unusually ugly turn-of-the-century building housing 100,000 objects, treasures from many millennia of Egyptian history: tiny scarabs; bulging, powerful stone statues of the almighty pharaohs; and, on an upper floor, in Room 52, twenty mummies, arranged according to age and sex, first the men and then the women, all exhibited in glass caskets for the benefit of the paying public. (There are people who cannot bear the sight of the smiling mummies with their bared teeth. They dash out of the room dripping with sweat.)

"So you really aren't sure there is a curse?" I asked.

Mehrez hesitated. Clearly he was weighing his answer carefully. Then he said, in the guttural Cairo English most Egyptian archaeologists trained at Oxford or Cambridge speak, "If you add up all these mysterious deaths, you might well think so. Especially since formal curses do crop up in ancient Egyptian history. But"—and Mehrez smiled painfully —"I simply don't believe in it. Look at me. I've been involved with tombs and mummies of the pharaohs all my life. I'm living proof it was all coincidence."

Four weeks after our conversation, Gamal Mehrez was dead at fifty-two. Doctors blamed circulatory collapse.

The strangest circumstance was this: Mehrez died on the day Pharaoh Tutankhamen's golden mask was once again disturbed. Furniture movers went to the museum on Marietta Street and packed jewels, ornaments, and the mask. Insured for about $55 million, this treasure was loaded aboard two RAF bombers and flown to London, where it formed part of an exhibit commemorating the fiftieth anniversary of the discovery of Tutankhamen's tomb by two Englishmen, Howard Carter and Lord Carnarvon.

Tutankhamen is the key figure in the curse which has, to date, cost the lives of at least three dozen scientists, archaeologists, and scholars. The pharaoh reigned only nine years, from 1358 to 1349 B.C., and he is of relatively little historical interest. Though he presided over a kind of Egyptian counterreformation that toppled the monotheism his father-in-law, Ikhnaton, had introduced, Tutankhamen was only the front man for a cabal of priests. His real importance stems from the relatively late discovery of his tomb, which, unlike those of other pharaohs, had not been plundered, and from the fact that a series of mysterious deaths followed the grave's excavation. The curse of the pharaohs then began to excite scientists for the first time.

The Life of Lord Carnarvon

Archaeologists had died mysteriously before. That was accepted as fate until Lord Carnarvon, who helped open Tutankhamen's tomb, died on April 5, 1923, amid unusual circumstances.

Why would a wealthy British lord bother with mummies and buried treasure in the first place? The life and personality of George E. S. M. Herbert, fifth Earl of Carnarvon, provide some clues.

Born in 1866, Carnarvon was a typical child of his time and position. He spent his early years at Highclere, his parents' country estate. After private tutoring he entered Eton. Later, at Trinity College, Cambridge, he became known, among other things, for his above-average performance as a horseman and for keeping a live snake in his desk drawer during an entire semester.

His father died when he was twenty-three, and he took over management of the family's vast estates. He also began to lead the life of a playboy.

Carnarvon was a car nut; in fact, he helped develop the sport of auto racing, and he owned several cars in France before automobiles were legal in England. That his passion for cars would turn his interests toward Egyptian archaeology, making him a co-discoverer of Tutankhamen's tomb and thus a victim of that spectacular curse, is both ironic and in need of some explanation.

"Motoring was bound to appeal to one of his disposition," his sister, Lady Burghclere, noted.

Though Carnarvon enjoyed a reputation for recklessness he was in reality far too collected and had too much common sense to woo danger. When the present writer reproached him for taking unnecessary risks, he replied: "Do you take me for a fool? In motoring the danger lies round corners, and I never take a corner fast." This was probably true, but the "best-laid schemes o' mice and men gang aft a-gley," and it was on a perfectly straight road that he met with the accident that materially affected his whole life.

It was on a journey through Germany that disaster overtook Carnarvon. He and his devoted chauffeur, Edward Trotman, who accompanied him on all his expeditions for eight-and-twenty years, had been flying for many miles along an empty road, ruled with Roman precision through an interminable Teutonic forest, towards Schwalbach, where Lady Carnarvon was awaiting their arrival. Before them, as behind, the highway still stretched out, when, suddenly, as they crested a rise, they were confronted by an unexpected dip in the ground, so steep as to be invisible up to within 20 yards, and at the bottom, right across the road, were drawn up two bullock carts. Carnarvon did the only thing possible. Trusting to win past, he put the car at the grass margin, but a heap of stones caught the wheel, two tyres burst, the car turned a complete somersault and fell on the driver, while Trotman was flung clear some feet away. Happily for them both, the latter's thick coat broke his fall, and with splendid presence of mind he lost not a second in coming to his master's rescue. The car had fallen aslant across a ditch. Had it fallen on the road, Carnarvon must have been crushed to death, instead of being embedded head foremost in mud. With the energy of despair, Trotman contrived to drag the light car aside and to extricate Carnarvon, who was unconscious, his heart even appearing to have stopped. The bullock drivers knowing themselves in fault had bolted, but Trotman saw some workmen in an adjoining field, saw they had a can of water, and without pausing to apologize seized the can and dashed the water in Lord Carnarvon's face. The shock set the heart beating anew, and meanwhile the workmen, who had followed hot-foot in pursuit of their can, arrived on the scene. They had no common language, but the awful spectacle and the chauffeur's signs were sufficient explanation and they brought a doctor to the spot. He found a shattered individual, evidently suffering from severe concussion, his face swollen to shapelessness, his legs severely burnt, his wrist broken, temporarily blind, the palate of his mouth and his jaw injured, caked in mud from head to foot.[1]

Lord Carnarvon underwent several operations, but they could not fully restore his health. He had trouble breathing, especially in the damp English winters, and in order to escape them he traveled to Egypt during the cold months, first in 1903 and for every winter after that. (The humidity rarely rises above 40 percent in Egypt, and the climate is salubrious for convalescents.)

It was natural that a man versed in the arts and forced to spend long stretches of time in Egypt would develop an interest in archaeology, and Carnarvon began digging the third winter. His efforts met with no success whatever. Discouraged, he asked Sir Gaston Maspero, then Cairo Museum director, for advice, and Maspero introduced him to Howard Carter.

Carter was a British painter and archaeologist who had been in Egypt since 1890. He had had a checkered career, during which he had acquired great knowledge, on top of his native idealism, but little money. Employed at various times as administrator for antiquities, he had already discovered two tombs in the Valley of the Kings, west of Luxor, for his wealthy American patron, Theodore Davis, a retired lawyer and financier from Newport, Rhode Island, who had been puttering about Egypt since the 1880s.

After several years of looking for hidden treasure, Carter and Carnarvon published their modest findings up to that time with pomp and pride in a book entitled *Five Years' Explorations at Thebes*. And they kept on digging; a forgotten pharaoh's tomb had to be hidden somewhere in the valley, Carter was sure. This conviction was based on solid if fragmentary evidence. As James Henry Breasted, a noted American archaeologist, has explained:

During the season of 1907–1908, Mr. Davis's workmen had found a cache of large baked clay jars containing funerary equipment consisting mainly of bundles of linen but including many of the things used in funeral processions. He dismissed the discovery as unimportant, and it might have been forgotten altogether had not Herbert E. Winlock of the Metropolitan Museum noticed that seal impressions in the closures of the jars, and a marking on one of the pieces of linen contained the name of Tutenkhamon.[2]

Davis had also discovered a pit grave with remnants of a wooden chest—it contained gold platelets with the name Tutankhamen inscribed on them—and had decided that he had discovered Tutankhamen's resting-place. Carter was dubious. An Egyptian king would not have been buried in so modest a grave during the XVIIIth dynasty. After all, mighty piles of rock had been erected in honor of the Middle Kingdom's rulers. There was no reason to shovel Tutankhamen into a pauper's grave. But where was his tomb?

Davis had done much of his digging in the general area where Carter suspected the royal tomb to be located, having been given an excavation license by the Egyptian government in 1902. Cairo authorities didn't expect Davis to come up with much—after all, the Italian adventurer and explorer Giovanni Battista Belzoni had given up that site as a lost cause way back in 1820—and by the time Davis threw in his spade in July, 1914, he agreed.

Carter and Lord Carnarvon, however, did not, and they snapped up Davis's digging concession. Both men wanted to start right away, but World War I fighting interfered, and it was three years before the great adventure in the Valley of the Kings could begin.

Until that time, no one had kept any records of who had dug where, when, and for what. Carter drew a map and, beginning in 1917, went through the area systematically, literally foot by foot. Huge masses of debris, accumulated during all the years of earlier digging, were removed. Yet the explorers found nothing. By the spring of 1922, Lord Carnarvon was about to give up when Carter asked for one last chance. Just below the tomb of Rameses VI, he told his patron, there remained a small triangular area whose clearance —since digging would stop tourists from visiting the Rameses tomb—they had postponed for some later off-season time. But it was precisely in this area that Carter had noted the foundation remains of a row of crude stone huts, evidently built by ancient workmen, which he would first have to remove. The foundations were made of large slabs of flint—and in the past such an accumulation of flint had been a sure sign of the proximity of a tomb.

For six years the two men had looked for something they weren't even sure existed, for six years they had been tortured every day by the fear that the whole enterprise had been in vain, but for six years they had been driven to go on just the same. And then everything happened in just a few weeks:

October 28, 1922. Carter arrives in Luxor without Carnarvon. He hires a crew of diggers.

November 1, 1922. Carter begins new excavations in the

Valley of the Kings. Starting in the northeast corner of the Rameses VI tomb, he has a ditch dug southward that leads directly through the flint foundations of the huts he discovered earlier.

November 4, 1922. As he does every morning, Carter rides his mule out to the excavation site. He is surprised at the unusual silence. The foreman runs up excitedly: "Sir, we hit a step hewn into the rock below the foundation of the first hut!"

November 5, 1922. By afternoon, four steps have been uncovered. No further doubt is possible; they must lead to a tomb hewn out of the rock. But is it a pharaoh's tomb? Will it be plundered? By evening twelve more steps have been cleared. A sealed stone gate appears. The seals show a jackal and nine stylized prisoners. It is the seal of the city of the dead in the Valley of the Kings. The tomb—so it seems —has not been plundered.

November 6, 1922. Back in Luxor, Carter sends a telegram to his patron, Lord Carnarvon, in England: AT LAST HAVE MADE WONDERFUL DISCOVERY IN VALLEY. A MAGNIFICENT TOMB WITH SEALS INTACT. RE-COVERED SAME FOR YOUR ARRIVAL. CONGRATULATIONS.

November 8, 1922. Lord Carnarvon sends two telegrams, back to back: COMING SOON, IF POSSIBLE and SHOULD BE IN ALEXANDRIA ON THE 20TH.

November 23, 1922. Lord Carnarvon arrives in Luxor, accompanied by his daughter, Lady Evelyn Herbert.

November 24, 1922. The tomb entrance, which has been reburied under the original debris, with a squad of Egyptian soldiers as guards, is again cleared.

November 25, 1922. The seals are photographed and broken. A passage sloping downward comes into view. Broken alabaster jars and seal clasps are scattered through the debris that fills the passage. It looks as if the grave has been broken into after all and then resealed.

November 26, 1922. Thirty feet behind the first stone gate, the diggers come upon a second. In addition to the seals of the city of the dead are seals with Tutankhamen's insignia.

Carter described the final hours in his book *The Tomb of Tutankhamen* this way:

Slowly, desperately slowly it seemed to us as we watched, the remains of the passage debris that encumbered the lower part of the doorway were removed, until at last we had the whole door clear before us. The decisive moment had arrived. With trembling hands I made a tiny breach in the upper left hand corner. Darkness and blank space, as far as an iron testing-rod could reach, showed that whatever lay beyond was empty, and not filled like the passage we had just cleared. Candle tests were applied as a precaution against possible foul gases, and then, widening the hole a little, I inserted the candle and peered in, Lord Carnarvon, Lady Evelyn and Callender [one of his assistants] standing anxiously beside me to hear the verdict. At first I could see nothing, the hot air escaping from the chamber causing the candle flame to flicker, but presently, as my eyes grew accustomed to the light, details of the room within emerged slowly from the mist, strange animals, statues, and gold—everywhere the glint of gold. For the moment—an eternity it must have seemed to the others standing by—I was struck dumb with amazement.[3]

Carnarvon was the first to speak.

"Can you see anything?" he whispered excitedly.

"Yes," Carter replied, "wonderful things."

What the flickering light revealed no human eye had seen for thirty-five hundred years. They were the most beautiful and most precious things archaeologists had ever dug out of the earth. There was a "beautiful lotiform cup of translucent alabaster; . . . a confused pile of overturned chariots, glistening with gold and inlay; . . . two life-sized figures of a king in black, facing each other like sentinels, gold kilted, gold sandalled, armed with mace and staff, the protective sacred cobra upon their foreheads"; [4] also, three great gilded couches, strange black shrines, and a golden inlaid throne. There was not a trace of a coffin or a mummy, but of course all this was only the antechamber to a labyrinth that must be filled with inexhaustible treasure.

Without knowing what else awaited them in the tomb's other chambers, Carter and Carnarvon agreed: This was the most sensational find in history.

As a responsible archaeologist, Carter had carefully prepared everything down to the smallest detail. He closed the opening again, had Callender and a detachment of armed men guard the tomb night and day, and ordered a massive grated steel door specially built in Cairo and brought to Luxor by train. In the end, he thought none of these measures safe enough and had the entry buried under debris again.

Lord Carnarvon and Lady Evelyn went home to England on December 4 to meet other obligations and prepare for the impact of the discovery, returning to Egypt early in February.

The Ominous Find

Howard Carter had not wasted the intervening weeks; he had collected every expert he could lay his hands on. The Metropolitan Museum of Art in New York lent him Harry Burton, its top photographer, and two draftsmen, Hall and Hauser, to make extensive and detailed sketches of the anteroom, as well as Arthur C. Mace, the Met curator in charge of the museum's excavations of the Lisht pyramids. Alan Gardiner, a top hieroglyphics expert, offered to help, as did James Henry Breasted, an old friend and an expert in ancient seals. Alfred Lucas, experienced as director of the chemical department of the Egyptian government, offered his help too.

First, they broke through the wall into the tomb's antechamber so they could examine it more closely than Carter had been able to on November 26. Close examination of the seals had already shown that the grave had been broken into. However, the robbers had hacked only small openings through the rocky walls and consequently taken only small objects from the treasure trove. Moreover, the robbery must have taken place a short time after the pharaoh's burial. Otherwise there was little point in replacing the broken seals.

The discovery, of course, could not be kept secret for long. Carnarvon decided to give the London *Times* world rights to the official story, but almost every other paper in the world scrambled for details. The tomb was guarded night and day as news spread that the excavations had only begun.

Carter noted that "by the time the Antechamber was finished our nerves, to say nothing of our tempers, were in an extremely ragged state."[5]

Every object in the room was photographed where it stood, sketched, and prepared for conservation, a laboratory having been set up in an empty tomb. Letters and telegrams flooded the excavation site: advice on preservation, requests for souvenirs ("I'd be grateful for a few grains of sand"), congratulations, offers of assistance, and even suddenly rediscovered family relationships ("Surely you must be the cousin who lived in Camberwell in 1893, and whom we have never heard of since," someone wrote Carter).

Those at the site, however, especially the scholars, were less euphoric. In fact, they became increasingly nervous. The reason for their concern was an ordinary clay tablet Carter had found in the antechamber. He had it catalogued, as he did the other objects. Then, a few days later, Alan Gardiner decoded the hieroglyphics on it. The inscription read:

> *Death will slay with his wings*
> *whoever disturbs the peace of the pharaoh*

Neither Carter nor Gardiner nor any of the other scholars present feared the curse then or took it seriously. But they worried that the Egyptian laborers would, and since they were dependent on native helpers, mention of the clay tablet was wiped from the written record of the tomb's discovery. Even the tablet itself disappeared from the artifact collection—but not from the memory of those who read it. (The tablet and the curse on it are cited everywhere, but it was never photographed and is considered lost.)

Significantly, the curse was found a second time, in a somewhat changed form, on the back of a statue: *It is I who drive back the robbers of the tomb with the flames of the desert. I am the protector of Tutankhamen's grave.* This magic figure was discovered in the main chamber of the tomb. Once that had been cleaned out, the archaeologists no longer needed to worry about frightening the Egyptian helpers. They had reached their goal.

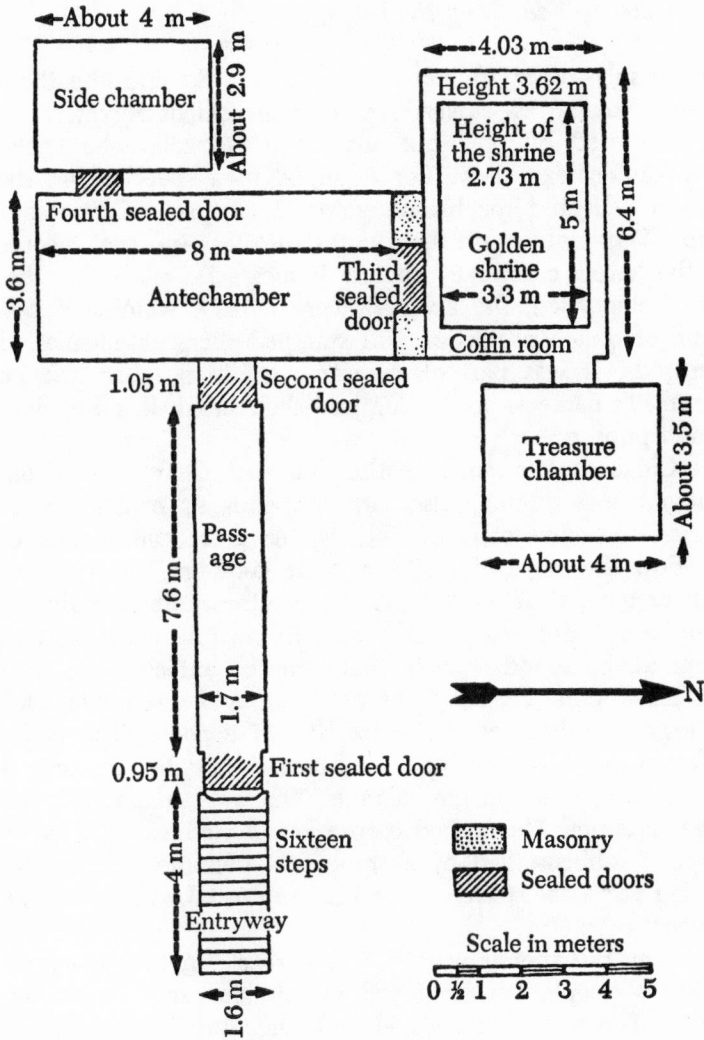

The ground plan of Tutankhamen's tomb. Steps and a passage ten meters long lead to the antechamber in which Howard Carter found the tablet with the fateful curse on it. To the right, next to the antechamber, is the room with the young pharaoh's coffin.

Curses: Older Than the Bible

Unlike such other oriental cultures as the Semitic—the Bible teems with curses—curses were rare in ancient Egypt. They were uttered by only one man, the pharaoh, who spoke with divine legitimacy. For example, in a speech from the throne delivered for his daughter Hatshepsut, Thutmose I said, "Those who curse their king shall die." And trial records of the harem conspiracy against Rameses III show that, before being tried, the accused were cursed, which stripped them of divine protection and stamped them as enemies of the gods. It was part of the same tradition to scratch an accursed's name on a clay jug and then smash it, an ancient proscription rite.

Curse tablets, such as the one that disappeared from Tutankhamen's tomb, also cite the gods as originators of curses: the curse of Osiris-Sokaris, the great god, master of Abydos; the curse of Isis, the great goddess. When an inspector general of the Egyptian antiquities administration, a man named Engelbach, discovered a tomb near the Medum pyramid, he found a curse tablet in the antechamber with the inscription, *The spirit of the dead will wring the neck of a grave robber as if it were that of a goose.* The tablet referred to the spirit of one dead person only, but the official found two corpses in the chamber. One was mummified; the other was not. The second corpse was a victim of the curse, a grave robber killed by a stone that plummeted from the ceiling just as he stretched out his hand to take the mummy's jewelry.

Why did the stone fall? The earliest Egyptians were a religious people who believed in miracles and ghosts and spirits. Those who understood and could predict the seasons of the Nile seemed like gods to their simpler brothers, not scientists. And since the pharaohs surrounded themselves with wise men, they were the first to know when the Nile would flood and enrich the earth.

But belief in gods and ghosts weakened as scientific knowledge spread and even common people learned something of the calendar, mathematics, geometry, astronomy, and artificial irrigation. Indeed, the demystification of the kings began toward the end of the Old Kingdom, when Djoser, Khufu (also known as Cheops), and Teti were still considered supermen, until the gods finally disappeared from the golden thrones.

As a result, enlightened Egyptians, though they believed in a life after death, were no ·longer convinced of the omnipotence of their dead. So priests and magicians used the technical knowledge of their day to maintain the power and fear the curses had once inspired. Thus a stone would not drop by accident from a tomb's vaulted ceiling when the mummy was touched but as part of a simple yet effective trap to keep grave robbers from the richly draped corpse.

Much more effort, of course, was expended on securing a pharaoh's last resting-place than that of a plain citizen. Unlike ordinary mortals, the pharaoh could plan lavishly for his own burial and make sure that his body would be surrounded by worldly pomp and properly embalmed for posterity.

And if the curse of the pharaohs proved most effective in the case of Tutankhamen, a king who had done the least to prepare his own last resting-place, there is a simple explanation: King Tut's burial was a matter for the priests and magicians. He was only eighteen when he died and, as we shall see, his end was a violent one.

Opening the Sealed Door

But all that was still unknown on February 17, 1923, when Howard Carter and Lord Carnarvon were ready to open the main chamber of Tutankhamen's grave.

None of the twenty-man staff gathered at 2 P.M. on that hot February day in the passageway of the tomb knew if they would find a pharaoh's mummy in it. And surely no one suspected that thirteen of them would shortly die.

Carter has described the scene:

Friday, the 17th, was the day appointed, and at two o'clock those who were to be privileged to witness the ceremony met by appointment above the tomb. They included Lord Carnarvon, Lady Evelyn Herbert, H. E. Abd el Halim

Pasha Suleman, Minister of Public Works, M. Lacau, Director-General of the Service of Antiquities, Sir William Garstin, Sir Charles Cust, Mr. Lythgoe, Curator of the Egyptian Department of the Metropolitan Museum, New York, Professor Breasted, Dr. Alan Gardiner, Mr. Winlock, the Hon. Mervyn Herbert, the Hon. Richard Bethell, Mr. Engelbach, Chief Inspector of the Department of Antiquities, the representative of the Government Press Bureau, and the members of the staff—about twenty persons in all.[6]

There are only thirteen names on Carter's list, an understandable oversight given the events surrounding that memorable day. Among those he overlooked were the provincial governor, Bey Fahmy, and the commander in chief of the Egyptian army, Sir Lee Stack Sirdah. Other members of the archaeological staff included three assistants, Messrs. Astor, Bruère, and Callender, and Alfred Lucas and Arthur Mace.

A dramatic sense of expectancy hung over the scene. Chairs had been set up in the antechamber. The two life-sized statues that guarded the entrance were encased in planks. Electric lights had been strung in the cave. Carnarvon and Mace stood on a specially constructed platform near the gate, alternately taking the stones Carter hacked out of the wall with hammer and chisel.

After he had chiseled a hole into the wall the size of a child's head, Carter pushed an electric lamp into the darkness. Gold sparkled back, a wall of gold, gold as far as the eye could see.

With the removal of a very few stones the mystery of the golden wall was solved. We were at the entrance of the actual burial-chamber of the king, and that which barred our way was the side of an immense gilt shrine built to cover and protect the sarcophagus [Carter wrote]. . . . The fall of a single stone might have done irreparable damage to the delicate surface of the shrine, so, directly the hole was large enough, we made an additional protection for it by inserting a mattress on the inner side of the door-blocking, suspending it from the wooden lintel of the doorway. Two hours of hard work it took us to clear away the blocking, or at least as much of it as was necessary for the moment; and at one point, when near the bottom, we had to delay operations for a space while we collected the scattered beads from a necklace brought by the plunderers from the chamber within and dropped upon the threshold.[7]

Howard Carter had put on a dark suit in honor of the occasion but had shucked his jacket when he began to chisel into the wall. After the opening in the wall was wide enough to allow a man to enter, Carter descended into the main burial chamber. Lord Carnarvon and Lacau followed.

It was, beyond any question, the sepulchral chamber in which we stood, for there, towering above us, was one of the great gilt shrines beneath which kings were laid. So enormous was this structure (17 feet by 11 feet, and 9 feet high, we found afterwards) that it filled within a little the entire area of the chamber, a space of some two feet only separating it from the walls on all four sides, while its roof, with cornice top and torus moulding, reached almost to the ceiling.[8]

Had thieves gotten to the shrine first? That question was uppermost in Carter's mind.

Here, on the eastern end, were the great folding doors, closed and bolted, but not sealed, that would answer the question for us. Eagerly we drew the bolts, swung back the doors, and there within was a second shrine with similar bolted doors, and upon the bolts a seal, intact.[9]

No doubt about it, the grave robbers had not penetrated any farther. Hidden behind that door was something no man had seen since the pharaoh's death.

I think at the moment we did not even want to break the seal, for a feeling of intrusion had descended heavily upon us with the opening of the doors, heightened, probably, by the almost painful impressiveness of a linen pall, decorated with golden rosettes. . . . We felt that we were in the presence of the dead King and must do him reverence, and in imagination could see the doors of the successive shrine open one after the other till the innermost disclosed the King himself. Carefully, and as silently as possible, we re-closed the great swing doors.[10]

These are the words of a man who was witness to, and discoverer of, a piece of history.

Preparations for bringing out the dead pharaoh proved complex and difficult. Once again the entrance to the tomb was buried under debris. Lord Carnarvon drove back to Cairo, where he rented a suite at the Hotel Continental for the duration of the excavations; Carter stayed in Luxor.

Lord Carnarvon's Death

Early in April Howard Carter received word that Lord Carnarvon was seriously ill, but he did not attach any great importance to the message. Only after he received a second telegram, LORD CARNARVON GRAVELY ILL, HIGH FEVER, did Carter go to Cairo.

"Yes, it's quite a story," Lord Carnarvon's son, the powerfully built, broad-shouldered, self-assured sixth earl, told me. The young man had been traveling in India while his father excavated Tutankhamen's tomb, but when he learned of his father's illness he boarded the first ship for Egypt.

The sickness began strangely. "I feel like hell," the fifty-seven-year-old earl said one morning at breakfast. At the time he already had a temperature of 104 and shook with chills. The next day his condition improved. Then the high fever returned. It went this way for twelve days. The doctors determined that Lord Carnarvon had cut himself shaving, opening an old wound with his razor. But that would hardly have caused the fever to linger so long.

"When I arrived in Cairo," the younger Lord Carnarvon remembered, "I drove at once to the Hotel Continental. My father was unconscious. Howard Carter was there, and my mother, Lady Almina. I was awakened during the night. It was ten minutes before two. The nurse came and told me Father had died. My mother was with him. She closed his eyes. As I stepped into his room all the lights suddenly went out. We lit candles. I took my father's hand and prayed."

Lord Carnarvon's sister, Lady Burghclere, wrote in her memoir, "Lord Carnarvon was very tired. . . . 'I have heard the call,' he said to a friend, 'I am preparing.'" [11]

"There was no explanation for the power failure all over Cairo," Carnarvon's son said. "We asked the Cairo electric company, and they knew of no rational explanation for the lights going out and then on again."

Carnarvon's son reported one other curious incident. "Father died shortly before two o'clock Cairo time. As I learned later, something very strange happened here in Highclere about the same time, shortly before four A.M. London time. Our fox terrier bitch, who had lost her front paw in an accident in 1919 and whom Father loved very much, suddenly began to howl, sat up on her hind legs, and fell over dead."

A Puzzle from the Second Millennium

For the first time, scholars and newspapermen began talking seriously about the curse of the pharaohs and about the tablet that had been found and then lost. Other men involved with the Tutankhamen excavations began to die, and panic spread.

The American archaeologist Arthur Mace, who had been asked by Carter to help open the tomb and who had ripped out the last chunk of wall blocking the entry to the main chamber, complained about growing exhaustion after Carnarvon's death. Finally he fell into a deep coma that doctors were unable to diagnose and died in the same hotel as had Lord Carnarvon.

Carnarvon's death brought a long-time friend to Egypt, George Jay Gould, son of the American financier. Gould traveled from Cairo to Luxor and to the Valley of the Kings, where Carter showed him the sensational discovery of the pharaoh's tomb. The next morning Gould was stricken with a high fever; that evening he was dead. Doctors were at first unable to diagnose the fatal illness but concluded later that the cause of death was bubonic plague.

The mysterious deaths continued unabated. While Carter

kept up his archaeological exploration of the tomb, a British industrialist, Joel Wool, visited the grave site, returned to England by ship, and died of a high fever. Archibald Douglas Reid, a radiologist who was the first to cut the cords around the mummy of the dead pharaoh in order to X-ray the body, suffered strange attacks of debilitating feebleness shortly thereafter, and in 1924, upon his return to England, he died.

By 1929, twenty-two people who had been directly or indirectly involved with Tutankhamen and his tomb had died prematurely. Thirteen of them had taken part in opening the grave. Among the dead were Professors Winlock and Foucrat, the archaeologists Garry Davies, Harkness, and Douglas Derry, and the assistants Astor and Callender.

Lord Carnarvon's wife, Lady Almina, died in 1929, allegedly as a result of an insect bite, and Carter's secretary, Richard Bethell, died that year too. The circumstances surrounding Bethell's death were the strangest in this sinister chain of events. One morning Bethell was found in his bed, dead of a circulatory collapse. When his father, the eighty-seven-year-old Lord Westbury, heard of his son's death, he plunged from the seventh story of his London house. Then, on the way to the cemetery, the hearse ran over a little boy.

Death will slay with his wings whoever disturbs the peace of the pharaoh.

What does the curse signify? Can any man, even a deified being, really influence the life rhythms of others, perhaps even stop them altogether? Were there once ways to do this in ancient Egypt, discovered by religious mystics or highly talented scientists and since forgotten? Were there poisons or disease-producing organisms, able to keep their potency across the millennia, with which the seemingly immortal pharaohs hoped to protect their disemboweled and gilded bodies from human touch? Was there a deadly radiation from rare chemical elements or metals which these demigods knew and used to protect their palatial rock graves? Or are these strange interlocking deaths only a matter of sheer coincidence?

2   Death and Chance

THERE ARE two ways of accounting for the set of facts described in the first chapter. One is to attribute them to simple chance. The second, and more difficult, is to develop hypotheses to explain them. These phenomena are so unusual that they don't seem to fit into any scientific frame. However, we'd like to opt for the second method.

What we generally call chance is known among scientists as "coincidence." Parapsychologists, especially, have studied coincidence. Carl Gustav Jung, the father of depth psychology and one of the first who analyzed scientifically things outside sensory perception and physical experience, wrote in *Die Dynamik des Unbewußten* (Structure and Dynamics of the Psyche), "I was often confronted with such phenomena and learned how much they mean to the inner experience of human beings. They are, after all, mostly matters people do not talk openly about lest they risk the thoughtless ridicule of others."

There were other early pioneers. The Austrian biologist Paul Kammerer was one of them. His major work, *Das Gesetz der Serie* (The Law of Series), was published in 1919, after he had spent a decade investigating chance and determination of death. Other milestone books in this field include Ernst Mally's *Wahrscheinlichkeit und Gesetz* (Probability and Determination), published in 1938; Warren Weaver's

Lady Luck: The Theory of Probability; and Arthur Koestler's *The Roots of Coincidence.*

Scientific research into coincidence and probability is still in its infancy, however, even though man has been interested in both for thousands of years. That interest can be traced back to Egyptian and Babylonian astronomers, who first discovered the regularly recurrent rhythm in the course of the stars and recognized the existence of certain relationships between the path of a star and the life of man.

Even if their early findings were sketchy and imprecise, the ancient Egyptians do deserve credit for first cataloguing the constellations and for devising astronomical almanacs with tables showing the position of each heavenly body on a number of dates in regular sequence. Sirius, or Sothis as the ancient Greeks called the star, announced the flooding of the Nile when it appeared in the morning sky. At first the Egyptians viewed this heliacal rising of Sothis as an inexplicable providence of the gods. But after centuries during which the Nile floods regularly followed the rise of Sothis, the Egyptians recognized the connection.

Tellurian observations have long posed questions of chance, some of which conventional science was able to answer. Others, however, remain a puzzle to this day.

Pre-Christian antiquity, for example, was already acquainted with the phenomenon of the regular rhythm of waves. Aeschylus and Euripides used the term τρικυμια, which corresponds roughly to "triple wave." This triple wave can be observed on ocean beaches as well as on the shores of large lakes: After ten waves of approximately equal height wash ashore, the next three are visibly higher. Although as far as I know there is to this day no full explanation for this phenomenon, few are likely to label it pure coincidence merly because physics has not come up with a scientific answer.

Mathematical Coincidence

If chance is examined mathematically, it loses much of its unpredictability. Toss a quarter and it will either come up heads or tails. The chance of its coming up heads is one in two. Two tosses, however, could lead to any of four results: heads-heads, heads-tails, tails-heads, or tails-tails. No other combinations are possible.

With three tosses, eight different results are possible: heads-heads-heads, heads-heads-tails, heads-tails-heads, heads-tails-tails, tails-heads-heads, tails-heads-tails, tails-tails-heads, or tails-tails-tails.

In his book *Die Gleichförmigkeit in der Welt* (Uniformity in the World), Karl Marbe described the first and last result of the series—three tosses that come up heads or tails—as a "pure series" and the odd results as "normal series." The closer the results of a set of tosses are, the closer they come to being a pure series, but they are also rarer and more improbable.

Theoretically, a coin could come up heads ten times in succession. If we put a letter for the number of tosses, the probability would be expressed as $1:n$, i.e., a single toss of a coin produces a relationship of $1:2$. The number of possibilities can be expressed in the formula 2^n.

Three tosses mean 2^3 possibilities, or eight possible solutions. Chances for a coin coming up heads 28 times, according to this formula, would be: $1:2^{28} = 1:268,435,456$.

The procedure becomes much more complex when there are more than two possibilities. Warren Weaver reported one such case that occurred on March 1, 1950, in Beatrice, Nebraska. A choir rehearsal scheduled that evening in the small village church was due to begin at 7:20 P.M. As chance would have it, however, none of the fifteen choir members had turned up by 7:25 P.M. The pastor and choir director wasn't there because he was waiting for his wife to finish pressing their elder daughter's dress; the girl, too, sang in the choir. Two women were unable to start their cars, independently of each other. One girl hadn't finished her homework; two others found a radio play so exciting they forgot the time. A mother had to call her daughter twice to wake her. All these are very simple reasons to explain why no one went to the church on time.

But these simple reasons suddenly are made to appear

in quite a different light, for at 7:25 P.M., five minutes after choir practice was scheduled to begin, a gas explosion blew up the Beatrice church and completely destroyed it. Was the fact that all fifteen people were late due to divine providence? Did they sense something? Or is it really just an accident that these people are still alive?

Weaver calculated that the odds against all ten reasons for being late coming up at the same time that night are a million to one. His argument is empirical. For an average choir practice, members were late one out of four times. But since all the choir members were late on that same day, the probability of being late for each one was in a relationship of $(1:4)$ [10].

Life Rhythms

The harmony of fateful characteristics is often attributed to the stars. Certainly that is the simplest and most popular theory. Though to date twelve men have taken giant leaps on the moon, the moon's influence on the earth has been left largely unexplored. The relationship between the moon and the tides of the ocean are accepted as fact, but little is known about the moon's influence on human life. The correlation between sunspot activity and climate has been determined, but only Russian cosmic biologists have claimed that sunspots influence the outbreak of epidemics or other natural disasters.

Two Russian scientists discovered solar cycles with a rhythm of seven, eleven, thirty-five, and eighty years. During these periods magnetic storms can knock out whole power systems, and statistical investigations have shown a noticeable increase in the incidence of psychoses, traffic accidents, suicides, and "natural" deaths.

On October 2, 1970, a prominent German actress and her doctor husband died in a traffic accident in Bavaria. Their tragic death is of interest here because on that October 2 both were in particularly bad physical shape—at least that's what scientists claim who have specialized in biorhythm.

An amazing and controversial theory developed by Wilhelm Fliess, a Berlin doctor, biorhythm is based on the following hypotheses: At birth man's life rhythm begins, a rhythm of his physical, emotional (or spiritual), and mental (or intellectual) abilities. The parameters of these rhythms are marked by a "high" and a "low" that express themselves in the individual's moods and performance. What complicates the life-rhythm theory is the fact that each of the three rhythms has a different time cycle: The physical cycle lasts twenty-three days, the emotional twenty-eight days, and the mental thirty-three days.

According to this theory people are particularly fit every twenty-three days, in fine emotional form every twenty-eight days, and at the peak of mental efficiency every thirty-three days. At the same time the high-low cycle must perforce result in nadirs of physical, psychological, and intellectual behavior. After the accident that killed the actress and her husband, biorhythmic researchers did some calculations—based on the birth dates of both and on their life-rhythm curve for October 2, 1970—and found their theory confirmed: The couple drove to their death on a day when "by chance" both had reached a physical low. An accident?

The biorhythm theory is controversial. Opponents dismiss positive and negative evidence as products of autosuggestion, saying that those who are aware of their alleged emotional nadir will feel particularly depressed that day, while those who know when to expect a psychological high will dare a great deal. That, however, says nothing about the life rhythms of people who are unaware of the biorhythm theory.

Human failing is considered the major reason for the amazing number of crashes of American-built Starfighter jets piloted by members of the new Luftwaffe. Through early 1973 a total of 156 Starfighters crashed. But when birth dates and life rhythms of twenty-three pilots were studied, it was found that thirteen had reached a life-rhythm "low" the day they crashed.

The Japanese are paying some attention to the theory of biorhythm. Taito Kokusai, Japan's largest taxi fleet owner, has his three thousand drivers write down every day, before starting work, the state of their life rhythm. And the fifty motorcycle messengers who work for the Yokohama cable office tie red or yellow pennants to their handlebars on certain days. Red means "Careful, driver on his low," while yellow signals "Take care, driver before or after a low."

Switzerland has put the Japanese experience to use. In Zurich the life rhythm of the automobile club's road service drivers is taken into account in assigning them jobs, and, as a result, the number of accidents for which drivers are responsible has dropped 30 percent. A taxi fleet owner in Basle, Switzerland, was able to cut accidents among his drivers by 40 percent as a result of observing life-rhythm curves. Jack Günthard, the trainer of the Swiss gymnastic team, fields his athletes at international meets according to their most favorable life rhythms.

If individual destiny is not the product of pure chance, these phenomena become all the more disconcerting when the fates of several people who have no contact with one another appear linked in some strange manner. Take the case of a Viennese physicist who, in a lecture on radioactivity, concentrated on the work of Pierre Curie. As he spoke, Curie died in a traffic accident. Another time the same professor lectured students on the gas theory of Austrian physicist Ludwig Boltzmann. During the lecture, Boltzmann committed suicide.

That seems more than coincidence; at the very least it raises serious questions about the role of mere chance. Are there psychic or parapsychological ties between people with similar interests, feelings, and problems? Could the curse of the pharaohs too be no more than the result—or the failure—of a thought process by individuals with similar feelings and interests?

We are sober, enlightened people who live in the last third of the twentieth century, yet we must accept the fact that the step from sensory to extrasensory perception can at times be so small that we do not notice the difference at first and only wake up to it, astonished, after we stand in front of an impenetrable wall. True, physiologists have an explanation as to why hysterics sometimes become deaf though they continue to "hear" with their fingertips; that is, how these people can transfer the perceptive ability of one sense to another. But they have no answer as to why some people get cancer and some don't.

Synchronizing Minds

The plethysmograph is an instrument for making brain activity visible. Its principles are much simpler than one might think. Highly sensitive sensors register pressure and volume of the brain's blood vessels. Pressure and volume rise when a thought process begins. A measuring instrument registers these changes and records them much as an electrocardiogram records heart action.

A Czech researcher named Figar tested two persons with analogous emotional makeups. He put them in separate rooms, attached plethysmographs to their heads, and then asked one of them to solve a fairly complex mathematical problem. The other knew nothing about the problem. Both measuring instruments began recording the brain activity of the two test persons at the same time. The incredible—and, for empirical science, inexplicable—happened: Both graphs recorded the same kind of brain activity, even though one subject did not know that the other had to solve a math problem.

Russian scientists slaughtered young rabbits in a submarine and at the same time measured the brain activities of the mother rabbits, which were in a laboratory several hundred miles away. At the moment of the young rabbits' death the measuring instruments attached to the mother rabbits recorded sharp fluctuations of brain activity. The mothers obviously reacted to some kind of stimulus. But what? Radiation, electromagnetic waves, current?

Leonid L. Wassiliew, a Soviet parapsychologist, by using a relatively simple physics experiment to prove his point, was able to show that paranormal phenomena and skills are not a result of waves, currents, or radiation. Test persons were locked in lead chambers equipped with hatches encased in mercury—the tightest screening against electromagnetic waves. Gamma rays, or very short waves, and very long waves

35

could penetrate such a "Faraday's cage," but the very long waves require an unusually high expenditure of energy which no human brain is able to produce, while very short waves produce brain damage. Waves could not have been the sourse of energy, because telepathic experiments with these test persons locked in their lead chamber succeeded.

Dr. Hans Bender, a Freiburg University parapsychologist, believes that deeply emotional components of the subconscious can act as a trigger mechanism in borderline cases involving life and death situations. Not surprisingly, most of the case histories of such abilities, derisively dismissed as "clairvoyance," are derived from wartime experience.

One classic example is the case of Rosa Schödl, an Austrian peasant. On the night of November 14, 1941, she was awakened by the creaking of her bedroom door. The wind had pushed it open. But as the woman tried to get up in order to close the door she had a strange vision. "I thought there was snow out in the hall and that a bier stood in the snow and that my son lay on the bier."

Frightened, the woman awakened her daughter-in-law and told her what had happened. It was about one thirty in the morning. For three weeks Rosa Schödl lived with the conviction that her son, Leopold, had died in Russia. Then her worst fears were confirmed: Her son's company commander wrote from Smolensk that Leopold had been hit by shrapnel in the head. After the medics had pulled the badly wounded soldier to safety, they had to abandon the stretcher in the snow and duck for shelter to protect themselves from renewed Soviet bombardment. As they did, Leopold Schödl called out twice, "Mother! Mother!" and died. The letter gave date and time of death as November 14, 1941, at 1:30 A.M.

The All Clear in the Operating Room

The fact that in borderline situations animals communicate with people does not contradict the theory of an unknown source of energy transference. On the contrary, it limits the hypothesis only to the extent that it precludes technological intelligence as a prerequisite of such transference.

Listen to what Mrs. Ida Loni H from Kreuzau in the Rhineland has to say:

"In 1944, a time of the heaviest air raids against Germany when our town, on the west side of the Rhine not far from Aachen, already had suffered a good deal and we had to spend just about every night in an air raid shelter, I visited a patient at the city hospital, and afterward I talked to Sister Ursula, a very easygoing, motherly nun. I told her that it must be awful to have to take the seriously ill patients from surgery down to the shelter every time there was an alarm. But Sister Ursula told me it wasn't that bad because she didn't always take her patients down to the cellar. She relied on a small neighborhood dog who began to bark shrilly whenever real danger threatened. That little dog was simply infallible and always knew whether the bombers were flying into our area or if they were turning off into the Ruhr."

Thus seemingly small circumstances can take on life-and-death significance. If the death of a man can be determined by so many apparently inconsequential factors, it is high time to explore them.

On a certain date and at a certain hour, for example, why is a person so careless as to stumble downstairs and break his neck? Why does a man suffer a heart attack on a certain day and at a certain time? And the question can be turned around: Why does one person survive a plane crash in which all the other passengers die?

The worst disaster in German civil aviation history occurred in December, 1972, when 156 persons were killed on a plane they had chartered from the Spanish airline Spantax which crashed shortly after taking off from the airport in Tenerife. An investigation showed that "human failure" was responsible for the accident. Why did the pilot fail so tragically on that particular morning? More importantly, why did the wife of bus line owner Josef Artmeier from Leithen in Lower Bavaria suddenly throw a hysterical fit just before the plane's departure and refuse to stay aboard? She and her husband got off when the aircraft was already on the runway.

"I just had this premonition," Hildegard Artmeier explained later. This is a typical example of precognition—to use the scientific jargon. But scientists have no real explanation for precognition either. If they did, aviation disasters would be a thing of the past.

A total of 140 children in the village of Axbridge (population 1,200), near Bristol, lost their mothers on April 10, 1973, when a British charter plane with 146 people aboard slammed into a snow-covered mountain near Basle. The local women's club had arranged the outing to the Swiss city. Marian Warren, forty, had also planned to go along on the shopping trip, but a few days before the planned departure she had a dream. "I saw the plane streak towards the trees and fall into the snow. Everything was terribly realistic. The bodies of my friends were strewn about. . . . At the last moment I sold my ticket at half price for eight pounds."

The odds against a plane crash are 330,000 to 1; that's a statistical fact. Yet a meeting of the International Air Transport Association (IATA) revealed that twenty-five passengers had canceled various flights because of "premonitions of danger" and the planes on six of these flights had actually crashed. Those are only 4-to-1 odds against disaster.

Are there people who know more about death than you or I?

Predicting Death

Jeane Dixon's terrifying ability to see into the future has been well documented in Ruth Montgomery's book, *A Gift of Prophecy*. In 1952 Mrs. Dixon predicted that a blue-eyed man would be elected President of the United States in 1960 and would meet with violent death while in office. On Friday, November 22, 1963, she lunched with two women at a Washington restaurant.

What's the matter? her friends asked when they saw that she did not touch her food. "I'm too upset," she replied. "Something dreadful is going to happen to the President today." Moments later the bulletin flashed on radio and television: John F. Kennedy had been shot.

Jeane Dixon did not only predict Kennedy's death but the second letter in his assassin's name—*s* in Oswald. No matter how sensational this may sound, there is no doubt about the fact that she made these predictions well in advance of events; independent witnesses corroborated all of them. Moreover, Mrs. Dixon predicted U.N. Secretary General Dag Hammarskjöld's fatal crash, Marilyn Monroe's suicide, and Mahatma Gandhi's death.

Death, it would seem, is not a matter of chance; it can be predetermined by some kind of circumstances, circumstances specially gifted people can sense or feel. Strangely enough, the concept of "feeling" has moved some distance away from its original meaning, so that it has little to do with "touching" or "sensing" any more. Originally, "feeling" meant the "registration of matter or energy." Matter or energy—that would be the simplest explanation for Jeane Dixon's premonitions of death. The simplest. Note that well.

Bioenergy

The ancient Chinese believed that every man was a power plant that produced energy known as "life force." This vital force continued in space. As a result, kinetic relationships exist between space and mankind. Variations of this theory can be found in all cultures. The Hindus call this form of energy "prana" and say it can be charged by breathing oxygen, almost as if one were "ionized." That's why breathing plays such a key role in yoga.

New aspects of the life energy theory were not developed until the sixteenth century. Paracelsus credited it with the ability to let a man live or die. He even claimed it could be transferred from one man to another. Paracelsus called this energy "munis."

A century later Jan Baptista van Helmont, a doctor and chemist from Brussels who discovered chloric acid, suggested that this vital energy, which he called "magnale magnum," could influence the will of someone else in another place. That put Helmont on the track of telepathy.

Franz Anton Mesmer (1734–1815), a German doctor, studied the physical aspects of what he called "animal magnetism" and even prescribed magnetic cures in order to bring energy requirements back into balance. He was convinced that the cosmic-magnetic forces in man could have a healing effect; for example, if the doctor placed his hand on the patient. Disease, he argued, is a disruption of the harmonic circulation of electromagnetic forces in our organism, while healing is the reestablishment of this harmony, which, in turn, is effected through application of magnetic radiation.

Since then, bioenergy has appeared under a variety of different labels, such as odic force, N-rays, etherical force, or X-force. Modern science talks about psychosomatic or psychotronic energy, but both are considered frontier areas of science even though such prominent scientists as Joseph Wüst, a physicist and a medical doctor, and Ferdinand Sauerbruch, a famous Berlin surgeon, were seriously interested in them.

Karl von Reichenbach, a German chemist, did research on what he called the "aura," the human radiation field, during the middle of the nineteenth century. While Mesmer conceived of his "animal magnetism" as a fluid, Reichenbach believed he had proved that the body exuded a kind of tanning bark he called "od." According to proponents of the theory, this nervous energy—or whatever else one chooses to call it— was physical enough to be secreted in water and to impart a distinctive taste. Clairvoyants and other especially sensitive people were said to perceive this od as a kind of light.

Unfortunately, devotees of the mystic and the occult were quick to misuse any new findings, so that scientists were little inclined to do any serious research. Although a man named Heydweiler measured the electric field around human beings with a quadrant electronometer in 1902, twenty-six years passed before his work was taken up again by Sauerbruch and Schuman. These two scientists conducted their experiments inside a Faraday cage and proved with the help of a galvanometer the existence of tension fields within the body which change their intensity according to muscle reaction.

More recently, Dr. Wüst studied body radiation. Since wood is a nonradiant substance, the experiments were conducted on top of wooden tables. They showed that radiant materials (stones, metals, liquids) could be measured even after their radiant qualities were removed for experimental purposes. That would hint at ionization of the surroundings.

More controversial and without scientific proof is the idea of the existence of stimulus zones based on earth radiation. Because dowsers were the first to develop this theory, it has not been recognized by orthodox science, although animal and botanical experiments have produced undeniable proof of its basic validity. Even among human beings there are astounding indications of these geopathological zones. One need only cite cases of chronic insomnia cured by moving the bed from one place to another.

Death at Kilometer 23.9

As Sauerbruch demonstrated, bodily tension is also dependent on the energy circumstances of the physical surroundings. Karl-Heinz Jaeckel, whose book *An den Grenzen menschlicher Fassungskraft* (The Limits of Human Perception) deals with this phenomenon, reports on an interesting experiment conducted with a Westphalian dowser, Hans Danner.

There are many "streets of death" in Germany, roads where a large number of fatal accidents occur without any apparent reason. Since 1932 hundreds of traffic accidents have taken place on a straight stretch of road near Bremen at the 23.9-kilometer marker. Then Danner, with two other dowsers, was taken across the cordoned-off road one night. He did not know the road, and the markers were covered with sacks. Danner discovered a powerful disruptive source of earth radiation. A kilometer marker on the site where Danner localized the disruptive radiation had the number 23.9 written on it.

Experiments with Pyramids

If earth, body, and material radiation are energies, then these energies can be increased. And in fact there are experiments indicating that certain geometric bodies are able to

41

accumulate energy and then give it off in more concentrated form. Scientific concern about this question has focused on the Egyptian pyramids.

The English explorer Paul Brunton had himself locked into the royal chamber of the Khufu pyramid for a night (see chapter 13). According to trustworthy accounts, Brunton almost lost his reason. He experienced a split consciousness reminiscent of an LSD trip, had visions of his own death, and was completely apathetic when he was freed the next morning.

In 1959 a Prague radio engineer named Karl Drbal patented a small pyramid. Drbal had observed experiments by the French radiologist Jean Martial based on relationships between the shape of a pyramid and physical processes within it. Martial had experimented with pyramid models in which he observed the reaction of organic matter for days on end. His conclusion: Pyramids speed up the process of mummification. For example, a fish placed inside a pyramid model built to scale lost two thirds of its weight within thirteen days; the windpipe of a sheep shrank by one half in six days; in forty-three days an egg wasted away from 52 grams to 12 grams. Even the fish did not mold or smell.

Drbal, basing his work on the earlier experiment, used the physical impact of the pyramid shape to develop—of all things—a razor blade sharpener. Out of cardboard, he built a pyramid model with a base line of 24 centimeters and a height of 15 centimeters. The floor was left open. Then he began the following experiment: A dull razor blade was placed on a base of wood or cardboard about a third as long as the pyramid was high, about 5 centimeters. The pyramid was placed over the base and exposed to normal daylight. More important, however, was the exact alignment of the blade and of the pyramid on the north-south axis, putting the cutting edge of the blade crosswise to the east-west axis. The sharpening process lasted about six days.

These two examples of pyramid geometry are taken from experimental physics. They raise this question: Did the ancient Egyptians—or at least the educated men among them—

know about some applications of energy which modern science has still not rediscovered? Can certain geometric forms mobilize psychic forces able to cause death? And if so, do they provide a basis for solving the riddle behind the curse of the pharaohs?

Thirteen people present at the opening of Tutankhamen's tomb died mysteriously afterward. Ordinarily, death is not due to any accidental malfunction of certain organs. On an average, a fly lives seventy-five days, a queen bee five years, a cat ten years, a horse forty years. An elephant can live to be fifty, a crocodile a hundred, a whale three hundred. A few human beings live past a hundred, but by and large men barely reach seventy. When Tutankhamen's tomb was discovered, 10 out of 15 people in Europe were at least fifty-five when they died. But only 10 of the 23 persons involved in the tomb's excavation lived that long.

The Secrets of Science

It is hard to believe how much ancient civilizations such as Egypt knew of modern science. Despite their revolutionary discoveries, however, the Egyptians did not share their knowledge with anyone but the selected few. For the masses, science was as shrouded in secrecy as were the men who practiced it. What a small upper class saw as fact was for the rest of the people the work of the gods, a miracle, magic. That's the only explanation as to why Egyptian scientists were able to take the fruits of their labor to their graves: knowledge, in short, designed to fulfill a certain function for a limited time and then to disappear from the consciousness of mankind, perhaps for millennia, perhaps forever.

But still, the last testimony of this great era was significant enough to prompt wise and famous men to undertake voyages to the land on the Nile in order to complete their education. Among those said to have undertaken such trips are Homer, Orpheus and Euripides, the statesmen Lycurgus and Solon, the philosophers Thales and Plato, the mathematicians Eudoxus and Archimedes. Even if it cannot be proved that these voyages actually took place, the assumption that they did is surely proof of the importance assigned Egyptian culture.

Plato even went so far as to call his own people, the Greeks, children as compared to the Egyptians. In Timaeus, 22, Plato had an Egyptian priest from Sais tell Solon:

"O Solon, you Greeks have always been children. There isn't a single wise man among you. You have no tradition, and your legends of Deucalion and Phaeton are only a tiny fraction of those destroyed by fire and floods. Such catastrophes have afflicted humanity from time to time to destroy whole nations and with them all written records and scientific achievements. But the Nile has preserved our nation from such disasters. That's why we have preserved in our temples the historic testimony to our past while you must always begin your history anew, never knowing what happened in your own, let alone in other, countries."

3   Suicide for the Advancement of Science

WEDNESDAY, MARCH 10, 1971. On the huge archaeological digging grounds at Sakkara, 30 kilometers south of Cairo, laborers were getting ready to quit work. Though it was only two o'clock in the afternoon, the workmen, gray with the dust of the desert, noisily tossed their baskets, made from halved truck tires, into the sand. Since seven in the morning the men had brought sand, dust, and rocks to the surface from 10 meters below—not an easy job but a well-paid one. And where else can a man earn good money, here at the edge of the Libyan desert?

The village of Sakkara had become attractive in the years since 1935 when all those crazy archaeologists began coming. The cemetery of Sakkara, Memphis' ancient city of the dead, is 7 kilometers long and anywhere from 500 to 1,500 meters wide. It is dominated by the five-thousand-year-old pyramid of King Djoser, the oldest still-intact building in the world.

Walter Bryan Emery, an Englishman, professor of Egyptology, and head of the digging operations at Sakkara, stood at the edge of the shaft.

Bryan, as his friends and colleagues called him, held a small statuette, perhaps 20 centimeters high, of the death god Osiris. Again and again he inspected the statuette from all angles; then he walked toward the village with his Egyptian assistant.

The diggers had a small one-story house in Sakkara with an office and a washrom, but none of the archaeologists lived there. When Emery and his assistant, Ali al Khouli, arrived in the office, Ali, exhausted from the heat, collapsed on a couch. Emery walked into the washroom. The assistant told me what happened next.

"I sat here on the couch. Suddenly I heard moaning coming from the washroom. I looked through the door, which was ajar, and saw Emery holding onto the basin. 'Are you sick?' I called out, but the professor did not reply. He stood there as if paralyzed. I grabbed him by the shoulders and dragged him onto the couch. Then I ran for the telephone."

An ambulance rushed Emery to the British hospital in Cairo. The diagnosis: paralysis of the right side. He couldn't speak. Emery's wife, Mary, who accompanied him on most of his expeditions, stayed with him the whole night. The next day—Thursday, March 11, 1971—Walter Bryan Emery was dead.

A day later the Cairo newspaper *Al Ahram* wrote, "This strange occurrence leads us to believe that the legendary curse of the pharaohs has been reactivated."

Emery, of whom the native diggers said, "He wasn't an Englishman, he was an Egyptian," had always ignored the curse of the pharaohs. He knew about it, but when journalists asked him to comment, he always refused. Ali al Khouli said, "He talked about everything. But never about that."

Emery had not become an archaeologist by design. At first Egyptology was nothing more than a breathtaking adventure; the Liverpool-born scholar was trained as a naval engineer and worked on the construction of two battleships. But he had a different image of his life.

He returned to college in 1921 to study Egyptology with Professor Thomas E. Peet. The subject had fascinated him since his school days, but brooding over ancient texts, he found, was not what he wanted either. Two years later he again quit school to take part in an expedition to Luxor. By 1926 he had dug up more than a dozen ancient Egyptian graves, among them one of the most valuable of the XVIIIth dynasty, that of the vizier Ramose. Three years later, in 1929, he moved his activity to Nubia, where numerous monuments waited to be saved from the submersion due to follow the planned elevation of the old Aswan dam.

Emery was made director of the Sakkara excavations in 1935. His first job was clearing the huge cemetery that dated back to the first dynasty. He devoted most of the next twenty years of his life to that task—with time out to serve in World War II.

After the war there was little money for continued excavations; then the Suez crisis intervened. But since Emery had become accustomed to Egypt, he accepted a diplomatic appointment in Cairo. Finally he was named Professor of Egyptology at the University of London; as the Sakkara excavations continued, he commuted between his lectures in London and his research in Egypt.

On October 5, 1964, Emery began what he considered his life's work: a search for Imhotep's grave.

Imhotep was a most interesting man. He was, according to Emery, "the first doctor to emerge clearly from the fog of antiquity." He lived in the times of the very first pharaohs and had the kind of scientific knowledge that made people believe he was the god of healing. But he was also an architect, an adviser to Pharaoh Djoser, a vizier, and "director of public works for the King of Upper and Lower Egypt." He built Djoser's pyramid and is supposed to have invented the calendar and writing. In short, he was an all-round genius.

Since Imhotep's grave has never been discovered, it is fairly safe to assume that it has not yet been plundered. Imhotep's architectural abilities support that thesis, for Imhotep is sure to have built himself a tomb while he was still alive—different from that of his pharaoh, Djoser, but no less splendid. Imhotep's grave, Emery was sure, would have at least as much importance for the history of the Old Kingdom as the discovery of Tutankhamen's tomb had for the New Empire. Only where in this desert should he begin digging?

The first trial excavations made it clear that the whole valley was full of constructions from the early dynasties.

47

Many of the buildings, seldom higher than 3 meters, were preserved only because in Ptolemy's day rubble had been poured between the monuments. (This "macadamizing" freed the land for new construction.) Professor Emery wrote:

For some years I have been interested in the valley area at the extreme west of the archaic necropolis at North Sakkara because the whole ground area is covered with remains of Ptolemaic-Roman pottery in a manner reminiscent of Umm el Quab at Abydos. Before closing down the work of the Egyptian Exploration Society in 1956, I sank two test pits in this area, exposing some brick work of the 3rd dynasty and finding two burials of the sacrificed bulls and the remains of ibis mummies in lidded pottery vessels. The existence of ibis burials in underground passages was known to some explorers of the last century, but for some reason the significance of their association with tombs of the 3rd century was not recognized. . . . In view of the widespread belief that the tomb of Imhotep would be located somewhere in the archaic necropolis (Firth, Quibell and Reisner firmly believe this), the bull and ibis remains suggest that in some way this site might be connected with his burial. Anyway, the surface conditions point to this area being a place of pilgrimage in Ptolemaic-Roman times.[1]

Emery, his goal ever in mind, worked more and more feverishly. On December 10, 1964, he hit the shaft of a grave from the IIId dynasty 10 meters down. A many-branched labyrinth was spread out before him: passages, bricked-up gateways, and countless mummified ibises. Clearly, several generations had crossed paths here. A statue from the age of Ptolemy told Emery he was on the right track. On its pedestal he found a list of the feasts celebrated in honor of the god of healing. (One of those feasts takes place on the day Emery was to die.) In the rites Imhotep is described as he who "rests in the great Dehan, a cave dear to his heart."

It could be, Professor Emery believed, that the cave was this great underground labyrinth.

Emery had little doubt that he was on Imhotep's trail, but he did not know if it would be a matter of days or years before he made his great discovery. "I was a lot more dubious than Emery," Ali al Khouli said. "At the end he was almost certain that he would find Imhotep soon."

The archaeologists wound string around their wrists, as Ariadne had done in the Cretan labyrinth of Minos, in order to be sure of coming back to daylight from the maze of passages. Sketches were made. Explored tunnels were sealed. But after months of subterranean labor Emery was forced to concede that none of the passages led to the tomb of Imhotep.

He was disappointed but not discouraged. Their failure to find access to the tomb did not have to mean, Emery believed, that Imhotep's grave was not somehow connected to the labyrinth. Quite the contrary: It had been so ingeniously designed that systematic digging was pointless.

Emery began to dig at another site—but in vain. The greatest triumph of his life, the discovery of the Imhotep grave, was denied him.

A Curse and Its Past

I have followed the life stories of many archaeologists. I wanted to find out if there were any parallels in the way they lived and died. There was little in their lives, let me say right away, that was special, save a passion for their chosen profession. But there were a number of remarkable coincidences.

No doubt about it, archaeologists are hard to put into a single category. That was one thing I discovered over and over again during my research for this book. It's not just a matter of the different theories they hold, but of character and personality differences. Some German archaeologists dismiss the curse as plain nonsense, while others stubbornly refuse even to walk into a pharaoh's tomb. When I asked a Munich archaeologist just what he feared, he replied, like a Delphic oracle, "The gods."

If the curse is not a unique phenomenon linked—and limited—to the discovery of Tutankhamen's tomb, other archaeologists must have died mysteriously before King Tut's last resting-place was unearthed.

Libraries and archives contain detailed descriptions of archaeological discoveries and theories, but there is precious little in them about the personal lives of the scholars or adventurers who made the discoveries and formulated the theories. My own research into the lives and deaths of leading Egyptologists, however, has brought new facts to light which indicate at the very least that the curse of the pharaohs was at work a century and a half ago. And it always struck men who had spent long years in Egypt and were somehow involved with excavation.

Dümichen's Deliriums

Take Johannes Dümichen, for example. Born in 1833, a pastor's son from Silesia and a professor at the University of Strasbourg, he traveled widely in Egypt and Nubia. His work cannot be valued highly enough. He copied grave and temple inscriptions, often spending weeks underground or in a ruin. Gradually his personality underwent radical change. If his were a unique case it would not be worth discussing, but it is only one of many.

Dümichen was often delirious and showed symptoms of incipient schizophrenia. He talked for hours about experiences on archaeological sites he demonstrably could not have had. He would tell anyone who'd listen, for example, about his labors in a Theban tomb where "it stank so horribly of bats that I could make copies only by tying a piece of orange peel around my mouth." There is no record that Dümichen was ever in or near such a tomb as he described.

By the time the archaeologist returned to Germany he had become a pitiful sight. He could hardly finish a coherent sentence and would jump fitfully from one thought to the other. Worst of all, he wrote that way too.

His publishers were close to despair. Baedeker asked him to write a guide to Upper Egypt and then shredded the edition because the book was so bad. Nor did the editor of a multivolume world history fare any better. Dümichen, who had contracted to write the Egyptian section of the series, wrote and wrote. After 300 pages the astonished editor realized that the good professor had not yet finished his introduction.

These symptoms closely parallel those produced by drugs. Many normal people are latently schizophrenic without the disease ever surfacing. Massive doses of hallucinatory drugs, however, can trigger outbreaks of schizophrenia or schizophrenic behavior. Thus Dr. John Griffith, a U.S. amphetamine specialist, reported about one of his graduate students who took amphetamines, "One day I asked him a question he could not answer. He grew so furious he took a 453-page book on the subject and learned every word in it by heart." Another U.S. doctor told of a student who took an exam while on drugs and wrote his entire answer on the top line of a piece of paper.

The ancient Egyptians, as we shall see, knew a good deal about drugs. Moreover, we know today that only minimal contact, such as wiping one's mouth with the back of a dirty hand, will allow some drugs to enter and affect an organism. The "accidental" discovery of LSD in 1938 by the Swiss pharmacist, Dr. Albert Hofmann, is one such example. He was working in the Sondoz drug company's research laboratory in Basle when a few millionths of one gram came into his mouth; forty minutes later he had visions! It is literally enough to touch such a substance with the forefinger and then dab one's lips with it.

The Strange Deeds of Heinrich Brugsch

There are other ways of getting high. Digging, exploring, conquering have brought ecstasy to many. It seemed as if the curse of the pharaohs exercised some magic force on its victims. Outstanding scholars were committing suicide for the sake of science or at the least they were returning from Egypt somewhat mad.

One example of such madness is recorded in the autobiography of Professor Adolf Erman, the director of Berlin's Egyptian Museum. It concerns Heinrich Brugsch (1827–1894), one of the best of the Berlin archaeologists, who could read demotic script by the age of sixteen.

Brugsch came from a typical Berlin background;

his father was a sergeant-major and lived in the Kupfergraben barracks, where Heinrich was born. Yet Brugsch was never able to accept his lowly origins, and even after he had become a renowned scientst he told people that his father was a prince.

Brugsch once bragged that he had dug up a green king's head in Sais, although everyone knew that he had bought the head at an antique shop. Another time Brugsch and Erman were in the museum's coin room where the director had spread out some valuable Renaissance medals on a table. Erman recalled the following conversation:

BRUGSCH: What have you got there?
ERMAN: Italian medallions from the fifteenth century.
BRUGSCH: What does *Pisanus Pictor fecit* mean?
ERMAN: That's the artist's signature.
BRUGSCH: I had some of those once, when I dug in the Nile delta with Visalli. We found a heap of them.
ERMAN: What happened to them?
BRUGSCH: Oh, I don't know, I gave them away.
ERMAN: But that means you gave away a fortune.
BRUGSCH: Yes.

Erman believes Brugsch may have found a copper plate during one of his excavations, but nothing more valuable.

Were these just neuroses, or had Brugsch's senses been affected by some outside influence? Brugsch began to turn a little queer after spending long years in Egypt. Gaston Maspero, as the Director of Antiquities, claimed that Brugsch invented the sources he used to buttress his scholarly work. And Erman reported that Brugsch proposed two diametrically opposed theories about the so-called "sea people" in two of his works.

It is all the more surprising that, despite these schizophrenic tendencies, Brugsch is recognized as one of the great Egyptologists of all time. This giant of a man who could forget the world around him when on the trail of a historical problem, who treated mummies as if they were living men—was he, too, a victim of the curse of the pharaohs?

The fact is that the longer he stayed in Egypt the stranger he grew. Finally, he left Cairo suddenly, after informing authorities in Berlin that he would take up Richard Lepsius's succession at the university, although the latter still occupied his professorial chair. Moreover, Brugsch threatened that if he were not given the post he would take a similar position in Paris, an offer no one had ever made him.

Once in Berlin he complained to the press that he was being persecuted by other scholars. Like many of his colleagues, Brugsch became a victim of his obsession. Erman wrote in his memoirs, "We only remember the 'bit of earth' in Brugsch, which sticks to every man of genius, and if this 'bit of earth' was especially painful in Brugsch's case, we can certainly roll most of the blame on the unhappy stars."

The Short Life of François Champollion

If we look back a bit farther into the history of archaeology we come upon the almost legendary Jean-François Champollion (1790–1832), who succeeded in decoding the hieroglyphics, the prerequisite for all future research in Egyptology.

The word *hieroglyphic* in Greek is ιερο-γλυφικα, which may be translated as "holy pictures." And indeed from the days of Greek antiquity to Champollion's rediscovery of their meaning, these signs were believed to be secret, mystical, and holy. Until the end of the eighteenth century some scholars seriously believed in their magic content and refused to study them. The Danish archaeologist Jörgen Zoëga was one of the first who undertook a serious study of old Egyptian letters. Zoëga was unable to decipher the hieroglyphics, but he did reach one important conclusion on which Champollion based his later findings: He realized that the oval frames around certain signs indicated the name of a pharaoh.

Champollion's short but amazing life seems marked by fate. Even before his birth, a seer predicted that Jean-François's father, a bookseller in Figeac in the south of France, would sire a "light of coming centuries," and Jean-François, born in 1790, showed early talent. He was not even five when he had his mother read passages from the Bible out loud, which he would then repeat word for word.

Frightened by his youngest son's intelligence, the father forced his wife to stop reading to the child, which prompted the five-year-old to steal a Bible from his father's store and study it in secret. The little boy could neither read nor write, but he knew pages and pages of the Bible by heart, and he knew where to find those passages in the book. He compared the sounds of the language with the length of the printed word, found agreements, and determined that the French pronunciation often deviated from the written word. However, his father sent him to the local schools in Figeac, determined that Jean-François be a normal boy, not a child prodigy.

The Rosetta Stone

Jean-François's older brother, Jacques-Joseph, was himself something of a tragic figure. He had studied history and become interested in ancient Egyptian art, and when Napoleon set off on his Egyptian campaign in 1798, Jacques-Joseph tried in vain to have himself included among the scholars and historians Napoleon took with him. Bitterly disappointed, he gave up history, moved to Grenoble, and went into business.

In 1801 Jacques-Joseph, recognizing his younger brother's genius, sent for him in order to give him a better education in Grenoble. Jacques-Joseph had a subscription to the *Courier d'Egypte,* the last echo of a suppressed passion. This newspaper in his brother's home would determine young Champollion's future.

One day the paper published a report about a stone Napoleon's troops had found in the Nile delta in 1799, near the village of Rosetta. The stone was of basalt. Upon it were three paragraphs in different scripts: the first one hieroglyphic, the second presumably either Coptic or demotic (a simplified form of hieratic writing), and the third, finally, Greek.

The Greek was easy to translate. It was a thank-you note

Egyptian documents are preserved in three different kinds
of script. Top: Hieroglyphics with about 600 picture signs.
Middle: Examples of hieratic script in use since the Vth
dynasty. Bottom: The demotic script widely used since
the sixth century.

from the priests of Memphis, written in 196 B.C. to Ptolemy
V, who had just become king. Ptolemy had enjoyed wide
popularity because he remitted the priests' back taxes, made
new sources of income available to the temple treasuries,

and provided special protection for the temples in time of war. Also, he had made more generous gifts to the deified Apis and Mnevis bulls than Egyptian kings had done in the past. All this prompted the priests to have a stone sculpted for the king with this address:

Immortal Ptolemy, beloved of Ptah and of Epiphanes, the god, who has done so much for the temples and their dwellers, who live under his rule, because he is a god, and the son of a god and a goddess. He is like Horus, the son of Isis and Osiris, who protected his father from harm.

It seemed reasonable to assume that the first two texts were identical with the Greek. Consequently the Rosetta Stone was copied and sketched, and casts were even made from it. Scholars all over the world tried to decipher the characters.

Jean-François Champollion was eleven years old when he decided to decipher the Rosetta Stone. The boy's enormous energy and patience is documented by the fact that he spent twenty-one years trying to solve the riddle, years during which he came closer and closer to unlocking the stone's secret.

By the time Champollion left school in 1807 at the age of seventeen to enter the Academy of Sciences, he was studying Coptic, the development of hieratic script, and the demotic that was derived from it. He discovered that, unlike Coptic script, hieroglyphics had eight personal pronouns which corresponded to analogous sound signs. This allowed him to conclude that hieroglyphics were made up of sounds as well as symbols. Champollion counted 486 Greek words on the Rosetta Stone, but 1,419 heiroglyphics. He moved ahead as he had done when he could neither read nor write and had compared the written Bible with his memorized texts.

The names of pharaohs and proper names, he reasoned, would have to sound the same in all three languages. The English physician Thomas Young had already decoded Ptolemy's name on the basis of the largest number of repetitions in the text. Champollion took a detour. He ordered drawings made of an obelisk from whose Greek text he knew that the

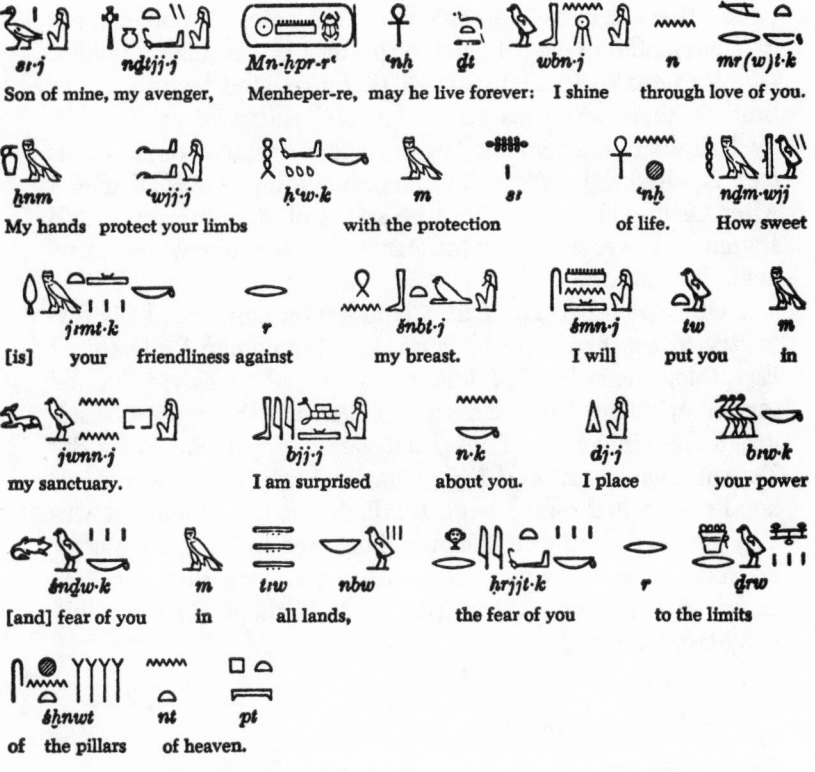

Son of mine, my avenger, Menheper-re, may he live forever: I shine through love of you. My hands protect your limbs with the protection of life. How sweet [is] your friendliness against my breast. I will put you in my sanctuary. I am surprised about you. I place your power [and] fear of you in all lands, the fear of you to the limits of the pillars of heaven.

Egyptian hieroglyphics are word and syllable symbols. This text example gives the phonetic spelling and its translation. (There are no vowels in the phonetic spelling because the Egyptians did not know them.)

name Cleopatra was used repeatedly. He integrated the sound signs into his own system, recognizing the letters L, P, and T, which are also part of Ptolemy's name. The symbol in front of the L in Cleopatra had to be either a K or a C.

When, on September 14, 1822, Champollion received copies of several pharaonic inscriptions, he was able to decode two of them at once: Rameses and Thutmose. No doubt about it—Champollion had solved the mystery of the hieroglyphics.

"Je tiens l'affaire [I've got it]!" he shouted joyfully to his brother, then raised his arms high and collapsed as if struck by lightning. He remained unconscious for five days. (This fact is cited by several authors, including Adolf Erman.) After Champollion recovered he spoke of strange visions and stammered over and over the names of pharaohs whose characters he had decoded.

On September 27, 1822, Champollion announced his discovery to the Academy in Paris. He was named Professor of Egyptology and in 1827 finally dispatched to Egypt "in the service of science" to head an expedition with Ippolito Rosellini of the University of Pisa that was jointly financed by the Tuscan government and King Charles X of France. His childhood dream had finally been fulfilled, but the fulfillment was also his death sentence. Champollion died in 1832, soon after his return from Egypt, seized with a paralytic disorder. The cause of death was never really established. He was only forty-two years old.

The Versatile Belzoni

No less mysterious was the death at an early age of Giovanni Battista Belzoni (1778–1823), probably the most colorful of early Egyptian excavators. The son of a Paduan barber, the huge Belzoni held many different jobs and tried many professions. His pious parents had wanted him to become a priest, but he was in turn a circus performer and strong man, actor, opera singer, engineer, and explorer. It is almost simpler to recount the things he was not.

Belzoni spent precious little time in Italy, the land of his birth, living instead in England, Portugal, and Africa. He went to England with a group of actors and, since he spoke only broken English, made a virtue out of necessity and performed as a mime. Later he advanced to opera singer and during a stay in Lisbon married the then well-known diva, Angelica Valabreque.

Belzoni could not explain even to himself his thirst for travel. Something kept pushing him from one place to another, and after he had tried out a dozen or so professions, he had calling cards printed up describing himself simply as "the celebrated traveler."

Belzoni adored Africa. He explored much of West Africa and tried to solve the riddle—much discussed at the time—as to whether the Nile and the Niger were really the same river. He first visited Egypt in 1815, not as a singer or archaeologist but as an inventor. He had constructed a waterwheel that was supposed to do four times the work of an ordinary one, and he offered his patent to the all-powerful sultan, Muhammed Ali. When his excellency gracefully declined the offer, the "celebrated traveler" turned to another business: archaeology.

The time was propitious. Since Napoleon's Nile expedition, things Egyptian were in demand all over the world. Drawings, paintings, and artifacts from the wonderland on the Nile sold for record prices. The strong man went to work. For five years he looked for hidden treasures; where his agile brain wouldn't do the job he used his muscle or, if need be, dynamite.

Through the intercession of Johann Ludwig Burckhardt, a Swiss traveler, he was referred to the British Consul General in Egypt, who hired Belzoni as forwarding agent and mover for the monumental bust of Memnon that had been found in Luxor. Belzoni took it to Alexandria, from where it was sent on to London. It was his start. The more antiquities he transported—an obelisk slipped into the Nile as he was trying to load it onto a wagon, but he fished it out of the river—the greater became his desire to dig on his own. Finally he was successful.

Belzoni wrote of conditions in the Theban City of the Dead in the early 1800s:

Once I was conducted . . . through a passage of about twenty feet in length, and no wider than that a body could be forced through. It was choked with mummies, and I could not pass without putting my face in contact with that of some decayed Egyptian; but as the passage inclined downwards, my own weight helped me on: however, I could not help being covered with bones, legs, arms, and heads rolling from above. Thus I proceeded from one cave to another, all full of mummies piled up in various ways, some standing, some lying, and some on their heads.[2]

In addition to countless mummies buried without the lavish trappings of the rich, or those whose treasures had already been stolen by grave robbers, Belzoni, after suffering many cruel disappointments, did discover some things of cultural significance. Even back in 1817 this wasn't easy. Many tombs, hewn into the rock, were home to the fellahin and their wives, children, and animals. Nevertheless, the professional traveler found a pharaoh's grave that year, to his great delight—that of Seti I, son of Rameses I. The tomb occupied Belzoni's attention a full year, for he had begun to develop a scholarly as well as a business interest in these excavations.

He copied reliefs and made drawings of what he found, writing in his diary that these discoveries made up for all the troubles of the explorations.

Belzoni became intoxicated with excavating, an intoxication that would prove his doom. He was particularly fascinated by the Khafre pyramid, the entrance to whose grave chamber was "lost." Feverishly the amateur archaeologist examined almost every stone in the 136-meter-tall structure. Yet he could not find a sign of any entrance. But Belzoni remained confident: If the chamber's door could not be found inside the pyramid (as was the case with the recently opened Khufu [Cheops] pyramid), then it had to be underground somewhere else.

Sand dunes towered to the north of the pyramid. Belzoni hastily hired labor battalions to remove them. And indeed, below the sand he found a passage obviously built by grave robbers later on. Then, halfway down the broad passage, a stone slab crashed into the entrance. Belzoni says the rock was 1.2 by 1.8 meters, about 4 by 6 feet. The stone trapped an Egyptian worker, but the knee-high sand in the passage saved his life and he was freed.

Tests on other rocks made it seem perilous in the extreme to continue; every boulder was loose. Belzoni found himself in a desperate situation. He spent days outside the somewhat larger Khufu pyramid, studying the huge hole in its side. He drew floor plans and sketches of the angles used. He compared the points of the compass and the direction of the blowing sand and finally came to the conclusion that the entrance to Khafre's pyramid had to be located farther east.

Three sand-covered granite blocks confirmed Belzoni's suspicion. A passage opened up behind them, which sloped down sharply and ended after 30 meters in front of a rock wall. It took Belzoni thirty days to break one stone out of the wall. Only then could he squeeze through the narrow opening.

He carried a torch of twisted wax candles. The passage ran horizontally. The orientation wasn't hard. The system of passages resembled that of the Khufu pyramid.

"As I walked further west," he reported, "I was surprised to find a grave in the floor. But I found only some stones and a few bones."

His disappointment grew when he found written in black script on one wall, "The stonemason Muhammed Ahmed opened this chamber. Master Osman was present; so was King Ali Muhammed, from the beginning to the end." Belzoni was a few centuries too late.

Even though this adventure was not crowned by complete success, Belzoni made a good deal of money from the graves he unearthed, as, for example, when he sold the sarcophagus from Seti's tomb. In 1820, when Belzoni returned to England from Egypt, he put his treasures on exhibit, and that earned him enough money to finance another expedition into Africa.

But he never saw Egypt again. Didn't the curse of the pharaohs follow him too?

In the spring of 1823 Belzoni and his wife left London for Tangier on a leaky old tub with a cabin for six people and one washroom. There were gaps in the planking so large that waves spilled through them during high seas. It was April when they landed. Belzoni wanted to cross the Sahara and push down to the Sudan. His wife accompanied him as far as Fès and then, as they had agreed in advance, she returned to England.

Soon afterward, Belzoni himself had to turn back—Tuareg tribesmen prevented him and his native bearers from penetrating any farther into the interior—so he decided to continue his voyage by ship in the direction of Sierra Leone. There he was ravaged by that mysterious disease seemingly suffered by other archaeologists, with its raging fevers and raving delusions.

A medicine man gave Belzoni resin oil and opium. "I feel the hand of death on me," the gravely ill explorer cried out. He was brought aboard his ship in the hope that the salty brine would help. His speech was confused and disjointed. Then he said, "I only have a few hours to live. I know it," and he pulled an amethyst from his finger. "Give this ring to my wife," he told his black servant. He died on the afternoon of that day—December 3, 1823—at the age of forty-five.

What Killed Professor Bilharz?

No less puzzling than Belzoni's early death are the circumstances surrounding the death in Egypt at age thirty-seven of the Swabian doctor and scientist, Theodor Bilharz. The son of a minor dignitary at a small German court, little Theodor began collecting stones, plants, and beetles while still in school. He wrote a catalogue for his collection and kept careful files. Except for math he was a model student. At eighteen he registered at the University of Freiburg in order to study medicine, zoology, the history of literature, archaeology, and classical art. Two years later he left Freiburg for Tübingen, where he planned to complete his medical education. As chance would have it, the dean of the medical school at Tübingen had organized a scientific competition. Bilharz took part, wrote about "our present knowledge of the blood of invertebrates," and won first prize. On passing his oral exams, the essay was accepted as his thesis (which medical students were then required to write), and he was granted his medical degree.

His first jobs were as a researcher in Tübingen and Freiburg. In Tübingen he worked with the internist Wilhelm Griesinger; when the latter was summoned to Egypt early in the 1850s to become the viceroy's personal physician and medical director, he took young Bilharz along as his assistant. Of course, Bilharz never imagined that he would succeed Griesinger as quickly as he did. But the older man had imagined his duties at court somewhat differently and he soon quit, leaving the field clear for Bilharz.

Now the young man could devote himself to all his early college interests at once. He took part in excavations, where his help was doubly welcome, partly because of his profound archaeological knowledge and partly because of a mastery of languages which allowed him to interpret among Arabic, English, and Italian teams.

Named Professor of Descriptive Anatomy at the University of Freiburg in 1856, Bilharz took great interest in autopsies of mummies, an interest sparked by his work in anthropology and pathology. Thus as an anthropologist he presented the university with a crate load of Egyptian skulls in honor of the school's 400th anniversary in 1857. As a pathologist, his gift was to mankind; he discovered the cause of a heretofore mysterious tropical illness which had scourged Egypt for thousands of years, a disease now named bilharzia for him. It is carried by a tiny parasitic worm, *Schistosoma haematobium*, found in the Nile's mud; the parasite's calcified eggs have been discovered in the kidneys of mummies dating back to the XXth dynasty.

At the time Bilharz conducted his research in Egypt, the people of the Nile lived in constant fear of disease; plague, typhus, and cholera still took the same toll they had in centuries past. But Robert Koch and Louis Pasteur's bacteriological discoveries had made cause and cure of such diseases a popular issue for the first time.

In the summer of 1858 four European tourists died within a few days of each other, after having visited the Giza pyramid and the pharaohs' tombs in the Valley of the Kings. No one mentioned the curse of the pharaohs but only talked about plague and typhoid. In order to allay the public's fears, an autopsy was performed on the four victims. For the record the causes of death were listed variously as the oriental plague, pneumonia with plague symptoms, petechial fever, and typhoid. But the Austrian surgeon Alexander Reyer and his countryman, anatomist Georg Lautner (both had joined the Alexandria health services after these deaths), attested later that the autopsy results had been altered. In any case, the two doctors could not give a medical explanation for the death of the four tourists.

The autopsy reports, however, prompted Alexandria's health authorities to put the port city under quarantine, which badly damaged Egypt's tourist-oriented economy. Only after Lautner and Reyer arrived on the scene and advised lifting these hasty measures were they removed. The incident illustrates the importance attached to the cause of death—as listed in death certificates.

In 1858 Bilharz was named a vice president of the Egyptian Society and found himself facing increasing social obligations. As linguist and art historian he was much in demand for showing Egypt's archaeological treasures to visiting VIPs. When Duke Ernst II of Coburg-Gotha came to Egypt in the summer of 1862 (the duke was interested in hunting; his wife wanted to see the graves of the Valley of the Kings), Bilharz was selected as the duchess's guide to Luxor. On the trip back to Cairo, Bilharz suffered violent feverish cramps. When Professor Lautner learned of his condition, he had Bilharz brought to his house, where he spent two weeks in a coma; then he died without ever regaining consciousness. Lautner was not able to establish a diagnosis as to cause of death. The official records show that Bilharz died of typhoid fever. Lautner disagreed, arguing that his friend and colleague had fallen victim to a mysterious fever. But where had it come from and what had caused it?

Three Basic Causes of Death

The list of Egyptian archaeologists who died mysteriously in the last century seems endless, but on closer examination three causes of death seem to predominate: fever with delusions and anticipation of death, strokes accompanied by circulatory collapse, and sudden cancers that were quickly terminal.

Richard Lepsius (1810–1884), the famous German archaeologist who shipped whole tombs from the Valley of the Kings to Berlin (among them a column from Seti I's grave), lived longer than most of his professional colleagues, but he too suffered a stroke which left him half paralyzed, and doctors diagnosed cancer as the immediate cause of his death.

The Egyptologist Georg Möller (1877–1921), who directed the excavation of the prehistoric grave field of Abu Sir and of the Theban City of the Dead near Deir el-Medina, was an expert in ancient Egyptian burial rites and spent much time inside tombs. Son of a German businessman, he was born in Caracas, but his parents returned to Germany when he was six in order to give him a good education. Like many Egyptologists he became fascinated by his future profession while still a boy and could decipher hieroglyphics in high school, and at twenty-eight was appointed scientific attaché at the German Consulate General in Cairo. He died at only forty-four while on a trip to Uppsala. Cause of death: feverish chills.

James Henry Breasted, professor at the University of Chicago whose research enjoyed Rockefeller support, was a veteran of many Egyptian expeditions, having gone there first as a young man in 1894 with a freshly minted Ph.D. from the University of Berlin. Over the years he began to suffer from fever. His son, Charles Breasted, reported that even before his arrival in Luxor he had begun to feel again the same feverish malaise. . . . This condition now grew worse.

Each afternoon a fever returned to plague him with an aching throat and with alternate chills and periods when his blood burned in his veins and throbbed in his head. He assumed that he was suffering a recurrence of malaria . . . but laboratory tests by the attending English physician failed to identify or quinine to allay the malady. The doctor ordered him to bed where he remained for more than six weeks throughout which with clocklike regularity the fever continued to return every noon and to recede in the early hours of the morning. He was permitted to get up only when Carter urgently required his presence at the tomb for consultations. On such occasions, with a linen mask over his mouth and nostrils to guard against dust, he would make the ten-mile round trip to The Valley in an open carriage (which had to be ferried across the river), to return utterly exhausted and shaking with the fever.[3]

Breasted had planned an expedition into the Sinai Peninsula and despite his illness was hard at work on the Edwin Smith surgical papyrus. In fact, he was so confident of making his trip that he said he'd go even if he had to be carried. But then fate interfered in the form of a Canadian professor of literature named La Fleur.

Quite by chance [Breasted wrote] he was given a room directly alongside my father's. We met him, were much attracted to him. He had letters to Howard Carter, which I delivered for him. Soon after his arrival he fell ill with influenza from which he was just beginning to recover when he received an invitation from Carter to come at once to see the tomb. He was still abed with a fever but being loath to miss such a rare opportunity, he got up and visited the tomb.

That night he became desperately ill.[4]

The next night, about three in the morning, the English doctor stepped out of La Fleur's room. Charles, who was still awake, approached him. The doctor nodded silently. La Fleur was dead.

As I stood waiting in the stillness, I thought: there is something especially sad about dying alone in the night in this strange country, beside the great, ageless river, in a hotel crowded with unknowing fellow humans. . . .

The doctor returned with two native servants carrying a long wicker basket in which the four of us bore La Fleur away. Afterward the doctor and I packed his things. When we had finished, he said abruptly, "We must keep your Pater from going on that journey—he might start, but he would never return!" . . .

The early morning sunlight was flooding my father's room and he had finished his breakfast abed when the doctor and I entered to plead with him again. . . .

"I know quite well what you're about to say." He smiled at us both. . . . "I think I appreciate your concern a little better after what occurred last night. . . . I heard our friend's silence. We'll abandon the Sinai venture—but only temporarily!" [5]

It never took place.

Although wracked by fever, Breasted continued to work with Carter on the as-yet-unopened Tutankhamen sarcophagus. He also acted as intermediary in the bitter fight between Carter and the Egyptian government about rights to the tomb. Next to Carter, he spent more time in Tutankhamen's tomb than anyone else.

Breasted, who recovered in Luxor from his illness, reported that Carter had appeared sick and feeble and that at times he had not seemed all there and had had difficulty making decisions. And yet Carter, for whom the tomb had become a second home, survived all the other excavators. His long life (he died at the age of sixty-six) is cited as an argument against the efficacy of the curse of the pharaohs. But I believe that this is one of those famous exceptions that proves the rule.

Breasted's wife, who had often accompanied her husband on his expeditions, died in July, 1934. Charles wrote about his mother's death that she had grown more and more tired until finally she fell into a sleep from which she did not wake.

Breasted survived his wife by only a year and a half. He was married again—to Imogene Hart, his wife's younger sister, whom he took to Egypt.

"I am as keen as a boy to get back to my desk and to

begin the revision of my *History of Egypt*," he wrote on November 21, 1935, from the harbor of Genoa. He was on his way home.

In mid-Atlantic [Charles wrote] a sore throat he had acquired in Italy flared up with a high fever which he mistook for a recurrence of his old malaria, and which the Italian ship's doctor treated as such. When the ship reached New York he was desperately ill with what was found to be a virulent hemolytic streptococcic infection which at this time, before the advent in America of sulfa drugs, was still invariably fatal. Though they marvelled at his magnificent refusal to surrender, the attending doctors, and the Rockefeller Institute for Medical Research which Mr. Rockefeller placed at their disposal, were helpless.[6]

Breasted died on December 2, 1935. The pharaohs, to whom he had devoted so much of his life, had called him home.

4   Graves and Gangsters

At 8:14 P.M. on February 8, 1973, the German news agency DPA carried a story from Egypt. It was headlined, FIVE THOUSAND ANCIENT EGYPTIAN GRAVES ROBBED. Few papers bothered to print the story; it seemed incredible. And yet, in eighteen lines DPA had reported the greatest Egyptian grave-robbing scandal in twenty years.

"There's shooting at Jebel Abu Sir." With these words a cotton worker stormed into the police station at Beni Suef, 120 kilometers southwest of Cairo on the west bank of the Nile, a small provincial capital noteworthy only because it did not have a railroad station. The Abu Sir mountain (*jebel* means mountain in Arabic) lies at the edge of the desert. Few people live near there.

It was dark when a police patrol drove out to the area. Lights could be seen far off between the rocks, and there was the sound of gunfire. As the police car drew near, the shooting stopped and the lights went out. The car's searchlight picked out a huge construction site. Here, at the edge of the desert?

There was no reply when the police shouted into the darkness. A ladder stuck out of a hole in the ground. When a policeman shone a flashlight into the shaft he saw three men about 20 meters down.

"What's up?" he asked.

"Don't shoot," was the answer from below.

Frightened, the three men climbed up the ladder. At first they assured the police that they had had nothing to do with the shooting. But once at the police station they came out with the truth.

Seven months ago one of them had discovered an Egyptian tomb on Jebel Abu Sir, a few days later a second, and soon a whole row of graves. He told some of his friends from the cotton plant about his find, and they decided to exploit the discovery together.

The longer the cotton workers dug, the more graves they found. Finally they quit work and did nothing but dig, at first in secret with guards posted for protection, later during day and night shifts without guards. Whoever stumbled on their activities was invited to join in, for the earth hid limitless treasures, did it not?

Business flourished for seven months. No one commented on the fact that several of the former factory workers, who still lived in clay huts, suddenly bought cars, albeit used cars. No one could comment, really, for all those who might have done so were themselves sharing in the business.

Then, early in February, two diggers opened a tomb whose content and furnishings surpassed the five thousand graves discovered so far.

"We've found a pharaoh's mummy!" The report spread like wildfire. The community of grave robbers demanded a share of the proceeds, but the two "finders" refused. They were summarily expelled from the syndicate.

When the two went back to "their" tomb at night in order to fetch the booty, shooting broke out and the whole enterprise collapsed. It may all sound like an adventure novel, but it actually happened in 1973.

The extent of the operation just described is unusual—five thousand graves aren't robbed every year—but plundering tombs remains almost an everyday occurrence in Egypt. Anyone who visits Biban al Moluk, west of Luxor, and shows any sign of archaeological curiosity, is surrounded by boys in rags and taken to dry gray huts at the rocky foot of the mountain. An unusually friendly Egyptian, at least for that region, pulls a small package wrapped in newspaper out of his burnoose and says piously, "Mummy, mister?"

The astonished tourist may feel a little queasy once the package is unwrapped: human hands, fingers, feet, and heads with skin, hair, and nails, shrunken and dried black. The price for a small black hand is often 50 marks ($17); a head costs more.

Mummies are still dug up today on the western bank of the Nile near Luxor—not kings, to be sure, but common people, buried with less pomp and circumstance, often in mass graves. These discoveries have little importance in terms of art history, but since the government requires that all such findings be turned over to the authorities, a black market flourishes. Often such illegal transactions take place under the benevolent gaze of white-clad Egyptian police. The dealer is quick to soothe tourist concern. "They belong to us," he will say in his halting English.

The Mummy Factory of Dr. Benam

In addition to illegal sales of mummies, forging them has also become lucrative.

Early in the 1950s Cairo police turned up the greatest mummy-forging scandal to that time. A well-known doctor, Ali Schükri Benam, M.D., was found to be the head of a gang with links to nearly every major Egyptian collection. In the seized correspondence of the mummy enterprise, police found names of many prominent private collectors as well.

Dr. Benam's secret was quickly revealed. He maintained good contacts with the city's gravediggers. For a fixed fee they brought him corpses, which Dr. Benam's staff spent weeks converting to likenesses of ancient Egyptian mummies, using the textbooks of Cairo University's Anatomical Institute, which had worked on royal mummies, as guides. Dr. Benam mailed out offerings wholesale whenever he had a new batch of mummies ready.

The "company" went out of business on June 2, 1952.

71

That was the day customs officials in the harbor of Port Said discovered four longish crates aboard the freighter *Enchantress*. When they asked what was in them, they were offered a large bribe to look at the rest of the *Enchantress* cargo instead.

The customs officials, however, remembered their duty and demanded that the boxes be opened. Thereupon they were presented with official customs declarations allowing the export of four ancient Egyptian mummies. The sudden appearance of "genuine" documents made the customs men even more suspicious. They had the boxes taken off the ship and opened. It turned out that not only had the customs declarations been forged but the mummies as well.

The police had long harbored such suspicions. The government Director of Egyptian Antiquities had been concerned for some time because mummies without traceable origins were being sold on world markets.

The exporter told police a man named Muhammed Nezlet Manauat had given him the commission to ship the forgeries. But the address turned out to be false. Then chance aided police. A truck ground to a halt with a broken axle near the great Khan el Khalili bazaar in Cairo. Several boxes slid onto the roadway. A policeman rushed up, anxious to get the traffic obstacle out of the way. As he did, he saw a mummified head of a corpse below the smashed box lid. The truck driver swore by Allah that he had nothing to do with the whole thing and told the authorities the name of the man who had given him the shipment: Dr. Ali Schükri Benam.

The last act of the drama proved spectacular. Police surrounded the whole district in which Dr. Benam's house stood. Then they stormed the building. Several of the doctor's employees were found busily embalming corpses and packing them in "genuine" sarcophagi. Other "prepared" corpses were stored in the attic.

A spokesman for Cairo's Egyptian Museum opined, after inspecting the forger's laboratory, "I believe that seventy percent of all the mummies which were shipped from Egypt during the last decade were forgeries."

Money has always played a large role in excavations in the Valley of the Kings: money, ambition, rivalry. Studious idealists were not the only ones who dug here; money-grubbing treasure hunters and naïve adventurers did too. Small wonder that the history of Thebes' City of the Dead is one long adventure story, beginning with its earliest monument on the eastern slopes of El Cocha, the grave of Princess Ihi (Middle Kingdom), down to the discovery of Tutankhamen's tomb.

The City of the Dead, west of Luxor, stretches for three kilometers in a north-south direction. Even today we don't know the real name of the splendid capital the Greeks called Thebai, on the eastern bank of the Nile some 500 kilometers below Cairo, but there is eloquent testimony of her past glory.

Thebes' rise began during the XIth dynasty. Powerful local princes of the Mentuhotep family built a temple in Karnak such as the world had never seen. It was dedicated to Amon, one of the eight original gods of Harmopolis, a city in Middle Egypt. Curiously, the city's graveyard on the west bank of the Nile did not contain very many graves, nor were the finds made in them very interesting. Indeed, from the XIIIth to the XVIth dynasty (1778–1610 B.C.) and during the rule of the Semitic shepherd kings, the Hyksos, Thebes sank into insignificance. But during the middle of the fourteenth century the kings of the New Kingdom sparked a renaissance that made Thebes the most beautiful city in the world. Memphis, for all its pyramids that ranged from Abu Roash in the north to Medum in the south, went into eclipse.

Thutmose III, the empress Hatshepsut, and Amenhotep III are the rulers who put their mark on the city—and on the Valley of the Dead on the other side of the river. A premature demise seemed to threaten "hundred-gated Thebes," to quote Homer, when Amenhotep IV shifted his official residence to Tell el-Amarna, halfway between Cairo and Luxor. But the heretic's reign would prove only a footnote of history, and the Theban City of the Dead remained a kind of mirror image of the centuries that had shaped Thebes itself.

The oldest relics at Thebes are found in the village of Qurna hard on the Libyan desert. Graves are hewn into the rocky ground for a distance of 1,200 meters and a width of about 200 meters. Presumably the graves of the XIth dynasty's first three kings—Intef I, Intef II, and Mentuhotep I—are to be found here. Auguste Mariette, a French archaeologist who dug in the 1860s, discovered pyramid remnants above the tombs, but they were modest in size, unlike the rocky vaults in the nearby Valley of the Kings. The higher court bureaucracy was buried near their rulers.

With the growing importance of the Theban kings as pan-Egyptian pharaohs, they sought more impressive surroundings for their last resting-places and picked the limestone-rich Deir el-Bahri gorge. Mentuhotep II built his tomb, topped by a pyramid, in the middle of the valley. Men close to Mentuhotep were buried in forty adjoining rock graves, among them his vizier, his chancellor, his eastern army commander, the head of his household, and the keeper of his bow. One singular aspect of this setup was three mass graves with sixty mummies—buried without coffins or embalming. They were soldiers who died in battle; their shrunken bodies were still pierced by arrows.

In order to pick up the significant historical strands we must now jump across four dynasties in time but move only about a thousand yards in space. With the advent of the XVIIth dynasty, the village of Abu'l Nega begins to win renewed importance because the Theban princes who drove out the Hyksos—some historians believe this is the source of the biblical Exodus—were buried there. One consequence of this "growth," however, was to make the Abu'l Nega tombs the most plundered in the valley. The antique Abbott papyrus reported that six pharaohs' vaults had been robbed. On the other hand, the grave of the relatively unimportant Nubcherper-re-Intef was not touched until 1827, when an Arab peasant (fellah) robbed it.

Mariette hit the jackpot in Abu'l Nega—to be sure, a questionable jackpot. Still unknown, but with a good record for discovering buried treasure, he was ordered by the viceroy Said Pasha to rebury several archaeological finds at some prominent spot. Said had learned from friends in Paris that Louis Bonaparte, Napoleon III's cousin, planned to visit Egypt, and as a special mark of respect the glory of past millennia was to be dug up in the visitor's presence and then presented to him. To his regret, Mariette had to scratch the artfully buried object out of the ground without the cousin from Paris present; the prince had changed his plans and didn't come. Still, Mariette sent his "find" to his grace, Louis Bonaparte, in Paris. The move didn't hurt his career. The influence of the Bonapartes in Egypt was still great enough that Mariette was named "Directeur de Service des Antiquités" by return mail.

Servants in the Abode of Truth

Even if we are to ignore the countless private graves of this region, where more people can allegedly be found below ground than above it, we must take a brief look at the grave field of Deir el-Medina. It was reserved for a special group: not kings or court officials or the wealthy, but the sculptors, masons, painters, and foremen who had created the magnificent subterranean buildings in the Valley of the Tombs of the Queens (Biban al Harim) and the Valley of the Tombs of the Kings (Biban al Moluk). These men were granted an honorary title: Servants in the Abode of Truth.

Since even then artists enjoyed writing down their thoughts, no other profession has left us more ample a record than the tomb builders in the Valley of the Kings. Artists' papyri are rare, but their records are legion. Even trivial or unimportant events were scratched onto limestone, sandstone, or clay, stuffed into a pocket, and tossed away later.

Servants in the Abode of Truth lived in an artists' colony in Gurnet Mura'i. It was the only settlement on the west bank of the Nile. The lists of the village registry have come down to us.[1] They cite not only all the inhabitants and their professions but also the number of people who lived in each house—and there were 155 houses.

These artists and artisans worked with deep faith in the divinity of the dead pharaohs. We know from various papyri, for example, that they did not consider themselves worthy of praying to the gods of the official religion and only called upon their own gods, the gods of the little people.

The treasures of Biban al Moluk have never been matched in history, neither the works of art which slaves and prisoners of war hacked out of the rock under conditions of incredible deprivation nor the dazzling wealth the court bureaucracy and the relatives of the kings stored there. Small wonder that a thousand years before the beginning of the Christian era and five hundred years after the first rock graves were built, most of the tombs had been robbed or plundered. The vault of Amenhotep II still sheltered the king's mummy but held no art treasures. And, as we have seen, ancient robbers twice tried to enter even Tutankhamen's tomb.

As a result, the New Kingdom pharaohs decided to stop erecting splendid buildings above the grave chamber. Temples and pyramids at the edge of the Libyan desert only served to attract thieves.

Amenhotep I and Thutmose I were the first to have their grave chambers hacked so deeply into the rock that they were invisible from the outside. Thutmose's architect, Ineni, reported on the construction in an inscription on his own grave —"I supervised the excavation of his majesty's rock grave all by myself without the work being seen or heard"—a statement that led the scholar Georg Steindorff to the somewhat controversial conclusion that prisoners of war who worked on the tomb "were sent to the happy hunting grounds after their labor was completed."

Pharaohs in Different Graves

But even if the graves of the pre-Christian era had not been plundered, few of them would have survived in their original form, since the rivalry among the divine kings did not halt at the stone tombs of their ancestors. Thutmose I was left to spend but a few years in his red sandstone sarcophagus before his daughter and successor, Hatshepsut—a woman who did everything she could to appear a man—kicked him out and put him in a tomb she had built for herself. (Her stone coffin had to be lengthened somewhat to fit its new tenant.)

Pharaohs could not be haled into court, however, while ordinary grave robbers could be and were. Trial records of these "ordinary" thieves describe how the tombs of Amenhotep III, Seti I, and Rameses II were plundered. First Rameses was put into Seti's grave. Then both mummies were taken into Queen Inhapi's vault. Later Rameses I would find his last resting-place there too. The French archaeologist Victor Loret's report compounds the confusion: In Amenhotep II's tomb he found Amenhotep III's mummy lying in Rameses III's sarcophagus, which, in turn, was closed with the lid from Seti II's sarcophagus.

Such cases were not rare. Here is a record from the XXth dynasty, about 250 years after Tutankhamen's death. It seems that a man named Peser, an official in the town on the east bank of the Nile (perhaps akin to our mayor), leveled a series of accusations against Pewer'o, who ran or managed the City of the Dead on the west bank. Peser accused his colleague of mismanagement and neglect. Expeditions to rob graves were the order of the day, Peser charged, and nothing was being done about them. Cha'emwese, the vizier (and regional governor), thereupon summoned a committee, made up of two priests, two scribes, and two police officers, to investigate the case.

Subsequently the committee delivered the following detailed report:

1. Re Peser's deposition addressed to the vizier and city manager Cha'emwese, to the Royal Lord High Steward, Nesamum, to the scribe of the Pharaoh, to the estate manager of the High Priestess of Amon-Re, to the Royal Lord High Steward Neferkere-em-per-Amon, to the Pharaoh's spokesman and to the Great Lord: The 120-ell-deep grave of Amenhotep I—located in the north of the Amenhotep temple—Peser claimed had been broken open was found to be intact.

2. The pyramid of Intef the elder, son of Re, was found undamaged. It lies in the courtyard of the Amenhotep temple, whose pyramid has been destroyed, but a memorial pillar with a picture of the king, his dog Behka between his legs, still stands outside.

3. The pyramid of King Nubcherper-re, son of Re Intef, was damaged by thieves. There was a hole at the foot of the pyramid, two ells wide. We discovered a second hole in the antechamber of the tomb of Jurai, director of offerings at the Amon temple. But the grave robbers had not been able to gain access directly into the graves.

4. We found the pyramid of King Sechemre Wepma't, son of Re Intef the elder, pierced in the same manner but not fully broken into.

5. The pyramid of King Sechemre Shedtawe, son of Re Sebekemsaf, was broken into from the outer hall of the tomb of Nebamun, Thutmose III's pantry director. The mummies of the king and of his wife, Chasnub, had been taken.

So much for the investigation and its report. The grave robbers were found and seized: eight stonemasons and servants of the Amon temple. After they were beaten they broke down and made the following confession:

We forced our way into the pyramid of King Sebekemsaf and his royal wife Chasnub, smashed their sarcophagi, and opened the shrouds in which they were bedded. The head and neck of the venerable mummy of King Sebekemsaf were covered with a long row of golden amulets and gold jewelry. The mummy was sheathed in gold, and the coffins contained gold and silver and magnificent diamonds. We ripped all the gold off the king's mummy and took the amulets and the jewelry on his neck and the shrouds. The mummy of the queen was furnished in the same way. We took everything we found and burned the mummification material. We also took all the gold, silver, and bronze household effects we could find. Then we divided the gold, the amulets, the jewelry, and the mummy shrouds into eight parts.

At that time the vizier was also chief judge. He oversaw six courts and their judges. The pharaoh appointed all judges, as he did the vizier Cha'emwese himself. All the evidence submitted at the trial was forwarded to the pharaoh for final disposition. Meanwhile, the thieves were held in a prison attached to Amon's temple. There are no records extant as to how the pharaoh disposed of this case, but grave robbery carried the death penalty.

Eight executions in Thebes, however (it is a safe bet that the robbers were killed), would have had no deterrent effect whatever. The temptation was too great. A single night's work promised a simple man wealth for life.

In the course of the millennia pharaohs' graves were discovered over and over. Diodorus wrote that records existed in Thebes for forty-seven royal graves there, but that during a journey to Egypt in 57 B.C. he could find only seventeen of them. Thirty years later Strabo said he had found forty worth seeing.

This raises an interesting question: Are there pharaohs' graves still waiting to be discovered?

I have asked this question of English and French archaeologists; they don't rule out the possibility but emphasize that discovery of an intact tomb is highly unlikely. Georg Steindorff and Walther Wolf, noted archaeologists both, have several graves on their "missing" list: those of Thutmose II and Smenkare, for example, and, above all others, Imhotep. As Walter B. Emery's assistant, Ali al Khouli, once told me while we stood on the spacious Sakkara grave field, "Look, somewhere out here the great Imhotep lies buried." And his arm swept across the horizon. "I just don't know exactly where."

The First Excavators

It is all Napoleon's fault: If it hadn't been for him, all Egypt including the Valley of the Kings might have spent another century as Sleeping Beauty, its rest only occasionally disturbed by bold adventurers like Richard Pococke, who discovered and described fourteen graves in the Valley of the Kings in the year 1745. But Napoleon discovered the land on the Nile not only for France (even though the French understood best how to take the greatest advantage of the discovery); his melodramatic pronouncement—"Soldiers, more than three thousand years of history look down upon you"— was heard all over Europe: by adventurers, scientists, and archaeologists.

The last were hardly scholars in the academic sense. Thus Giovanni Belzoni, whom we have already met, wrote about one of his trips into the Valley of the Kings that the close air in many of the tombs made many people faint; "A huge cloud of dust rises up that penetrates throat and nose; the lungs have trouble absorbing it all and to fight against the stench of the mummies." Furthermore:

> The entry or passage where the bodies are is roughly cut in the rocks, and the falling of the sand from the upper part or ceiling of the passage causes it to be nearly filled up . . . not more than a vacancy of a foot left. . . . Surrounded by bodies, by heaps of mummies in all directions; which, previous to my being accustomed to the sight, impressed me with horror. The blackness of the wall, the faint light given by the candles or torches for want of air, the different objects that surrounded me, seeming to converse with each other, and the Arabs with the candles or torches in their hands, naked and covered with dust, themselves resembling living mummies, absolutely formed a scene that cannot be described.[2]

The black walls point up the fact that modern explorers and their pitch torches did more damage to the tombs than ancient grave robbers, who generally did no more than take gold and utensils, whereas soot from the torches attacked the wall paintings and in some cases destroyed them.

The old Egyptians did not use torches in building and decorating the tombs, for one thing because they knew that soot would cause damage, for another because torches would have taken the last oxygen out of the rocky labyrinths hundreds of meters below ground and asphyxiated the workers. Instead, the Egyptians used something the native guides still use today: mirrors. Mirrors have no trouble conducting sunlight hundreds of meters into the rock. Extra mirrors, placed at the correct angles, can conduct light around corners or up and down. This procedure guaranteed the artists daylight and allowed them to judge the luminosity of colors with great accuracy. The Egyptian Antiquities Administration has learned from the ancients and uses white neon light in tombs open to the public. Only untutored laymen consider this a stylistic perversion.

Belzoni remarked about his daylight activities underground, not without pride, that

when my weight bore on the body of an Egyptian, it crushed it like a bandbox. I naturally had recourse to my hands to sustain my weight, but they found no better support; so that I sunk altogether among the broken mummies, with a crash of bones, rags, and wooden cases, which raised such a dust as kept me motionless for a quarter of an hour, waiting till it subsided again.[3]

The Warehouse of the Mummies

There are special reasons why a total of fifty-two royal mummies, some of which may be seen to this day in Room 52 of the Egyptian Museum of Cairo, survived in the rocks of Biban al Moluk despite organized armed efforts to steal them.

Guards protecting the treasures in the tombs were first attacked during Rameses III's reign (1197–1165 B.C.). As these attacks mounted, the priests of the XXIst dynasty put a carefully considered plan into action. They broke into every grave they knew of and took out all the royal mummies, forty-nine in all. Thirteen mummies were taken to the secret grave of Amenhotep II. The remaining thirty-six were carried by the priests in secret procession to a gully where a nine-meter-deep tube had been drilled into the rock. A passage led from the end of that shaft into a chamber seven meters by seven meters. The embalmed bodies of earlier rulers were placed in the room and walled in.

Their hiding place remained undiscovered for almost three thousand years, until one day in February, 1871.

Ahmed Abed el-Rasul was a fellah who lived in the village of Qurna, eking out a precarious existence by selling artifacts he found in illegal diggings. That day, however, he decided to dare more and had his brother Muhammed lower him on a rope into a mysterious labyrinth. He had known about its existence for a long time and had done some "acoustical" exploring by tossing rocks down the shaft. Now, once inside, he had to break through a stone wall. This done, he stood before the mummies the priests had brought here a thousand years before Christ's birth.

"Pull me up!" he shouted, terrified, to his brother, who dragged him back out into daylight.

"I've seen ghosts," Ahmed stammered, which prompted his accomplice to flee in terror.

Ahmed went back several times before he dared a second descent. Only then did he realize that the mummies still wore their jewelry, including the uraeus, stylized symbol of the asp, denoting sovereignty, on their foreheads. As a veteran grave robber he knew that he had discovered the mummies of pharaohs.

Illegal excavations were subject to heavy punishment even in the late nineteenth century. He could not afford, therefore, to let out the secret. Only Ahmed and his family knew. He reasoned, correctly, that he could not sell the mummies whole but had to mix up the valuables and fence them one by one.

In fact, Ahmed Abed el-Rasul told the secret to only one man outside his family: the Honorary Consul Mustafa Aga Ayat, who represented England, Belgium, and Russia in Luxor and enjoyed a reputation for absolute integrity. Ahmed had once briefly worked for him as a butler. For ten years the consul sold what Ahmed brought up from the labyrinth. They were such valuable finds and of such high quality that they puzzled the experts.

Sir Gaston Maspero, then Director of Antiquities for the Egyptian government, was the first to become suspicious. Sir Gaston had discovered several gems on the black market which he attributed without hesitation to the XXIst dynasty. A grave from that period must have been discovered somewhere, he reasoned. He bought several of these finds and traced their orgin. All trails led either to Consul Aga Ayat or to the Abed el-Rasul brothers.

Since he enjoyed diplomatic status as consul, Aga Ayat could not be arrested. Ahmed Abed el-Rasul denied everything and even when beaten did not reveal his secret; he was jailed for two months and then set free. Finally he had a fight with his brother, Muhammed, and his brother betrayed the mummy warehouse to the provincial governor.

Several years later the American archaeologist James Henry Breasted visited the hiding place. Here is his report:

"Habeeb and a guide begged me not to go down, but I ignored their nonsense and stripped myself of all superfluous clothing. As I could not trust them to let me down safely into the thirty-eight-foot shaft, I stationed them behind some projecting rocks, made them lie down, brace their feet as in a college 'tug-of-war' and hold fast to the rope. With a candle and some matches in my pocket, I swung over the edge and, hand over hand, let myself down to the bottom.

"I lighted my candle and began crawling along a very low passage, rendered smaller still by pieces which had fallen from the ceiling. After two right-angle turns, the passage led 195 feet into the mountain. The air, heated by the suns of thousands of years, was suffocatingly hot, and the perspiration poured from me. Behind and before me was inky darkness, and a silence so deep that even the burning of the candle flame became loudly audible.

"Suddenly there was a rushing sound, the candle went out, and in the first instant of darkness, something struck me full in the face. It was only a bat, but match after match failed to strike, and though there was nothing to be afraid of, it seemed an eternity in that horrible blackness till the candle flickered again.

"The passage ended in a chamber about twenty feet square. Here the priest kings of the Twenty-first Dynasty had concealed the bodies of the great kings of the Eighteenth and Nineteenth Dynasties. For even as far back as that time it had been impossible to protect their tombs against grave robbers. But here in this secret, rock-hewn chamber they had lain secure and undisturbed for nearly 3000 years, till modern natives—the descendants of those same early tomb robbers—in 1881 discovered them. . . .

"Huge blocks had fallen from the ceiling till it was difficult to move about in the chamber (a small piece came down while I was there). A few years will see it completely choked. If I was not the last visitor, there will be few after me. I put the candle on a fallen block, and sat down for a few minutes while my mind tried to envisage the strange scene which took place here 3000 years ago—first when the workmen cut this shaft and chamber into the limestone mountain, next when the most trusted men of the priesthood secretly brought the mummies (which to them already seemed very old) to this hiding place. If these walls could give out the voices which once reverberated against them, if by some miracle the full knowledge of a single member of that trusted group could be imparted to us, what a superlative chapter in the history of human development it would make! My heart thumped at the thought.

"I took up my candle again, crept back along the passage to the shaft, and pulled myself up into the heavenly brightness and relative coolness of the outer world."[4]

In the 1800s archaeology still held the promise of adventure and romance, especially in Egypt where, before the turn of the century, anyone who wanted to could begin digging. No one bothered about education or professional qualifications. As a result, merchants and circus performers, professors of literature and playboys pushed their spades into the sands of the Libyan desert or dug outside Nubia's gates. Charles Breasted gives a vivid account of how this was handled:

Assignment of sites and permission to excavate then rested with a government "Committee of Antiquities" which met only once a year. The chief condition it exacted of an excavator was that he must give half of his finds to the government. But if a site proved unfruitful or worthless, the excavator had no choice but to wait a year for the Committee to grant him a new one. At this time the least promising sites were assigned to European excavators, while the richest sites were given to native antiquity dealers who were permitted to carry on haphazard digging solely for commercial purposes.[5]

This practice and the great heat between March and September are the reasons why some excavations dragged on for many years.

The discovery of the remaining thirteen mummies hidden by the worried priests was the work of Victor Loret, who uncovered the tomb of Amenhotep II in 1898. The royal mummy was in excellent condition; evidently the tomb's location had been forgotten centuries ago. Loret moved the thirteen mummies who had lain here undisturbed for three thousand years to Cairo. But he left the pharaoh in his sarcophagus and posted armed guards outside the tomb, which was subsequently opened to visitors.

The guards proved unequal to their task. On November 24, 1901, thieves opened fire and the guards fled. The modern grave robbers, just as their forerunners had done several thousand years ago, tore the mummy apart, stole jewels and amulets, and even took a ship that was part of the tomb's treasure.

The robbery brought a man to the fore who had not yet made his mark: Howard Carter. Charles Breasted has described what happened:

He [Carter] had come out to Egypt a dozen years before as an archaeological draughtsman, had gradually been drawn into excavational work under both British and French auspices, and in 1899 had been appointed . . . as Inspector-in-Chief for the Monuments of Upper Egypt and Nubia, with headquarters at Thebes . . . and it had been at his suggestion and under his personal supervision that Mr. Davis had in 1902 undertaken the systematic exploration of the entire Valley of the Kings' Tombs. . . .

Though the chief guard had been absent, Carter held him responsible, immediately dismissed him, rounded up all suspects, forced the return of the loot, and brought the men to trial in Luxor. As this was unavoidably before a native court, the case dragged on interminably. Despite flagrant obstruction of justice and repeated threats upon Carter's life, the suspected parties were proven guilty beyond the slightest doubt. But the native judge finally declared them innocent, dismissed the charges.[6]

Carter had made himself unpopular with the Egyptians and was transferred to the Inspectorate of Lower and Middle

Egypt, with headquarters in Sakkara. He lost that job, too, after a scuffle with a group of drunken French tourists, and spent some time poor and penniless until, finally, Davis employed him as a draftsman. (We have seen that Carter left Davis when he found a more congenial patron in Lord Carnarvon.)

Theodore Davis dug steadily for twelve years, and he dug in an area where three others had stopped before him, being convinced there was nothing left to find. The result? Davis uncovered another seven graves: the tombs of Thutmose IV, Queen Hatshepsut, and Juja and Tuju; the grave of Amenhotep III's parents-in-law; the tomb of Horemheb and Siptah; an anonymous grave which harbored the jewels of Siptah's wife, Tewosrat; and another anonymous vault that contained jewelry and effects of Amenhotep IV, and of his mother, Teje.

When Davis turned in his digging license in 1914 he was convinced, as had been the men before him, that his discoveries in the Valley of the Kings would be the last. He could only shake his head in wonder at Lord Carnarvon and his ambitious English archaeologist, Howard Carter. If Davis had known what Carter and Carnarvon would discover, he would never have left them his digging license.

5 Autopsy of a Pharaoh

THE BODY in front of Professor Douglas Derry on November 11, 1925, had been dead for more than thirty-three hundred years. Tension inside Cairo University's Anatomical Institute mounted as the clock moved toward 9:45 A.M. Derry and Howard Carter stepped up to the white-shrouded figure on the autopsy table. The sheets hid the corpse of Tutankhamen.

On November 11, at 9:45 A.M., the examination of the royal mummy was commenced [Carter wrote]. There were present H. H. Saleh Enan Pasha, Under-Secretary of State to the Ministry of Public Works; H. H. Sayed Faud Bey el Khôli, Governor of the Province of Keneh; Monsieur Pierre Lacau, the Director-General of the Department of Antiquities; Dr. Douglas Derry, Professor of Anatomy in the Faculty of Medicine, Egyptian University; Dr. Saleh Bey Hamdi, Director of the Sanitary Services, Alexandria; Mr. A. Lucas, government chemist, Department of Antiquities; Mr. Harry Burton of the Metropolitan Museum of Art, New York; Tewfik Effendi Boulos, Chief Inspector of the Department of Antiquities, Upper Egypt; and Mohamed Shaaban Effendi, Assistant Curator, Cairo Museum.[1]

The autopsy had created intense excitement because so old and well preserved a pharaoh's mummy had never been dissected before.

Douglas Derry had scruples about performing the autopsy; perhaps he was afraid. He wrote in his notes—and it sounds like a thin excuse—

A word may fittingly be said here in defence of the unwrapping and examination of Tut-ankh-Amen. Many persons regard such an investigation as in the nature of sacrilege, and consider that the king should have been left undisturbed. [But given] the persistent robberies of the tombs . . . it will be understood that once such a discovery . . . has been made . . . to leave anything whatever of value in the tomb is to court trouble. The knowledge that objects of immense value lay hidden a few feet below ground would certainly invite the attempt to obtain them, and while the employment of a strong guard might suffice for a time to prevent any such attempt . . . any remission of vigilance would be instantly seized upon.[2]

Tutankhamen's mummy, incidentally, was taken to Cairo for the autopsy, as all pharaohs' mummies were, but was then buried again in his sarcophagus in the Valley of the Kings. He rests near Luxor to this day.

The external ornaments and inlaid gold trappings . . . having been removed [Carter continued his account], the king's mummy lay bare with its simple outer coverings and gold mask. . . .

The other wrappings consisted of one large linen sheet, held in position by three longitudinal (one down the centre and one at each side) and four transverse bands of the same material. . . . They were doubled, and varied from 2-¾ to 3-½ inches in width. The central longitudinal band, beginning the middle of the abdomen (in reality thorax), was passed under the lower layer of each of the three transverse bands, over the feet, under the soles, and doubled back below the second layer of transverse bands. . . . The mummy lay at a slight angle, suggesting that it had been subjected to some shock when lowered into the sarcophagus. There was also similar evidence to imply that unguents had been poured over the mummy and coffin before they were lowered into the sarcophagus—the liquid being at different levels on the two sides, suggesting the tilting of the coffin.

In consequence of the fragile and carbonized condition of the linen swathing, the whole of the exposed surface was painted over with melted paraffin wax of such a temperature that when congealed it formed a thin coating on the surface, with minimum penetration of the decayed wrappings beneath. When the wax had cooled, Dr. Derry made a longitudinal incision down the centre of the outer binding to the depth penetrated by the wax, thus enabling the consolidated layer to be removed in large pieces. Nor did our troubles end here. The very voluminous under-wrappings were found to be in even worse condition of carbonization and decay. We had hoped, by removing a thin outer layer of bandage from the mummy, to free it at the points of adhesion to the coffin so that it might be removed, but in this we were again disappointed. It was found that the linen beneath the mummy and the body itself had been so saturated by the unguents which formed a pitch-like mass at the bottom of the coffin and held it embedded so firmly, that it was impossible to raise it except at risk of great damage. Even after the greater part of the bandages had been carefully removed, the consolidated material had to be chiselled away from beneath the limbs and trunk before it was possible to raise the king's remains.[3]

Jewelry, 143 pieces in all, each bedded in a small linen pillow so as not to disturb the outer shape of the mummy, appeared between individual sheets of bandage as they were unrolled. The closer the linen bandages were to the body, the more decomposed. One could see clearly that the torso had been bandaged crosswise. Arms, legs, and penis were wrapped separately first and then pulled into the whole bandage system. The right hand lay on the left hip, the left hand on the right ribs, so that the arms were crossed. Fingers and toes were wrapped in cloth with gold pods laced over them. Straight and diagonal strips of linen enclosed the head; below them appeared a kind of pillow crown, like Osiris' tall crown, or atef. Presumably the pillow was designed to protect Tutankhamen's face from the heavy golden mask placed over it.

An amulet—a semicircle atop a stalk supposed to represent a neck support—lay on this pillow. It is worth special attention for two reasons: first, it was made of iron, a material found nowhere else in the tomb; second, there was a symbolic meaning in its presence, as explained in Chapter 166 of the Book of the Dead:

"Awake from the swoon in which you sleep. You will triumph over everything done against you. Ptah has overcome your enemies. They no longer exist."

Radiologists have long puzzled over this strange amulet. The theory that radioactivity explains the deadly curse of the pharaohs will be examined in chapter 11; it is startling enough to note here that what may be interpreted to be a pronouncement of doom in the Book of the Dead should come true so quickly for two of the scientists present at the autopsy.

Tutankhamen wore twenty-one other amulets around his neck, but their meaning and symbolism are easier to divine. Basically, their function had to do with the burial process: in part they were technical devices, such as balances, in part pure decoration.

As the strips of linen were removed, an Isis symbol, two golden Osiris symbols, and a scepter of green feldspar appeared. Next came three gold pendants in palm and snake shape, a feldspar thoth, a snake head of red chalcedony, a Horus pendant of lapis lazuli, an Anubis of feldspar and a papyrus scepter made of the same material. The eight amulets on the bottom sheet included a winged snake with human heads, a royal snake, a double royal snake, and five vultures.

These amulets around the neck of the dead pharaoh had only one purpose: to protect him on his journey to the empire of the dead. The people had great faith in these amulets. The only question is whether the priests who represented the intellectual upper classes of ancient Egypt believed in the magic power of these amulets too, or if, knowing their own impotence in these matters, they used scientific discoveries to reinforce the amulets' power.

For that purpose it was not necessary to know the *theory* of a science such as, say, radiology or virology. Its effectiveness alone was important. A curious example of this is the small bags of sand which were sold in Bohemia's Joachim Valley as headache and rheumatism remedies long before the discovery of radiation therapy. Doctors threw fits about this "occult nonsense" of putting bags on the areas of pain. But the patients claimed they helped. Who was right? The answer is startling. It was certainly not the doctors. The bags contained earth with radium in it, uranium pitchblende, and thus were slightly radioactive. And radium, for example, dissolves uric acid into hydrochloric acid and ammonia. A seemingly senseless bag of sand, therefore, was in a position to trigger physiological reactions, although this seemed scientifically impossible and although the corresponding scientific methodology had not yet been discovered.

None of this is intended to make general acceptance of superstition and the occult easier; on the contrary, it is designed to explore methods that might explain the hitherto inexplicable.

It is a fact that the Greeks incorporated mystic healing methods and the Egyptian faith in miracles into their own science. Despite their critical observation of natural phenomena and the analytic research of men like Hippocrates, the idea of "demons of disease," which came from Egypt, played an important role in Greek thought, an indication of the great influence Egyptian culture had on other peoples even as it declined. Nor did the mysticism practiced by the Egyptian priesthood prevent the priests from using the great discoveries of natural science—discoveries perhaps forgotten soon after they were made and only being dug out of the rubble of the past in our own day, discoveries perhaps still buried under the dust of centuries.

What is the T?

Twenty-one amulets had appeared, and Dr. Derry was still unwinding bandages from arms and legs before getting to work on the rump. As Carter wrote in his three-volume study of the tomb's discovery:

Both the forearms were smothered from elbow to wrist with magnificent bracelets, seven on the right and six on the left forearm, composed of intricate scarab devices, granular gold-work, open-work carnelian plaques. . . . Their diameter shows that they had encircled a very small arm, none of them was of sepulchral nature, but all were obviously once personal ornaments that had been worn during life.

Each finger and thumb, having been primarily wrapped in fine strips of linen, was enclosed in a gold sheath. Upon the second and third fingers of the left hand was a gold ring. . . .

We now come to the abdomen, distributed over which, in almost as many layers, were ten objects. . . . At the left flank, within the first few outer bandages, was a curious Y-shaped amulet of sheet-gold and an oval gold plate, placed one immediately above the other. The meaning of the Y-shaped amulet is not clear. A similar object depicted in the Middle Kingdom coffin texts carries the name *abt* or *abet*, which seems to convey something of the nature of a baton, but as this symbol forms in shape part of the hieroglyphic determinative *mnkh* for clothing or linen, it would seem more likely to have some reference to the bandages, or bandaging of the mummy, the more so, as the second object—the oval metal plate found with it—has direct relation with, and was intended to cover, the incision in the left flank of the mummy, through which the embalmers removed the internal organs for separate preservation. The next object in sequence was a T-shaped symbol made of sheet-gold resembling a draughts-man's T-square. It was placed in the wrappings over the left side of the abdomen and extended down the upper part of the left thigh. So far as I am able to judge it has no parallel and its meaning is unknown.[4]

In addition other, more typical, ornamentation of the dead was found: for example, eight golden bands around abdomen, thigh, and upper arm. A few more layers of bandaging later, "which were in a very decayed state, another chased gold waist-band or girdle was exposed. Tucked under it obliquely . . . was a most interesting and handsome dagger. It has a handle ornamented with bright yellow granulated gold"; the blade, in contrast, of hardened gold.[5]

Then Professor Derry lifted the last bandages. Tensely, those around him watched the proceedings. Derry reported:

The skin of the legs, like that of the rest of the body, was of a greyish-white colour, very brittle and exhibiting numerous cracks. Examination of a piece of this showed that it consisted not only of the skin but of all the soft parts down to the bone, which was thus laid bare when such a piece came away, the whole thickness of skin and tissues in this situation being not more than two or three millimetres.[6]

The limbs, Derry continued,

appeared very shrunken and attenuated, but even when due allowance is made for the extreme shrinking of the tissues, and the appearance of emaciation which this produces, it is still evident that Tut-ankh-Amen must have been of slight build and perhaps not fully grown at the time of his death. Direct measurements made him about 5 feet 4-¼ inches in height, but . . . an estimate of living height from the measurements yielded by the principal limb bones calculated according to the formula devised by Professor Karl Pearson gives a stature of 1.676 metres (5 feet 6 inches), which is probably very near the actual truth.[7]

That the pharaoh did in fact not live to be very old was recognized by Derry when he exposed the lower end of the femur (knee joint). He found the epiphysis

to be separate from the shaft and freely movable. [The epiphysis is part of the bone which ossifies separately before fusing to the main section.] . . . In the limb bones the epiphyses form the chief part of the upper and lower ends. During early life they are attached to the main bone by cartilage which finally becomes completely converted into bone and growth then ceases.[8]

In other words, the status of cartilage fusion can be a measure of age. The lower femur usually unites with the shaft "about the age of twenty. At the upper end of the thigh bone the prominence known as the great trochanter was almost entirely soldered to the main bone, but on its inner side a definite gap showing the smooth cartilaginous surface where union was still incomplete, could be well seen. This epiphysis joins about the eighteenth year." Thus, according to the evidence of his leg bones, the pharaoh "would appear to have been over eighteen but below twenty years of age at the date of his death." [9]

The dissection of the arm was conducted with equal care and produced the same anatomical results: grayish skin, some cartilage fusion.

The heads of the humeri, or upper-arm bones, which join about twenty, are still not united [Derry wrote in his autopsy report], but the lower ends are completely joined to the shaft. . . .

The lower ends of the radius and ulna in modern Egyptians show little or no union in most cases until the age of eighteen, after which date they fuse fairly rapidly. The union begins on the inner side of the ulna and proceeds laterally, gradually involving the radius. In Tut-ankh-Amen fusion appeared to have begun in the ulna, but the distal end of the radius is entirely free. . . . From the state of the epiphyses . . . it would appear that the king was about eighteen . . . at the time of his death. None of the epiphyses which should unite about the twentieth year shows any sign of union. There is evidence that in Egypt the epiphyses tend on the average to unite somewhat earlier than is the rule in Europe.[10]

Osteology, the science of bones, today can provide detailed explanations about the age and the diseases suffered by men who died centuries ago. However, there is a large margin for sensational error.

The famous French surgeon Paul Broca (1824–1880)—he discovered the speech center in the brain named after him —astounded paleopathologists around the globe when he contended in 1876 that syphilis had been found in Europe before the discovery of America; until then it had been accepted as fact that Christopher Columbus and his crew had brought the disease home across the ocean.

Broca offered proof that this was not so. He examined human skeletons dug out of the ruins of a thirteenth-century lepers' home whose skulls clearly showed syphilitic symptoms. Paleopathology was—or so it seemed—one illusion the poorer.

No one would ever have dared doubt the great surgeon's

findings had a Danish medical historian, Vilhelm Möller-Christensen, not come to an entirely different conclusion. Director of the History of Medicine Museum in Copenhagen since 1964, he had examined skeletons found in old cemeteries all over Europe. And his osteological research confirmed the original thesis; syphilis had first appeared in Europe around 1500. Could Broca have been mistaken? Möller-Christensen decided to check his work.

There was nothing wrong with the conclusions the French surgeon had drawn: the heads did show syphilitic symptoms. But the Danish scientist went a step farther and did something Broca had failed to do; he checked their age. And that made the case into a paleopathological scandal.

The syphilitic skulls had indeed been dug out of the ruins of a thirteenth-century building, but the skeletons themselves dated from 1792 to 1818. Apparently they had been taken to the ancient site after a cemetery was plowed under, in order to avoid any fuss.

The anatomist Elliot Smith spent years researching diseases prevalent in ancient Egypt, often becoming so involved with his research that he forgot that his "patients" were really mummies. (One day he was seen riding in a taxi with the mummy of Thutmose III (1502–1448 B.C.). He was taking it from the Egyptian Museum to a clinic where he planned to X-ray the pharaoh.)

After examining five hundred skulls found at the Giza excavations, Smith determined that the old Egyptians had suffered as much from receding gums as we do. Smith looked for syphilitic bone deformation on no less than 25,000 skulls without finding any.

The French bacteriologist Armand Ruffer, who taught at Cairo University and served as president of the Egyptian Red Cross, discovered bacteria in mummies that responded to chemical tests. He also found an unusually large number of bacteria in lung and liver—in direct contrast to the findings of the government chemist, Alfred Lucas. Ruffer also came upon eggs of the bilharzia worm in the kidneys of two mummies from the XXth dynasty and even diagnosed a case of black lung disease in an ancient Egyptian miner.

Such diagnoses made from mummified inner organs are rare, because the organs were removed and placed in canopic jugs and often lost or not preserved. Circulatory ailments, in contrast, are relatively easy to recognize. Rameses II (1301–1234 B.C.), for example, who built the mighty rock temple of Abu Simbel, died of arteriosclerosis, a fairly common cause of death then as now.

Clearly, archaeological examinations frequently demand the cooperation of several sciences. If one analysis is not made correctly chances for error increase in proportion. Certainly that proved to be the case during the examination of Tutankhamen's mummy.

The skin of Tutankhamen's abdomen was less well preserved than on his legs and arms. Professor Derry's autopsy report states:

The abdominal wall exhibited a marked bulging on the right side. This was found to be due to the forcing of the packing material across the abdominal cavity from the left side where the embalming incision is situated. This opening, which had a ragged appearance, is roughly 86 mm. in length.[11]

The pharaoh's abdominal organs were pulled out through the incision; they were not embalmed together with the corpse but preserved separately in the tomb.

The old Egyptians believed that the god Osiris weighed each heart at the last judgment, and therefore the heart had to be kept in a special jug. In place of the heart the priests generally placed a scarab, a reproduction of *Scarabaeussacer*, the dung beetle, an insect the Egyptians considered holy and whose symbolic importance was as strong as that of the Cross for today's Christians. Reasons for pulling the other organs out of the body make good sense. For one thing the Egyptians knew they would deteriorate first; for another, they took their symbolism into account—these organs trigger hunger and thirst, feelings the dead were not allowed to have on their journey into the underworld. That's why they were divided and placed into four jugs. The covers were sculpted as heads of the god Horus's four sons—Amset, Hapi, Duamutef, and

Kebehsenuf—and were designed to ward off hunger and thirst. In the Old and Middle Kingdoms "food and drink" were placed in the tomb—wine jugs of wood and roast goose of alabaster—as well as miniature kitchens and bakeries.

People of the Middle and New Kingdoms, however, already believed that removal of the organs improved preservation. By Tutankhamen's day, therefore, all the dead were cut open before mummification. It was not always thus. The best-preserved mummies, found in Mentuhotep's temple in Deir el-Bahri, did not show a single incision; they dated from the XIth dynasty (2050–1991 B.C.). However, incisions for organ removal were made on mummies as early as the XIIth dynasty.

Laying bare Tutankhamen's head proved most difficult of all. Dr. Derry had to proceed very carefully to make sure he would not damage the—as all hoped—perfectly preserved face. As more bandages were cut away from the pharaoh's head, the clearer its unusual shape became, a shape already commented on in the paintings and statuary of the tomb. Tutankhamen had a well-developed occiput, something archaeologists had also noted about his father-in-law, Ikhnaton. Carter wrote:

The removal of a few layers of wrappings revealed a magnificent diadem completely encircling the king's head—an object of extreme beauty and of simple fillet type. In design it comprises a richly ornamented gold ribbon of contiguous circles of carnelian, having minute gold bosses affixed to their centres, with, at the back, a floral and disk-shaped bow, from which hang two ribbon-like gold appendages similarly decorated. On both sides of the fillet are appendages of a like but broader kind, and having a massive pendent uraeus attached to their front margins. The insignia of northern and southern sovereignty of this diadem . . . were found lower down, separate, and on the right and left thighs respectively, and as the king lay within the sarcophagus, east and west— his head turned towards the west—the uraeus of Buto being on the left side, and the vulture of Nekhebet on the right, the insignia took their correct geographical position [i.e., Upper and Lower Egypt].[12]

There was a good deal of guesswork about the diadem's meaning. It was definitely not the "king's crown" all pharaohs wore but which was made separately for each. One thing is sure, however: The diadem was more than only an ornament on the king's head. The Golenischeff papyrus, a find of dark origins but unquestioned authenticity, contains ten hymns glorifying the diadem "that shone frighteningly on the brow of the sun god and on that of the earthly king, and brings destruction to their enemies."

Papyri are the oldest written documents of mankind. The Egyptians used these scrolls since the third millennium before Christ. The oldest letter that has survived into our time dates back to about 2400 B.C. In it, an Egyptian soldier complains about his bad uniform.

In order to produce papyrus scrolls, the stalk of the papyrus bush was cut into strips which were plaited, placed one on top of the other, and then pressed together. The viscous material in the plant glued the fiber plait. Shells and fish bones were used to polish and smooth the papyrus. Then it was ready for reed pens to write upon it.

The Egyptians shipped their papyri to Greece and Asia Minor, to Italy and to Spain. The Ostrogoths, Lombards, and Vandals wrote on papyrus. Old Egyptian papyri, which have been found by the bales in the tombs, were popular during the baroque period—as frankincense. Only in 1788 did the Italian cardinal Stefano Borgia submit a papyrus brought him by a traveler from Egypt to scientific examination.

That was before Napoleon's Egyptian campaign, before Egyptology became a science, and before Champollion had deciphered hieroglyphics. But luckily the Danish scholar Nikolaus Schow, who studied the papyrus for the cardinal, did not need to understand hieroglyphics since the "Charta Borgiana" was written in Greek. Dated 192 B.C., it was a list of inhabitants in a Fayum village who had taken part in dam and canal construction work. This disappointing find was one reason why interest in Egyptian texts faded so quickly.

The Russian collector Waldemar Golenischeff gave the diadem papyrus to Adolf Erman for brief study. He had bought it from someone in Russia who, in turn, had purchased it in Egypt. The piece was in excellent condition and probably traveled one of the many tortuous paths that were the fate of so many Egyptian treasures after smart grave robbers had taken them from hitherto unexplored depths.

We know neither the author nor the age of the papyrus. Archaeologists assume that the 571-centimeter-long strip, made up of fifteen separate pieces and written on only one side, dates back to the seventeenth century B.C. The text was probably written by a priest of Sobk, who worshiped the crocodile god in the Fayum.

However, Erman concluded that the name of Sobk should be understood in symbolic terms and was to be equated with pharaoh. He cites as proof that not once in the whole six meters of text is there any mention of a "god."

The ancient Egyptians paid special reverence to diadems, which leads us to conclude that they believed diadems had special magic powers. The asp, which every pharaoh wore on his diadem, was supposed to have "the power to destroy enemies"—at least that interpretation is found in various sources.

What kind of power? Was the diadem a source of radioactivity? That would certainly be one explanation as to why so many died who were involved in excavating Tutankhamen's tomb; he was the only pharaoh who still wore a diadem when his grave was discovered.

During the course of the autopsy, Dr. Derry came upon a delicate linen cap, with gold and pearl stitching, which fitted tightly around the clean-shaven head. Howard Carter reported:

The removal of the final wrappings that protected the face of the king needed the utmost care, as owing to the carbonized state of the head there was always the risk of injury to the very fragile features. We realized the peculiar importance and responsibility attached to our task. At the touch of a sable brush the last few fragments of decayed fabric fell away, revealing a serene and placid countenance, that of a young man.[13]

The unguents poured over the mummy before burial had triggered a chemical reaction which, in turn, produced heat. Thus the pharaoh's skin was literally burned and blackened in spots.

According to Dr. Derry's autopsy report:

The plugs filling the nostrils . . . were . . . of some woven fabric, impregnated with resin. . . . The eyes are partly open and had not been interfered with in any way. The eyelashes are very long. The cartilaginous portion of the nose had become partially flattened by the pressure of the bandages. The upper lip is slightly elevated revealing the large central incisor teeth. The ears are small and well made. The lobes of the ears are perforated by a circular hole measuring 7.5 mm. in diameter. The skin of the face is of a greyish colour and is very cracked and brittle. . . .

The skull cavity was empty except for some resinous material which had been introduced through the nose in the manner employed by the embalmers of the period, after they had extracted the brain by the same route.[14]

The general excitement of the day probably contributed to the short shrift given an injury on the pharaoh's left cheek. Carter does not mention it, and Dr. Derry writes laconically:

"On the left cheek, just in front of the lobe of the ear, is a rounded depression, the skin filling it, resembling a scab. Round the circumference of the depression, which has slightly raised edges, the skin is discolored. It is not possible to say what the nature of this lesion may have been." [15]

How Tutankhamen Died

The mystery surrounding Tutankhamen's head wound was only cleared up forty years later when an anatomy professor from Liverpool, Dr. Ronald Harrison, examined the mummy in the Valley of the Kings with a portable X-ray machine. That was not the first X-ray examination made of the pharaoh but it was the most thorough.

Fifty X-ray pictures finally confirmed the following diagnosis: King Tutankhamen died a violent death. The wound on the left side of his skull was the result of a fall or a blow.

The actual cause of death was a blood clot under the meninges (brain membranes). That settled all the guessing about the pharaoh's early death, for which scientists had variously suggested brain tumor, tuberculosis, and inflammation of the arteries as causes.

Professor Harrison's assistant, the serologist Dr. R. C. Connolly, was able to determine Tutankhamen's blood group—with the help of a pin-sized piece of tissue. It was A2, subgroup MN. Tutankhamen, therefore, was indeed "rare blooded" and most probably was descended from an old and "pure" aristocratic family.

The rare A2 blood group provides evidence for another hypothesis as well. Howard Carter had contended that the most remarkable thing about Tutankhamen's face was its extraordinary resemblance to his father-in-law, Ikhnaton, which he had first noted in their statues. Carter, who did not know that Tutankhamen and Ikhnaton had the same blood group, assumed correctly that the former, about whose heredity nothing was known, was an illegitimate son of the latter. Since Ikhnaton's wife, Nefertete, had borne only daughters, one of whom the future pharaoh took as his wife, he married—and he must have been all of twelve at the time of the wedding—his own half sister. His father-in-law was also his father. Harrison and Connolly were thus able to prove in 1959 what had been pure conjecture in 1925.

Alfred Lucas, government chemist employed by the Department of Antiquities, examined the mummy along with Dr. Derry. However, Lucas's results are so questionable they can hardly be used as evidence or explanation for the curse of the pharaohs. For example, he writes about fungi found in the tomb and their chemical impact on the organic particles of the membrane and on the bones of the mummy, but he also calls the grave free of germs.

The thick fungus growth on the walls of the tomb, however, and the many dead insects found on the floor do seem significant evidence to support the "poison theory" suggested in chapter 10. The entomologist of the Royal Agricultural Society in Cairo, A. Alfieri, identified some of them as "small beetles who lived off decayed organic matter." This beetle species allegedly has existed in Egypt for the last three thousand years. Moreover, holes in wooden grave furnishings resembled those made by our woodworms. And finally, spiders were found which had left huge webs behind them.

Flowers had been put in Tutankhamen's tomb, as in tombs of other pharaohs. They were strange plants. For example, there was wild celery (*Apium graveolens*), whose leaves had been wound into wreaths. Such wreaths were also found in the tombs of Amenhotep III and the architect Cha, as well as in an unmarked Theban grave from the XXIId dynasty (950 B.C.).

Perhaps the most touching bouquet was placed on Tutankhamen's coffin, inside the sarcophagus. It was a small bunch of flowers which his fifteen-year-old widow must have plucked from the Nile shore and sent as a last greeting to her beloved.

The corpse itself was decorated with various plants. At the head of the second coffin lay wreaths of olive blossoms and leaves. Professor P. E. Newberry identified this bundle as a "justification wreath." It is also described in a special chapter in the Book of the Dead and, since the beginnings of the New Empire, had been placed on the coffin while the priests uttered magic incantations.

On the second shrine of the tomb lay a garland of flowers, and a collar of flowers was found in the third one as well. The degree of plant preservation differed sharply. Some turned to dust at the slightest touch; others still retained their color and could be identified without difficulty.

Cornflowers were found most often in pharaohs' tombs. Small wonder, for flowers grow luxuriously along the small fertile strip of land between the shore of the Nile and the desert. Lotus flower and papyrus shrub, the two symbols of empire, were of course used as decoration for tomb and coffin.

The Mysterious Demon's Apple

The origin of one plant, which does not grow in Egypt but was found in Tutankhamen's tomb and in those of other pharaohs, remains unexplained. It is the mandrake (*Mandragora officinarum*). Wall paintings in the tombs of the XVIIIth dynasty often depict baskets of fruit with its bulbs in them. The meaning is under dispute, since the bright yellow fruit was best known as an aphrodisiac. The country nearest Egypt where mandrakes grow is Palestine. Henry B. Tristram noted that fact in his book *A Natural History of the Bible*. The Arabs call the mandrake fruit *tuffah al-jinn*—demon's apples. With careful dosage, "demon's apples" are known as a stimulant, but taken in larger quantities they can drive men to frenzy, producing reactions akin to hallucinogenic drugs.

Professor Newberry believed the mandrake fruits found in the tombs and shown on paintings to be identical with the so-called didi fruit. Called *dudaim* in Hebrew, it is often mentioned in the writings of the New Kingdom. On the Nile island of Elephantine, near the present Aswan, it was even used as a narcotic.

Neither the chemical nor the anatomical examinations of Tutankhamen's mummy brought any new archaeological knowledge to light. It would have been preferable for the advancement of science if the tomb had been discovered in the 1950s or 1960s; Professor Harrison's investigations show that clearly. Even though he had to work with partially destroyed mummies, his findings have greater scientific significance than those of all the scholars who worked before him put together.

Tutankhamen's autopsy at the Anatomical Institute of Cairo University on November 11, 1925, had tragic consequences: Alfred Lucas died soon after from a heart attack, and a little later Professor Derry died of circulatory collapse.

The deaths of two scientists who dealt with the pharaoh's mummy so briefly spread concern among scholars around the globe. Their sudden demise made even skeptics who had dismissed the curse of the pharaohs as a matter of chance sit up and take notice.

6 Kings and Magicians

WHAT KIND of man was Tutankhamen? Why was his grave secured so strongly that the curse of the pharaohs was more potent in it than in any other pharaoh's tomb?

Howard Carter said about the pharaoh who died so young that the only noteworthy thing about his life was the fact that he died and was buried. That judgment, of course, is one-sided. Tutankhamen was not a big wheel in the clockwork of Egyptian history, but small wheels too have their importance.

The XVIIIth dynasty of the New Kingdom ended with Tutankhamen. We are able to talk of dynasties and place the 360 pharaohs, and the foreign kings, into a dynastic framework because of existing fragments of a historical work that an Egyptian priest, Manetho, wrote in Greek about 305 B.C. The thirty dynasties Manetho counted between Menes (3200 B.C.) and Alexander the Great (332 B.C.) encompass the Old Kingdom, the Middle Kingdom, the New Kingdom (or Empire), and finally the Late Period, which begins with Psamtik (about 715 B.C.).

The Old Kingdom lasted from 2850 until the end of the Heracleopolitan era (2052 B.C.) and saw such great pharaohs in power as Djoser, Khufu, Khafre, Menkure, Unas, Teti, and Pepi. The Middle Kingdom began with the reign of Mentuhotep (2052 B.C.) and ended with the XVIth dynasty and the termination of Hyksos rule. Historians put the beginning of the Empire at about 1610 B.C. and its end with the XXIVth dynasty in 715 B.C. Most of the historical testimony we have comes from those nine hundred years. Pharaohs like the Amenhoteps, Thutmoses, and Ramessides put their stamp on the age.

These Egyptian dynastic divisions, which are not very precisely drawn, are constantly being modified by new scholarship. Originally, the ancient Egyptians counted time according to the year of a pharaoh's reign or a particular event: for example, "Tutankhamen's third year" or the "year of the battle and victory over the northern peoples." And a new dynasty began when a royal family died out and was replaced by another.

Egyptian Plural Marriages

As Adolf Erman and Hermann Ranke have shown, polygamy was an accepted practice in ancient Egypt, even though it was not the rule. We know that Emeni, one of the ten grandees of Upper Egypt, was married to a woman called Nebet and to another named Henut. With Nebet, Emeni had two sons and five daughters, with Henut one son and three daughters. The two wives were not rivals; quite the contrary. Out of respect for the other, Nebet named one of her daughters Henut, while Henut, in turn, called all three of her daughters Nebet.

An Egyptian could have several wives because there was no such thing as marital law. A marriage contract was concluded. Men were usually fifteen years old, women twelve or thirteen. The contract included a "year of eating," a test year at whose conclusion the marriage could be dissolved without any formalities. Concubines and their children, who lived in the harem, had no rights whatever. They were supposed to be beautiful and to dance and sing well.

There were some pharaohs, though, who had several legitimate wives. Naftera-mernemut, Rameses II's first wife, for example, was not the mother of Nenephta, the heir to the throne. His second legitimate wife, Ese-nofre, was; he was married to both at the same time. The two wives finally welcomed a third, the daughter of the Hittite king, whom Rameses II probably married for reasons of state, after he made peace with her father. Such political marriages were customary. Thus Prince Neheri married the daughter of the ruler of the sixteenth district, and Neheri's son, Chnemhotpe, did his part when he married Cheti, the heiress of the seventeenth district. Thus within two generations Neheri's district had increased threefold. We know that Chnemhotpe's marriage was not a love match, for his heart belonged to Zata, the beautiful "sealer of all the treasures."

Keeping blood lines pure was important to the ancient Egyptians, one reason why sibling marriages were so common, especially among pharaohs. Even the gods did not make an exception: Osiris had married his sister Isis, Seth his sister Nephtys. Sibling marriages were so "normal" that finally the word "sister" took the same meaning as "mistress" or "beloved"—which did not make unraveling the complicated family relationships any easier.

The divine pharaohs did not enjoy any special legal rights. Aside from religion, the common man could do as the pharaoh. This was also true of marriage.

There was always only one woman who was the legal wife, "the mistress of the house." But if the pharaoh had concubines and a harem, so could the ordinary citizen also —provided he could afford them.

Despite this, the social position of women in ancient Egypt was not as inferior as in many other civilizations. For example, even the oldest Egyptian pictures show men and women the same size; it is only children and servants who are depicted as smaller.

A papyrus preserved today in Leiden, Holland, gives real insight into married life in old Egypt. It is the letter of an army general from Memphis whose wife died while he was away. The man became very ill after her death and believed that the ka—the spirit who watched over his wife and, indeed, protected all Egyptian dead on their journey into the underworld—had sent the sickness. Therefore he put this letter to his wife into the grave of another dead person:

What evil thing have you done to me so that I find myself in this miserable situation? What have I done to you, that you vex me so where I have done you no harm? What have I done when I was your husband, and even to this day, that I would need to hide? Through the words of my mouth I will go to trial before the nine gods, who sit in the West. Then they will have to decide between you and me. What have I done to you?

You became my wife when I was young. Later I assumed several offices. I never left you nor gave you any cause for sorrow. But you won't let me be happy. I will call you to account, for right shall be separated from wrong.

Remember how when I trained the pharaoh's officers and charioteers, I made them come and throw themselves down before you. They brought presents and put them at your feet. I hid nothing from you as long as I lived. Not once did I go as an adulterer into another house. I let no man tell me what to do with you. When I was moved to my present post, it was impossible to come home as I had done before, so I sent you my oil and my bread and my clothes, and they were brought to you.

You don't know how much good I have done you. I always asked how you were. When you were ill I had the head doctor come and he prepared the medicines and did everything you asked. When I traveled south with the pharaoh, my thoughts were always with you. I spent the eight months without eating and drinking like a real man.

When I returned to Memphis I asked the pharaoh to excuse me and came to you and grieved over you with my men when I learned of your death. I gave clothes and linen for your wrapping. I had clothes made for you and left nothing good undone.

Now I have been alone for three years and I have not visited another house. This is not seemly for a man like me. But you cannot distinguish between good and evil. Someone will have to decide between us. And as for your sisters—I have not gone to any of them!

More XVIIIth Dynasty Relationships

Marriages and family ties were especially complicated during the XVIIth and XVIIIth dynasties. The XVIth dynasty had started with Sekenjen-Re, who had Ahhotep as wife and whose son Ahmose—he drove the Hyksos out of Egypt—married his sister Ahmes-Neferteri. Their daughter Ahmes married Ahmose's son Thutmose, again a sibling marriage.

Ikhnaton (Amenhotep IV) had three daughters. Meritaton, the oldest, was married off to Sakere during Ikhnaton's lifetime. (Sakere shared the throne with Ikhnaton for a short time but died before his father-in-law.) Ikhnaton's second daughter, Maketaton, also died young. That left the youngest, originally named Ankhesenpaaten. She was married to Tutankhamen (first named Tutankhaton) in order to document her hereditary claim. That happened very quickly. Ankhesenpaaten, born during the eighth year of her father's reign, was only nine at the time of her marriage, an age that was extremely young for marriage even in Egypt. The child wife had to pay bitterly for it; she suffered two miscarriages and the badly needed heir did not materialize.

The gray eminence at Ikhnaton's court in Tell el-Amarna was the almighty high priest and court chamberlain, Ay. His wife, Teje, had been Queen Nefertete's nurse. Ay held all the strings of power in his hand, and it was in his own interest to prevent a strong man from succeeding Ikhnaton. The youthful Tutankhamen seemed just right.

Tutankhamen's most important accomplishment was his break with the monotheistic sun religion his father-in-law had introduced into Egypt. A result of that decision was the abandonment of the new residence in Tell el-Amarna and the return to Thebes. As an outer sign of obeisance to the Theban city god Amon, the pharaoh changed his name from Tutankhaton to Tutankhamen (or Tutenkhamon). And his young wife no longer called herself Ankhesenpaaten but Enhosnamon.

A memorial tablet from Karnak, today stored in Cairo's Egyptian Museum, deals with this restoration. The inscription reads:

I found the temple in ruins, the holy places destroyed and the courtyards overgrown with weeds. I restored the shrines and the temples and gave them jewels. I made pictures of the gods out of gold and amber, decorated with lapis lazuli and precious stones.

Tutankhamen died, as we have seen, from a blood clot in the brain, the result of a head injury. That left Enhosnamon a widow at fifteen and without an heir to the throne—perfect conditions for Ay to seize power.

He plotted cleverly; the fifteen-year-old queen was putty in his hands. As queen of Egypt she knew very well what was at stake. The process of mummification lasted seventy days, after which the new pharaoh had to conduct the "mouth-opening" ceremonies at the burial. Within seventy days—the time between the pharaoh's death and his funeral—she had to find another husband who could succeed Tutankhamen. Who would it be?

Enhosnamon could not find a suitable man in all Egypt. In her despair she finally turned to the King of the Hittites, Shuppiluliuma, writing him, *My husband is dead and I do not have a son. I am told that you have many grown sons. Send me one of your sons and I shall take him as my husband because I do not want to marry any of my subjects.*

Just seventy days, that was all the time the fifteen-year-old queen had. It took a courier fourteen days to travel from Egypt to Asia Minor where the Hittites lived. That meant she could expect an answer in a month at the earliest. And if the king had any questions an agreement would take sixty days, provided he replied at once.

The king didn't know what to make of the message. Was it a trick? Was one of his sons to be taken as hostage? Shuppiluliuma was unsure, but he sent his chancellor, Hattu-Zitish, to Egypt with an answer.

Numbly Enhosnamon listened to the letter his courier read to her: *How will you prove to me that you have no prince to marry? Perhaps you wish only to deceive me. Perhaps you do not want one of my sons as regent.* Nevertheless, she managed to convince the chancellor she was telling the truth. And if she had one small glimmer of hope left for getting a husband before the seventy days were up, her last pleading letter was it. *Why should I deceive you? I have no son, and my husband is dead. Do you really believe that if I had a son I would approach you in this demeaning way? Nor have I written such a letter to the ruler of any other country, only to you. Give me one of your sons, and he shall be king in Egypt.*

After Shuppiluliuma received that letter he believed the young queen's sincerity and sent his son Zannanza to Thebes. But the road was long and there were two men in Egypt who had hopes for the throne. Ay was one. He was almost certain that the young prince would not be able to arrive in Thebes within the seventy-day limit. The other was a young general, Horemheb (or Haremhab). He too knew of Enhosnamon's plans but was less sure than Ay. In any event he took no chances and decided to send an escort to "greet" the prince. Zannanza was murdered, and the father saw his early suspicions confirmed; the Egyptian queen's letter had been a trap. From then on he regarded the Egyptians as mortal enemies.

Back in Thebes, Ay had planned more carefully than Horemheb. On the evening before Tutankhamen's solemn funeral he declared himself heir to the throne, and on the next day he performed the mouth-opening ceremonies to allow the ba, the dead pharaoh's soul, to leave the body. That made Ay the new pharaoh.

Ay and Enhosnamon sat on the Egyptian throne together. Their reign passed without any memorable event being recorded; Ay died within four years and the fate of young Enhosnamon is lost in the darkness of history. It is certainly possible that Horemheb murdered her and covered up the crime.

Certainly Horemheb felt that his time had come after Ay's death. He had won the support of Amon's priests. And during a great feast Horemheb was enthroned as the new pharaoh. In order to preserve the illusion that he wished to continue the tradition of the XVIIIth dynasty, he married Mutnedjemet, Nefertete's sister. But under Horemheb's rule the marriage was the only thing to remind anyone of the XVIIIth dynasty.

A vengeful dictator, he tried to destroy all statues and

pictures of his predecessors. Wherever Tutankhamen's name appeared, Horemheb had it chiseled out or scratched off. Statues were decapitated. Every intact relic of the Aton epoch was destroyed. Horemheb used the stones of the Tell el-Amarna temples as the foundations for three mighty pyramids which he had built in front of the Amon temple in Thebes. He did everything he could to imprint his image on history and erase that of his predecessors. Even the graves did not stop him. He destroyed many tombs of Tutankhamen and Ay's courtiers. Every vestige of their reign was to be eradicated.

A leading expert on the age, the French Egyptologist Christiane Desroches-Noblecourt, wrote in her biography of Tutankhamen:

Everything Horemheb did seemed to have been carefully weighed and balanced. This "virtuous" restorer proceeded with the fanaticism that bred so much crime to win the support of the originators of the counter-reformation. But despite the clear logic of his actions he made one mistake: Although he did everything to strike Tutankhamen, who loved Thebes more than the God of the city himself, from the annals of history, he inexplicably did not plunder his tomb.

The question has bothered Egyptologists for a long time. There does not seem to be any valid reason why Horemheb, who destroyed every memory of King Tut, left his tomb untouched. This is all the more surprising because everyone knew at the time how opulently the young pharaoh had been buried. And Horemheb had never missed a chance of enriching his treasury. He had the priests on his side, so that they would never have held him back. No, there is only one explanation for Horemheb's restraint: Before it was sealed, the priests secured the tomb with secret and mysterious powers that could not be destroyed. Otherwise the curse would have struck the pharaoh himself.

The Dark Power of the Priests

The office and dignity of a priest in ancient Egypt was surrounded by secrets and mysteries. Priests were an intellectual elite. They had the knowledge the masses lacked. And knowledge was power, even five thousand years ago.

Unlike other offices, the priesthood could not be inherited. The office had to be earned, and those who would hold it had to work for it. And then there was rank within the priesthood itself. In the New Kingdom there were five stages. The life of the priest Beknechons, whose records have survived from the twelfth century B.C., shows the long way from *we'eb*, the lowest priestly rank, to head priest. Beknechons was trained as a horseman in the pharaoh's army. He distinguished himself, exhibiting above-average intelligence, and when he turned seventeen was accepted as a "reading" priest in Amon's temple in Thebes. After four years he rose to the next rank in the hierarchy of Amon priests; he became a "father of the god." He had to serve in that capacity for twelve years. By the time he had climbed up to the third rank of the priesthood, Beknechons was thirty-three. He spent the next fifteen years as third priest; then he moved up to second priest, an office he held for twelve years. When he was sixty years old, Rameses II named him head priest of Amon. Beknechons lived to be eighty-seven.

Such a man represented a source of real authority for other priests, courtiers, and scientists. But for the people he was a magician who knew everything and could do everything. It was not only his age and career that placed a head priest so far above the common people; above all it was the extent and scope of his power. As head priest, Beknechons presided over a kind of university. The Amon temple harbored an art academy, a music school, and an engineering college. The temple district was larger and richer than the pharaoh's palace. And even if the pharaoh exercised all visible power, the priests held its invisible strings.

Doctor, priest, and magician—often he was one and the same. Pentu, Ikhnaton's personal physician, was not only the pharaoh's closest adviser, he was the first temple servant of the god Aton. These magicians were powerful men. They were courted by the pharaohs because they had scientific knowledge no one else had. They formed a kind of mysterious cult or class which shared its knowledge with no one else.

Their occult, scientific, and medical discoveries were written on papyrus rolls and consulted when needed.

Such secret texts have come to us from the Vth dynasty (2500–2350 B.C.) When vizier Wesh-Ptah dropped dead before his pharaoh, Neferirkare, presumably after suffering a stroke, the king called in the priests and doctors and had a wooden box brought in which contained a papyrus roll with diagnoses and secret medication. In the Ebers papyrus, a kind of magico-medical textbook, there is frequent reference to the "secrets of the doctor," mostly in discussions of certain treatments where medicine and mysticism seem to fuse.

If a pharaoh was satisfied with the achievement of his priests and magicians, the whole class benefited. After a victorious battle, Rameses III (1197–1165 B.C.) gave the priests of his temple 86,486 slaves and 32 tons of gold. In the 11th century B.C. the Amon priests owned 2,400 fields, 83 ships, 46 shipyards, and 420,000 head of cattle.

Slaves were completely at the priests' mercy. Priests had the right to condemn slaves to death, which ordinary citizens did not. And it was certainly tantamount to a sentence of death, for example, when doctors "tried out" an operation on a slave first. Such surgical procedures included everything from filling a tooth to brain surgery. Magicians and doctors recorded the results of such experiments in their secret books.

Medicine and Magic

The Egyptian priests faced a difficult task in coordinating the many gods of the districts united into kingdoms and then of the kingdoms brought together into an empire. Small wonder that magic enjoyed growing popularity. Every town or region had its own local godhead. Every political union was followed by a theological one. It was up to the watchful priests to let gods die or meld one into another. Thus Re and Atum became one god, as did Shu and Onuris, Ptah and Sokaris. Osiris was later added to the last two, so that one talked of a godly trinity. It was important to silence doubters and to reinforce the will and omnipotence of the gods.

In order to accomplish this, the priests made use of

scientific knowledge whose existence the people at large did not even suspect, and which still amazes us today. Information about the state of medicine and magic in ancient Egypt is contained in seven major medical papyri. They are clearly differentiated according to size, content, and date.

The largest and most famous is the Ebers papyrus. It was written at the beginning of the New Kingdom. With its 108 pages and broad coverage of subject matter, it is almost a medical classic. The Berlin papyrus—its twenty-four pages make it the second longest—was written toward the end of the New Kingdom. The Edwin Smith and Hearst papyri, twenty-two and seventeen pages respectively, date back to about 1550 B.C. The two Kahun papyri, A and B, which must have been written about 1900 B.C., are the oldest. Both are incomplete: Kahun A is a treatise on female illnesses; Kahun B is a fragment of a comprehensive work on veterinary medicine. Finally, we have the eighteen-page London papyrus from Tutankhamen's day with its pharmaceutical prescriptions and magic spells for mother and child, more evidence of how closely medicine and magic were linked in ancient Egypt.

The medical papyri also list real pharmaceutical prescriptions, which, as a glance at the Ebers and Smith papyri will show, could well have worked. In the book of intestinal and stomach diseases, for example, we find the following diagnosis and therapy:

Examination directions for one who complains of stomach trouble. If you examine a man for stomach ulcers, a man who has trouble eating because his belly is narrow and his heart [sick], and if he feels like someone suffering from an inflammation of the anus, then you must first look at him stretched out on his back. If his stomach feels hot because of the ulcers you must tell the patient that he has congestion of the liver. You should prepare a remedy listed in the secret book of herbs, such as the doctors do. Grind the drug pachsett and date stones together and dissolve them in water. The man should drink it for up to four days in order to empty his stomach.

But if the right side of the patient's stomach feels hot

The Ebers papyrus. Named for its discoverer and interpreter, German Egyptologist Georg Ebers, the document contains medical prescriptions and directions for therapy from the New Kingdom (seventeenth century B.C.). It is written in hieratic script.

while the left remains cold, then you should tell him: Your illness is spreading. Later you should examine him again and if you find all of his stomach area cool to the touch you should tell him that his liver has split and his body accepted the medication.

The Edwin Smith papyrus also has directions for emergency surgery:

Examination directions for a wound on the gema bone [according to the papyrus this is "the bone between the corner of the eye, the ear lobe, and the lower jaw"]. If you examine someone with a wound on the gema bone, which is not a gaping one but does go down to the bone, you should look at it closely. If you find his gema bone intact without split, hole, or break, then you should tell him: You have a wound on the gema bone, an illness I will treat. On the first day he should put fresh meat on it, and thereafter treat it with salve and honey, and do that every day until he feels better. A wound that does not gape yet reaches to the bone is a small wound, one that goes to the bone without gaping and without lips on it we call narrow.

"You should"—that form of instruction corresponds exactly to the style the ancient Egyptians used in teaching science. Math books are written in the same didactic way. The "you" for the doctor is contrasted with "he" for the patient. The person of the doctor is hardly ever mentioned—at most "the doctor's knife" or the "secret methods of the doctor" or the "doctor's great book of heart secrets."

A doctor in ancient Egypt had to inspect the sacrificial meat for religious observances—just one of his many functions. He was magician and pharmacist, priest and healer. Certainly he was powerful, much more powerful, for instance, than the doctors in ancient Rome. Just compare their patron saints: Aesculapius, the Roman god of healing, was a second-rank godhead, whereas in Egypt it was the powerful Thoth who held a protective hand over doctors. Nor was Thoth the only divine doctor. Amon, Min, Chons, and Horus were also said to have healing powers. Amon was supposed to cure eye diseases without medicines. Min made the sick well and kept the living alive. Chons was the great god who drove out the demons. Horus's word lowered fever and healed the sick.

The Ebers papyrus cites some unusual therapies for eye diseases, widespread in both ancient and modern Egypt. Thus it suggests plucking eyebrows and lashes and smearing lizard blood on the body as treatment for trichiasis. Dioscorides, a Greek doctor who lived after Christ's birth, reports that the Egyptians also suggested chameleon's blood. He himself recommended burnt shoe soles as a cure for burns, medical advice that was given in the Ebers papyrus in somewhat changed form as burnt skins.

Bloodshot eyes should be treated with the milk of pregnant women. The London papyrus attributes weakened eyesight to demons and ghosts. That's why its therapy is not primarily directed at the illness but concentrates on magic spells for driving out demons.

Purely medical advice on treating eyes is also given. Thus the London papyrus recommends putting "beef liver over a spelt and barley fire and pouring the juice over the eyes," while the Ebers papyrus suggests placing "fried and squeezed ox liver" on them.

"Magic spells for mother and child" suggested that excessive salivation during teething of babies could be controlled by placing live mice in their mouths or having them eat chopped mouse.

Several Egyptian texts talk of secret powers. The Setne "novella" tells how Thoth demanded that Re return a magic book, which Ne-nefer-ke-Ptah had stolen, and how the god complied by sending down "a divine force from heaven" to make sure the robber would not safely return to Memphis.

The magic papyrus XI reports about "the divine powers" that "rest" in the town of Bubastis. The demotic Book of the Dead, the Pamont, also refers to them when talking about "divine forces of the city of Bubastis that come up from their crypts." And the name of the judge of the dead means, in translation, "the Bubastic who comes up from the crypts."

All these powers are never called upon to protect the living. Why do only the dead and the gods ask for them? The simplest explanation seems to be that they were lethal. And if we assume the pharaohs protected their tombs with them, we are directly on the trail of the curse of the pharaohs.

One other strange point: We have no documents that tell us where and how doctors were instructed in their art—surely proof that it was a most mysterious and secret business. Only in the late Egyptian period is there any record of medical schools. Such a school was opened in Sais during Darius I's reign (around 500 B.C.), but it had nothing in common with medical education in ancient Egypt; Darius sent his own head doctor, Udsha Harresnet, to found the school in the Nile delta.

Hospitals were unknown in Egypt during the entire

period from the Old to the New Kingdom. Such institutions would have been too prosaic, too lacking in mystic background. No, a doctor or magician was asked into one's house. And when he came he entered with suitable ceremony. For in the eyes of the people he was above all else an artist who could heal everybody and everything, even the lovesick.

The old Egyptian doctors knew three methods of treatment: surgical, medicinal, and magical. Surgical treatment included operations. "In order to quiet the blood," knives were preheated. "The doctor must take extreme care" when preparing to bleed someone. Bones and joints were set, wounds bandaged, and basic sterilization concepts understood. Broken bones were put in splints, and tubes—reeds wrapped in linen—were used for artificial nourishment. They even used the dental bridge; old teeth were placed in the hole between two healthy teeth and fastened with gold wire.

Medicinal treatment included prescriptions of juices, salves, powders, and even suppositories. Smoky powders were ignited and inhaled. Existing instructions for taking pills and drugs produced by Egyptian doctors do not differ markedly from those of modern pharmacology; "Take before going to bed," or "Take twice a day" were common directions.

Finally, doctors used magic treatments, which, however, often went hand in hand with the other two. We know about tricks that may have reinforced the common belief in magic but are easily explainable medically. For example, doctors would paint a god figure on a patient's hand who suffered from pain or poison and then tell him to lick up the picture. These "god pictures" must have been drawn not with paint but with a liquid drug, but if they helped it was considered to be an act of the gods.

The Secret Books

The education gap in ancient Egypt was a chasm. A small intellectual and social elite faced largely illiterate masses unable to account for scientific knowledge as anything else but magic—a fact of some consequence for subsequent

Egyptian history. The pharaohs' libraries housed books of magic alongside more traditional works, medical texts and so-called books of wisdom. Adolf Erman noted that even the educated stood in awe of the latter authors and considered them "earth gods" or "gods of wisdom." A seventh-century priest claimed to have found one such book of secrets in an animal grave. Others were found in jars placed next to mummies. The Egyptians would only recognize as the highest cherheb, or priest, someone who knew the old holy books by heart.

No doubt the transition from magic and superstition to scientific knowledge was often fluid. Thus a monthly calendar has been handed down from the Middle Kingdom which calls the eighteenth day of the month good, the ninth bad, and the third "half good." The basic conception here was simply that some days are happy and others unhappy; biorhythm resembles that theory.

Then as now, biorhythm was not a generally accepted science. But we know from a New Kingdom papyrus—a student's schoolbook—that the idea was taught to the young. The book says a day is happy or unhappy depending on what happened that day in the history of the gods.

Lines are hard to draw; not everything that points to the supernatural can be equated with crude magic. There is nothing magical about putting food in tombs and painting daily furnishings on the walls of the grave chambers or writing or reciting magic incantations. This was simply a matter of religion or tradition. But magicians and charlatans exploited this popular belief in order to turn it into a money-making business—with the help of scientific method.

Magicians were needed at every turn of life. They exorcised wind and rain; they protected men from lions in the desert and crocodiles in the Nile. A magic spell was said every morning to protect the pharaoh against his enemies. A clay shard found in Thebes shows how far these spells and magical invocations went, even at the beginning of the Middle Kingdom, about 2000 B.C. This one details the practice of "smashing the pots." A pharaoh of the XIth dynasty had all the names of people who were his enemies scratched onto different jars and pots: Bakuai, the ruler of Ubates, and all his relatives; all the inhabitants of Kosh, Meger, and Shaat; and in addition "all their strong, their runners, their allies, their friends, those who will become our enemies, who will plot, who will fight, those who say that they will fight, and those who will become our enemies in this whole land." That included the princes of Libya and Palestine and finally the high councils in his own country: All were named and condemned to death. It was still believed that people would die the minute the clay jars that had their names engraved on them were broken.

But gradually the pressure on the magicians to produce results grew. People realized that the expensive magic spells and formula needed outside help to work. And as the general educational level of the Egyptian people rose, the magicians' spells became more strident, more demanding, even threatening.

In the pyramid texts we find spells and incantations such as these:

O you gods of the horizon: So as you wish Atum to live, that you cleanse yourselves with oil, that you wear clothes and receive your food, so also take his hand and place him in fields of food.

There is little faith, conviction, or self-confidence left in such a sentence. It can more easily be explained as a perplexed magician's cry for help. His despair becomes even clearer:

But if you will not bring him to the ship, he [the dead] will tear the curls from your head like buds on the shore of the lake.

Is it any wonder that a priest who had been so bitterly disappointed by his gods would look to science for help in shoring up his own credibility? Or that priests and doctors became so deeply involved with magic?

In short, a study of available sources makes a strong case for the use of science as a buttress of Egyptian theology. Clearly, scientific secrets are part of the explanation for the curse of the pharaohs.

7 On the Road to Immortality

ON JANUARY 19, 1967, the American physicist James Bedford died of cancer in Los Angeles at the age of seventy-three. He was better prepared for death than anyone else before him.

Immediately after the fact of clinical death had been established, a team of three doctors and chemists began to implement a detailed plan: During an eight-hour operation the doctors drained all liquids from the body of the dead scientist and replaced the blood with a chemical solution. While the body was being deep-frozen, one doctor intensively massaged the heart in order to keep the brain cells alive as long as possible. Right after the last of the blood had been drained, the body was cooled down to minus 196 degrees centigrade, placed in a rust-free steel sarcophagus, and taken to Phoenix, Arizona, where it has been preserved in a so-called cryotorium—a deep-freeze mortuary—standing upright in a hivelike building with temperatures near 200 degrees below zero centigrade.

Dr. Bedford was the first deep-freeze man; he bought the prospects of immortality for some $30,000. Is the California scientist a dreamer or a visionary?

Deep-Freeze Men: Mummies of Today

Back in 1964 physicist Robert Ettinger published his controversial book *The Prospect of Immortality*. His theory proposed shock-freezing persons who have died of an incurable disease and bringing them back to life once a cure has been found for the illness that killed them. The medical profession received the idea with skepticism and puzzlement.

One thing seems sure, however: An organism can be brought back to life only if during the freezing process the temperature drops by 100 degrees centigrade per minute and if thawing out is equally swift. There is a good reason for this: Cold or heat shock prevents formation of crystals which would destroy vital molecules and makes the crucial protein and nucleonic acid molecules solidify so quickly that water in the tissues and cells doesn't crystallize but turns into a glasslike mass.

Plants and human sperm cells have been revived, but no human being has ever been brought back to life from the deep freeze. Nor is it certain that anyone ever will be. Nevertheless, several cryonic societies already exist in the United States which maintain cryotoria in Phoenix, on Long Island, and in the San Fernando Valley, where deep-frozen humans are stored for an annual rent of approximately $700. It has been three thousand years since men expended this much effort on their dead.

When Nerves Go Mad

What motivated the ancient Egyptians to prepare their dead in such a fashion that their remains have been preserved almost intact? What made them bury their pharaohs with a display of wealth neither possible nor customary in history before or since? Was it their unshakable faith in immortality or was it rather, as is the case today, the conviction that one day science would discover immortality?

The Egyptians of the Old Kingdom were, without doubt, more naïve than those who lived in the Middle or New Kingdoms. It is therefore likely, as we have said, that over the centuries their faith in miracles became altered by a greater scientific awareness. Even if burial rites remained largely the same, some things must have changed that had more than symbolic significance. An example may help clarify the point.

For centuries, acupuncture, the healing art from the Far East, was dismissed by Western medicine as charlatanism at worst or a curiosity at best. Today acupuncture is being hailed in Europe and America. How come?

The ancient Chinese believed that placing needles into certain parts of the body drove out demons and evil spirits that caused pain. They developed a theory that needle punctures—later they isolated 360 different treatment points—would allow putting into or taking out of the body any deficiency or excess of Yin and Yang.

According to Chinese wisdom, Yin and Yang are two dependent and complementary natural forces: male-female, light-dark, creative-receptive, joyful-painful. These alternately dominant basic forces, the ancient Chinese thought, are the final cause of everything that happens in the perceivable world and can be kept in natural balance with the help of needles, which act in the same way as antennas or lightning rods.

Even today there is little scientific agreement about acupuncture. Doctors and scientists began to take the Chinese "needle art" seriously when the English neurologist Henry Head proved in 1893 that organs can trigger pain at points of the body some distance removed from them. Some time later, exactly the reverse process was observed: Treatment of certain skin and body parts had an influence on the physiology of organs some distance away.

Today we have reached the point where the once-derided acupuncture method is credited with results that could revolutionize whole branches of medicine, especially anesthesia.

One modern scientific explanation for the pain-killing effects of acupuncture was developed by Dr. Godfrey Chin Wan Man of Michigan, during the Second International Congress for Toxicology, held in 1973 in Paris.

He postulated the existence of thick A nerve fibers, surrounded by a sheath of marrow, and thin C nerve fibers, both closely connected within the spinal cord. A fibers transmit exterior stimuli such as heat, cold, and touch to the central nervous system at high speeds. C fibers conduct dull pain sensations, but much more slowly. For example, we will pull back a finger from a hot stove very quickly without feeling pain; that sensation comes later.

Dr. Man contended that A fibers influence the spinal cord in such a way that it becomes less receptive to the pain reports transmitted by C fibers. A fibers report with lightning speed that everything is in order. If these impulses are missing—for example, in the case of an amputated leg—a patient can suffer a phantom pain. Acupuncture needles can help multiply the A fibers' pain-dampening impulse to the point where C fibers are completely blocked.

Clearly, what was regarded for hundreds and thousands of years as "needle attack" against "evil spirits" was, without anyone realizing it at the time, based on scientific principles. In the same way, it is probable that the ancient Egyptians developed effective methods to protect their tombs against grave robbers, methods whose effect they recognized but whose basic principles they did not understand.

That, of course, holds true only for the opulently buried pharaohs; the ordinary man was buried as miserably as he had lived. Despite Egypt's enormous territory, the country threatened to choke in its dead because bodies were only buried in the narrow, cultivated strip of land west of the Nile and in the Nile delta. There was a good reason for burying the dead in the west: The Egyptians believed that the entrance to the underworld was located where the sun sank behind the desert sands and the limestone plateaus.

Burial techniques for the poor had little in common with costly embalming rites. Ceremonious conservation for eternity was reserved for nobles and pharaohs, and the simple Egyptian was buried the same way at the end of the New Kingdom as his ancestors had been three thousand years before. Even today graves are found in the hot desert sand where the dead lie on their left side in embryo position, legs tucked up, covered with a bast-fiber mat, having survived the millennia without mummification, thanks to the low humidity. But the basic beliefs about death were the same for poor and rich: Even the poorest fellah was buried with a clay jug with food and drink, simple arms, and toilet articles such as the highly prized eye makeup.

Comparisons of early Egyptian graves show that over the years they were dug deeper and deeper in order to protect them from jackals. Primitive ditches later developed into rectangular pits and then into chambers. Side chambers were added as storage rooms for gifts given the dead. Finally, the tomb was made visible to the outside by building a wall around it and filling the area with building material, thus creating a monument shaped like a longish rectangle. This was called a *mastaba*, which means bench in Arabic. They were of different sizes, depending on the wealth and importance of the owner. The pharaohs of the Ist and IId dynasties (2850–2700 B.C.) had mastabas built for them in Abydos.

This structure gradually developed into the type of step pyramid the architect Imhotep built for his pharaoh, Djoser, in the IIId dynasty (about 2650 B.C.) by placing narrowing mastabas on top of one another.

The tomb not only was a place to store the corpse but was a home for the ka, the spirit who protected the dead. At first a fake door was built with the name of the dead and various prayers and magic incantations on it. Later, rooms were added behind the door. The doors were always placed on the east side, facing west, and the rooms and passages behind them soon developed into a regular labyrinth.

The Mummy Makers

The form of burial that best fitted the ancient Egyptians' faith and sensibilities did not emerge fully until the Vth dynasty (about 2400 B.C.): mummification, the effort to preserve the dead body's natural appearance.

Next to art historians and archaeologists, physicists and chemists have been most interested in mummification techniques. All the details involved have not yet been discovered, despite the application of every scientific tool available to us and the massive descriptions left behind by adventurers and explorers.

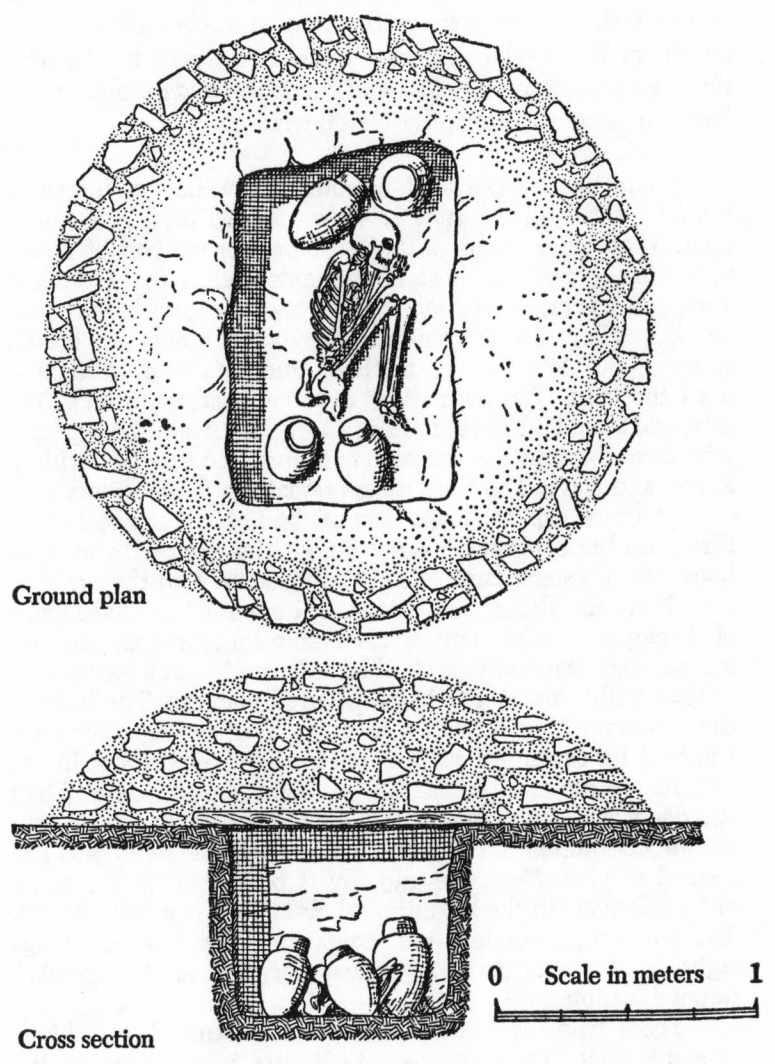

Ground plan

Cross section

0   Scale in meters   1

A grave from the Ist dynasty (about 3200–2800 B.C.).
The grave gifts in these "pauper tombs" were so modest
that securing them against robbers was unnecessary. The
dead were also buried without a sarcophagus.

The Greek historian Herodotus, who traveled to Egypt in the fifth century B.C., is the first and perhaps the best known of those who confronted the mystery of mummification. His reports are detailed and therefore, even if not always factually correct, historically very interesting:

There are professional mummifiers. When a corpse is brought to them they show relatives painted models of mummies. They claim theirs is the most perfect method of mummification, except for those of the gods themselves. I think it wrong, however, to mention the names of the gods in that connection. Then the mummifiers show the family a second, cheaper and less perfect method, and finally a third that costs the least. The mummifier explains everything and then asks what method should be used on the dead. The people who have brought the corpse name the price they are willing to pay and leave. The mummifiers remain in the mortuary.

The most expensive and best method of embalming is this: First, the brain is drawn out through the nose with an iron hook, though sometimes solvents are poured into the brain as well. Next, the abdominal cavity is slit open with a sharp knife of Ethiopian stone. The entrails and inner organs are removed and the body is flushed out with palm wine and rubbed with ground, pleasantly scented material. The body is then conserved by putting it into hydrated sodium carbonate [natron] for seventy days. The corpse may not be kept in the hydrated sodium carbonate longer than seventy days. Then the dead is washed and wrapped in linen bandages. A kind of rubber solution is coated over it, which the Egyptians use instead of glue. Next, the mummy is picked up at the home of its relatives. In the meantime they have had a coffin made. The mummy is put into that coffin and stored standing upright in the mortuary. So much for the most expensive mummification.

Those who can't afford it, settle for second best. This is how it is done: The corpse is not cut open in order to take out the entrails. Instead, the abdominal cavity is filled with an edema of cedar oil. The oil is injected up through the anus and in such a fashion that it cannot flow out again. Then the body must spend the obligatory seventy days soaking in natron. The oil has such a strong effect that it washes out flesh and innards so that only skin and bones remain. Once this procedure has been completed the body is returned to the family without any further treatment.

The third type of mummification, as used by the poor, is as follows: The abdominal cavity is flushed out with a laxative, cleaned, and salted. The mummifier then puts the corpse in natron for seventy days before having the family come to pick it up.

Diodorus Siculus, who reported on the same procedure some four hundred years later, provided this additional information:

When someone dies in Egypt, all his friends and relatives scatter earth on his head. During the funeral ceremony they march lamenting through the town. During that period they don't wash, don't drink wine, and abstain from all pleasure. They don't even wear beautiful clothes.

There are three types of burial: very expensive, medium, and modest. The first costs a talent of silver, the second twenty minen, while the third is very cheap indeed.

Mummifiers learn the art from their ancestors. They come to the deceased's house with pictures of various mummies, and ask how the bereaved wish the dead to be treated. When agreement is reached the dead is brought to the mummifier.

Once the corpse has been laid down, a man known as the demonstrator puts a mark on the left side of the body where the incision is to be made. Then the man who is called the dissecter takes a knife of Ethiopian stone and cuts through the abdominal wall, precisely according to the instructions. Then he runs away, and those present pursue him, throw stones after him, and curse him for what he has done. For in Egypt anyone is hated who injures or wounds or does some other damage to another. On the other hand, the embalmers enjoy dignity and honor. They are on the same level as the priests and are allowed into the temple as holy men without anyone hindering them.

When the embalmers have gathered to prepare the opened body, one of them puts his hand through the wound into the chest and takes out heart and kidney. Another cleans the organs and makes them fragrant with palm wine and incense. After the corpse has been washed, it is treated for thirty days with cedar oil, later with myrrh and cinnamon. That protects the corpse for a long time and also spreads a sweet-smelling scent.

The dead are then returned to their relatives. So carefully have the bodies been prepared that even eye lashes and brows are intact. The body exterior does not change and even facial expressions are recognizable. Many Egyptians keep the bodies of their ancestors in special chambers so that those who are born after them can see them. And when the old Egyptians study shape and appearance, even the facial expressions, of their dead, they feel one with them and with the times in which the dead lived.

The Latest Results

One man who has recently studied the conservation techniques used on mummies is Dr. Zeki Iskander, director of the Antiquities Administration in Cairo. He wrote that brains were first taken out of the skull during the XVIIIth dynasty (from 1570 B.C.). Chisel and hammer were used to cut through the nasal septum, and then the brain was drawn out through the nose with an iron fire hook. Chiseling open the skull from the side to get at the brain was done more rarely. The heart, which the Egyptians believed to be the seat of spirit and emotion, was not treated as were other organs, since it would be weighed during the last judgment. If it was not left in the body, it was replaced, as mentioned earlier, by a holy scarab.

The actual process of mummification dovetails pretty closely with Herodotus's description. It is worth noting that the corpse was stuffed during the drying process in order to avoid shrinkage or malformation. Herbs and straw were preferred as stuffing material, but often desert sand had to do. All the means of the then known cosmetic arts were used to prepare the corpse: milk, wine, mastic, and cedar oil were used to give the skin some color; cheeks were puffed up with linen balls, as were the eyeholes; the nose was corked with clumps of resin.

This complicated mummification technique was not limited to humans. The importance the old Egyptians assigned to the mummification of animals is documented in a demotic papyrus, Vienna No. 27. This fragmentary text, written in a mixture of demotic and hieratic, provides minute details about the ritual surrounding the burial of the Apis bull.

The paper has writing on both sides, in different hands. Presumably it comes from the Memphis Serapeum and was written during the age of Ptolemy, between 250 and 150 B.C. It contains precise directions to priests and servants of the dead for embalming and mummifying the animal:

They are to spread out a mat of papryus from Upper Egypt in front of him and to put a blanket upon it. After that they are to walk behind the conductor of the rites and the chanting priests. They are to be brought shaven. They are to be given clothes and sandals. They are to be washed. They should walk to the chapel and wail and gnash their tooth. Then they are to put a bandage on their neck and to sorrow over the god of the great house. A mat of papyrus is to be spread before the chanting priests, and the conductor of the ritual is to decide what objects he wishes to have in the chapel.

Among these objects was a board upon which, later on, human mummies were put, and stones and linen. The actual mummification process is described as follows:

Next, the conductor of the rites and the chanting priests are to prepare the cloth, covers, and bandages they need for head and limbs. The two rollers are to be six fingers wide and a finger and a half thick. The covering for the head is to be made of new bandages, four on top and four below. The length is to be six ells, the width two thirds. . . . After that the conductor of the ritual and the priests are to go to the place where the god [the Apis bull] is. They are to place the cloth between the front legs of the god, inside the right shoulder so that it comes out of the left shoulder. Then the bandage is cut and let go within the left shoulder so that it comes out on the right shoulder.

Strangely enough, the dead body is anointed only after the thigh has been wrapped. The ointment, it is emphasized, must be allowed to enter the body.

Then a man should sit in front of the conductor of the ritual. He should open the inside of the god's skull and push his hand into the skull as far as it will reach. He should take whatever he finds in the head and stuff it well. He must pay special care to the substances the priest has taken out.

Finally, he must remove the two canine teeth in the lower jaw as well as two other teeth. Wax, myrrh, and incense should be stuffed into the head of the god so that it cannot be closed. A large bag of myrrh is to be placed under the tongue, while the tongue itself is covered with a salve-soaked substance.

Three bandages are wound around the head. One is placed on the top, the other [sic] around the face. Then three pieces of cloth are to be put on the windpipe and the esophagus, two others on the gum, and two more on the two cheekbones. The inside of the head is to be well pillowed. Then the man is to stand in front of the eyes. He is to stuff the inside of the eyes and to anoint them and to put the material on the eyes—two bandages on each eye. Finally, he should take all the substance out of the nose and stuff the inside with linen.

After the head wrapping, the papyrus describes wrapping the bull's horns. Then a chanting priest steps in front of the abdominal cavity of the animal, spreads a large cloth over the dead body of the animal, and disappears under it. Instructions for mummification further state:

The chanting priest is to take everything out of the abdominal cavity he can find. He shall reach as far with his hand as he can. Then he is to cleanse the cavity with water and to stuff it with cloth.

The stuffed bull is finally set upright. In order to do that, the plank is shoved between his legs. Head and neck are bound high so that the animal takes on a natural position. In that position the Apis bull is lifted into a shrine that serves as a coffin. Only then can the actual burial ceremonies begin, for which all the priests and servants of the dead must be dressed in red.

Today we know a good deal about the botanical and pharmaceutical composition of the ingredients used in mummification, but we don't know everything. Resin drugs and natron—hydrated sodium carbonate—are cited most frequently in pyramid texts, the Book of the Dead, and various papyri.

Resin drugs were used not only in their natural state but in several other forms. The Harris papyrus, for example, says, *In your great courtyard in Memphis there are trees planted of incense and myrrh—such as my two hands have brought from Punt to make your divine face light up at the time of morning.*

There is a parallel to this prayer in the same papyrus, where myrrh from Punt is cited—not, however, the tree but the finished resin product. Imported incense cedars are also mentioned.

Punt is one of the most mysterious lands of antiquity. Phoenicians and Egyptians actively explored it and traded there as much as they could because of its valuable raw materials: turpentine, scents, ebony, gold, and poisons and minerals, which, however, had to be taken from the pygmy-sized natives by force. Punt, strange land of mystery and pygmies, was not a myth but actually existed, probably on what is now the Somali coast of Africa.

Pictures in Theban graves show how incense cedars and myrrh trees were dug up in Punt, put into huge clay jars, and dragged hundreds of miles through the desert. Poles were stuck through the handles of the jar, which was then carried by slaves. These "tree transports" reached their high point during the XVIIIth dynasty, especially under Queen Hatshepsut.

At the time of Rameses III, during the XXth dynasty, myrrh trees already grew in Thebes, but the climate did not allow them to flourish. After the birth of Christ, the Roman historian Pliny commented that myrrh trees "degenerated" in Egypt. Pliny used the word *degenerate* in its original meaning of changing, which a trained scientist would interpret as qualitative deterioration; by that time the myrrh tree had already mutated into a bush.

Scented drugs were used as solid resin for the preparation of the mummy and as smoke during the mummification ceremonies. Incense and myrrh in the mouth of the dead were supposed to clean him, scented resin to assure him of enough to eat in all eternity and of life after death. Incense and myrrh, the Egyptians believed, possessed such enormous power that they could overcome even the ka of the gods.

The smoke of scented resin allowed the dead to overcome the force of gravity; it freed him from earthly bondage. One papyrus commented:

> *They pull him to heaven*
> *to heaven on columns of smoke of divine scent.*

The Gods Nut and Tefnut drew the dead up on these clouds of scent, away from the material and into the spiritual world.

Alfred Lucas, the government chemist who attended the opening of King Tut's mummy, worked on a classification of

Slaves brought rare plants and trees from distant lands thousands of kilometers to Egypt. Here: Incense cedars from the magic land of Punt.

incense. He believed that in addition to the incense plant we know today, *Boswellia carteri*, the Egyptians may have used some of the following: myrrh (from *Commiphora pedinculata*), balsam (from *Balsamodendron africanum*), *Gardenia thunbergii*, labdanum (from *Cistus ladanum*), storax (from *Styrax officinalis*), and galbanum (from *Ferula galbaniflua*). Herodotus wrote about incense, myrrh, storax, laudanum, and galbanum. And in his *History of Plants*, Theophrastus made this point:

Some say that incense smells more fragrantly in Arabia but grows more beautifully on nearby islands [probably the Bahreins], for there it is formed on the trees in any desired shape. Perhaps this is not improbable, since form is shaped by the cuttings made into the tree.

While the various scented resins served the spiritual-idealistic and autosuggestive side of the burial cult, natron was essential for dehydrating the body and thus conserving it. Natron occurs naturally in the sea. A hydrated sodium carbonate, it is the basis for various compounds including chloric acid, caustic soda, and hydrochloric acid.

Natron is found in three places in Egypt. Seventy kilometers west of Cairo, in the Libyan desert, lies the Wadi el-Natrun. During the Nile floods small lakes form there, which evaporate as the floods recede. A white crust is left on the sand, which the inhabitants first identified as natron back in the Old Kingdom. Lucas also reported that natron is found in the lower Egyptian province of Beheira and in Edfu in Upper Egypt. (These sites, however, have different names in old Egyptian texts. One papyrus talks about "southern natron," which obviously means that brought in from Edfu.)

As Herodotus and many others reported, the dead in ancient Egypt were placed in natron for seventy days in order to completely dehydrate the body. Later observers, however, also cited a forty-day period, which, according to modern findings, is closer to the truth. But preparing the body sometimes took much longer: allegedly 272 days passed between the death of Queen Meres-ankh and her burial.

At the beginning of the Old Kingdom it was not customary to remove the inner organs and the entrails. But during the IIId dynasty the custom came into wide use, only to go out of fashion during the Middle Kingdom. Instead, a turpentine solution was injected into the anus and kept inside the body for several days. When it was allowed to flow out, the decomposed innards were flushed out as well.

Both methods were used in the New Kingdom, although the surgical method was preferred because of its greater cleanliness. The art of mummification reached its high point during the XVIIIth dynasty.

The Procession of the Dead on the Nile

When mummification was completed, the mummy was put into a coffin. In the Old Kingdom that meant a simple wooden or stone sarcophagus; later it would be decorated with hieroglyphics and pictures. Two eyes decorated the head side of the mummy coffin—slits for the ka. Fake doors were put on the sides of the coffin for the ka's benefit too. Still later, the coffins were covered over with death spells, so-called transfigurations. Since the dead were supposed to be given as many transfigurations as possible, there soon wasn't room enough to write them all on the coffin, so they had to be put down on papyri, which were then put into the coffin: This was the famed Book of the Dead.

The inscriptions asked the help of the gods. Anubis, Osiris, Nut, and Isis, but above all others the four children of Horus, were to protect the dead. The last opened Osiris's mouth so that he could again eat and talk. And Horus's sons were also supposed to keep hunger and thirst from the dead.

Once the mummy had been placed into the coffin and the rock tomb or earthen grave readied, a ghostly ritual took place. Those who could afford to do so arranged, while still alive, to have their mummy buried in Osiris's holy city, Abydos. But one could also have a fake tomb in Abydos or merely erect a simple tombstone there. It was also customary to take mummies down the Nile to Abydos, where they would take part in sacrifices to Osiris, and then carry them back and bury them at home.

The funeral procession regularly began on the eastern bank of the Nile, where the coffin was placed on a flat boat, thick with flowers, with a canopy in the middle. The wife and daughters of the dead man sat, bare-bosomed, on both sides of the coffin, crying and weeping, while the priest of the dead, a leopard skin over his shoulders, poured incense over the mummy.

A small boat with a male relative of the deceased aboard sailed ahead of the funeral ship, while the man shouted across the white-glistening river to the helmsman, "Turn to the West, to the land of the just. The women on the ship weep and wail. In peace to the West. You, O praised and adored one, come in peace. When this day has become eternity, then we shall see you again. Look, you walk to the land where men are mingled."

Depending on the number and importance of the deceased's relatives, many or few ships took part in the crossing. The flat boat with the coffin aboard was pulled out of the water on the other side by four cattle and dragged to the burial site so that "he can join his fathers and mothers and that the masters of the land of the dead may welcome him." [1]

A priest called the *sem* starred in this bizarre theater. Bandaged like a mummy, he lay in the grave as the mourning procession arrived. Three men awoke him, and he rose amid elaborate ceremonial. Then he performed the ritual of opening mouth and eyes, using his little finger. This allowed the deceased to see and eat again, vital prerequisites for immortality.

There was one cruel feature of this death rite: As the mourners took their leave of the dead, a live calf had one of its front feet cut off. This custom, whose import has not yet been explained, is reflected in wall paintings that often show a three-legged calf standing in the midst of a herd of cattle.

The thought that during his journey to the underworld the dead might suffer hunger was particularly painful for the ancient Egyptians and explains the models of roast goose, bread, or ox tail, made of wood and alabaster, that were placed in the grave.

Equally unbearable was the thought that someone might die without having prepared his burial place, or that he might die abroad. Those killed in war or during voyages of discovery into Nubia or to the Red Sea had to count on friends or relatives to ship them home.

Vanity of the Tomb

Noble Egyptians began laying out their tombs while still young. As soon as the architectural design was finished, the future tomb owner had himself and his family painted on its walls. That was often difficult, since family relationships as well as ranks and achievements tended to change during a lifetime. Therefore, the grave builders might leave room in front of the owner's name to accommodate titles yet to come, a space that as often as not remained unfilled.

Such blanks can tell an eloquent story: Chaemhet, master of the barns under Amenhotep III, had a grave built for himself in western Thebes. As a man of some distinction and honor, he wanted it completed while still alive. But although he enjoyed a harem befitting his station, he had not yet picked a wife. So he left room for his future bride's name to follow such inscriptions as "my dear wife ——" or "the lady of the house ——." The name was never written in. Chaemhet died before deciding on a spouse.

Death in Egypt was expensive. Many, including high court officials, found themselves reduced to taking over the tombs of older families that had died out. Grave inscriptions were painted over, reliefs covered with clay. Sometimes the pharaohs rewarded poorer officials with graves of their own. We know that Menkure (about 2500 B.C.), for whom the smallest of the three great pyramids at Giza was built, lent a man called Debhen, a palace official, fifty royal workers so that he could equip his own tombs. Pharaoh Sahure (about 2480 B.C.) gave an opulent fake door to his personal physician, Ne'anch-Sachmet, for use by the doctor's ka. However, the showpiece served only to make the good physician's grave seem all the meaner.

A people this concerned with the dignified burial of its dead certainly worried about preserving the graves and their valuable contents. As we have seen, this task was entrusted to the organizers of the burial ceremonies, the priests. As the curse of the pharaohs shows, they fully deserved this trust.

8 The Secrets of the Gods

SOMETHING MOVED under the microscope. Later, some scientists would dismiss what the German biologist Erwin Santo had seen; others hailed it as a miracle.

Santo had observed a new way of cell formation, the creation of new life. He had placed the remains of dead bacteria in a food solution containing traces of lithium. They were left in the food solution, at slightly above room temperature, for seventeen hours: by then they had fused into cells complete with nucleus and plasma. They resembled white corpuscles—and they were alive.

Biologists have known for fifty years that as plant and animal cells die tiny cell elements remain alive, a phenomenon that has been observed under the most sterile conditions. These cell remnants bear an amazing similarity to bacteria, but they are not fully developed and can best be categorized as "unidentified life carriers."

This means that while the death of a body's cells ends one human life, it does not end all life in the corpse. Bacteria-like life carriers can help build new life after individual death. They are building blocks which all organisms—bacteria, plants, animals, humans—can use to help form new life. Does that mean that life after death or reincarnation is more than an article of faith in various religions? Is it subject to scientific proof?

One thing is clear: These life carriers have greater powers of resistance than any known organism. They can be extracted from boiled, frozen, or chemically destroyed tissue, even from five-thousand-year-old mummies.

Back in 1951 the Russian biologist Lepeshinskaya carried out similar experiments—and earned the hostility of many colleagues because she believed she had proved that cells can regenerate. Specifically, she found that "life carrier" cells developed from decaying blood corpuscles.

Admittedly, this leaves many questions unanswered: Doesn't an organism absorb such cells in food? How does body metabolism handle them? Could they be necessary for regeneration? Why do we age if the body receives a steady supply of new life substances?

Such a line of thought prompted a University of California scientist, Elof Carlsson, to postulate the possibility of a mummy's scientific reconstruction, i.e., the genetic creation of an individual who looks, thinks, and feels like the descendant of an Egyptian mummy. He proposed isolating genes from mummified tissue and reactivating the nucleonic acid crystals needed to crack the genetic code. The nucleus extracted from a mummy tissue cell would have to replace the nucleus of a fertile cell.

Simple as it sounds, this is a procedure modern biochemistry is not even close to mastering. It is, of course, possible that someday a man with a pharaoh's heredity will be "born," three or four thousand years after his "ancestor's" death. But it is doubtful that even such an extraordinary event would bring us any closer to solving the mystery of the ancient Egyptians.

The ancient Egyptians were the most intelligent people who had yet lived, a fact friend and foe attested to throughout Egypt's thousands of years of history. Even the apostles admired Moses for having been taught "all the wisdom of Egypt." And despite the church fathers' criticism of Egyptian polytheism, they did not extend their attack to Egypt's science, then closely intertwined with theology.

These hypotheses do not, of course, offer any answers to

the riddle of life's origins, but they help demystify Egyptian religion and grant it a scientific base.

Reincarnation in a Lotus Flower

The early Egyptians believed in a life after death. Under no circumstances was death the end of a man. But there was no agreement as to how life continued. For some, life went on in the grave chamber; for others, among the birds on the trees, amid the beetles in the sand, or in the lotus flower that grew along the banks of the Nile. Still others looked for their dead among the stars of heaven or in the underworld traversed by the sun god at night.

One of the peculiarities of Egyptian religion was the tripartite division of man after his death. There was, first of all, the body; then the soul, known as the ba; and finally the ka. The ka was a kind of guardian angel who brought men happiness, joy, health, and a long life. Gods, pharaohs, and ordinary people all had their kas. Countless wall paintings and reliefs depict double figures, one just behind the other, in the same position and with the same appearance. The second figure is always the ka. The kas of the pharaohs were often equipped with special attributes and even with names of their own. Thus Thutmose III spoke of his ka as "a victorious bull who shone in the rings of Thebes."

It was not a man's soul, but rather his ka, that was responsible for life after death. The body was embalmed for the ka's benefit, so that he could use it any time he wished. Life-sized statues of the dead were placed in the tombs of the pharaohs so that the ka would always have their physical appearance before them. And, of course, the food and drink left in the tombs was to nourish the ka.

The ba, on the other hand, was a godlike element enclosed in the body during life and only liberated at death. The Berlin papyrus No. 3024 records a man's conversation with his ba. The Egyptologist Winfried Barta discussed this text within the context of the ba problem in his book *Das Gespräch eines Mannes mit seinem Ba* (Conversations of a Man with His Ba). He wrote:

The ba should resemble the deceased not only in physical appearance but in character, knowledge, and experience; he should know what the dead knew. His magic power to take on any shape he wished was a factor of his divine nature. He is magic and cannot be neutralized by other magic. The body, in contrast, is only shadow or transfiguration. A crucial difference between body and ba: Only the body must undergo transfiguration by having the living chant magic incantations so that he can attain the state of grace needed in the afterlife. The Ba, as incarnation of the life force, is not affected by death. At most, the ba requires sacrificial rites, not the magic of transfiguration, to assure his continued existence. And even though some New Kingdom texts talk of transfiguring the ba, it seems to be less a matter of the ba's transfiguration than its union with the transfigured—the corpse.

The ba emerges as an independent personality embodying the life force only after the body dies. Thus ancient texts speak of a "living ba" and promise the deceased that he too will become a living ba. The expression a "living transfiguration," would—since only the corpse has been transfigured—have to be interpreted as a transfigured corpse complete with a living ba. The forces that grant the ba constantly renewed life are embedded in his indestructible generative capacity, which he is said to possess in the hereafter just as the deceased had it in this life.

Every Egyptian, and especially the children of the dead, were duty-bound to care for the deceased by providing him with material possessions as well as spiritual gifts—curses and death spells to ward off grave robbers and a plentiful supply of food. They even thought about means of transport. Not everyone was given as magnificent a gilded carriage as Tutankhamen, but a ship was placed in every grave, even if it was only a small one made of clay. It served the ka for crossing the waters that enclose the heavenly fields of the blessed.

It is not easy to tell just where these fields of the blessed were located. Unlike many of the religions that followed it, the Egyptian theology is as peaceful and contemplative as the people were at the beginning of their history. The sun, the moon, and the stars were the first things to excite the Egyptian imagination. Later, strangely shaped stones, huge trees, dangerous snakes, and crocodiles were added, and all were assigned divine power.

Egypt was an enormous country, and to a stone- and iron-age people it must have seemed much larger than we can imagine today. This is one explanation as to why they gave the same god different names: For example, the protective god was named Seth in Upper Egypt, Horus in Lower Egypt.

Formation of the Horus empire, which united Upper and Lower Egypt under the leadership of Lower Egypt and was ruled from Heliopolis, was an event of the greatest historical importance. The Harris papyrus provides details about the wealth of Heliopolis temples which make for interesting comparisons. Under Rameses III Heliopolis was 160 times larger than Memphis, for example, with four and a half times as much cattle and four times the population. Ownership of 103 surrounding villages added to the capital's economic importance, as did the Nile measuring rod, located on the island of Roda in today's Cairo, because its tide gauge served as an orientation mark for helmsmen.

And the ancient Egyptian calendar, whose origins date back to 4240 B.C., was also oriented to Heliopolis.

As Kurt Sethe writes in his book *Urgeschichte und älteste Religion der Ägypter* (Basic History and Ancient Religion of the Egyptians), the sun was worshiped in Heliopolis as the highest and oldest divine being.

The first and oldest godhead was the personification of light, Re, which simply means "sun." Re emerged from the sexual union of earth and sky. Keb and Nut, Father Earth and Mother Heaven, must beget Re anew every night so that every morning he is reborn between Nut's thighs. This is the oldest version of the story.

But in Heliopolis it was decreed that the sun had neither father nor mother. Instead, the sun rose up from a hill and brought light, life, and movement into the world. The Heliopolis sun god Re was identical with the local god Atum (which means "the whole" and "the universe"). As a result the sun was also called Re-Atum.

Atum was depicted as an Egyptian king holding the

144

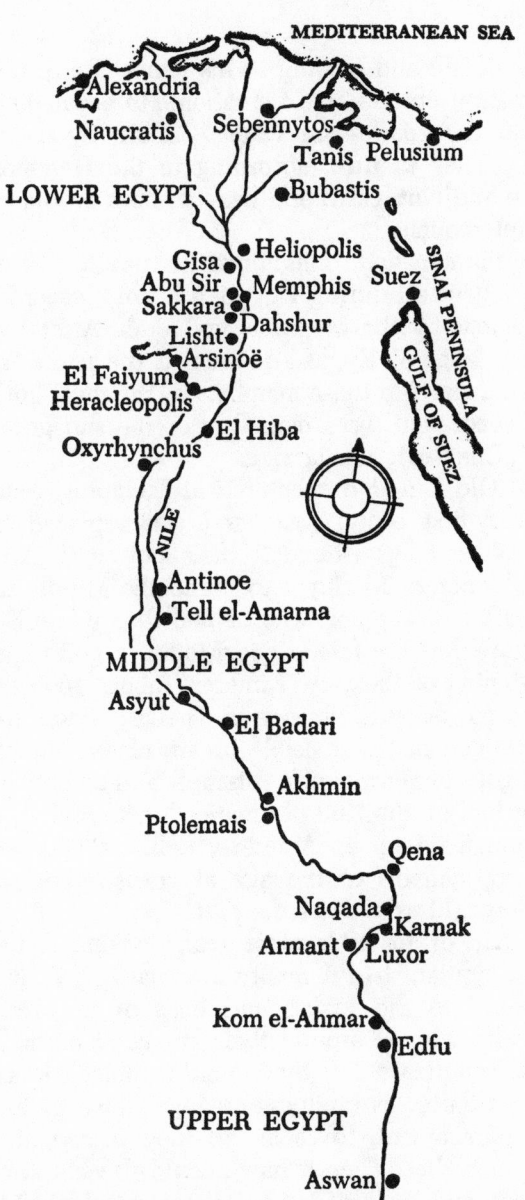

The old Egypt of the pharaohs. All the historic sites lie directly on the Nile or just a few miles from this vital artery.

symbols of life and healing in his hands! Re-Atum began his labors with a unique act of creation. He begat the god of air, Shu, and the goddess of water, Tefnut, by coughing them into life. They in turn, according to the Heliopolis version, had Keb and Nut, earth and heaven, both products of normal sexual intercourse.

Re, the sun god, maintained his position as creator and highest regent all during Egyptian history, except for a brief displacement by the Memphis god Ptah. After the IVth dynasty the kings of Egypt also carried the name "son of Re." Since Khufu's reign those members of the royal house selected for the succession were named after the sun god: Dedef-re, Khafre (Cha'f-re), Meukew-re.

The Old Kingdom, centered at Memphis, went under in the twenty-first century B.C. and was replaced by Thebes, whose minor kings extended their power to Abydos, Sint, and finally across all Egypt to found the Middle Kingdom in about 2050 B.C. The god who helped the middle Egyptians to this victory was the falcon god Montu, a god of war. But at the beginning of the New Kingdom, about 1600 B.C., another god won power and influence in Thebes: Amon, the "Hidden One," the god of the invisible breath of air, one of the eight original gods of Hermopolis. A temple and an oracle altar were built for him on the "hill of creation" in Karnak.

Amon lived on as Amon-re, unlike the other founding gods who, symbols of the age of chaos, were relegated to the underworld as gods of the past.

As one of history's most realistic-minded peoples, the ancient Egyptians had difficulty in visualizing their gods. First they looked to the snakes and lions of the desert, to the jackals who whined around their graves at night, and to the gently grazing cows. But they found it difficult to ascribe such human attributes as kindness or anger, love or hate, protection or punishment, to them. So they placed animal heads on human bodies. Then a hawk could use his arms to strike or protect, and even a crocodile was capable of human action.

There is nothing remarkable about faith in the divine nature of animals—animal worship is found in nearly all developing civilizations—but most of them tended to abandon their animal cults as spiritual and intellectual development progressed. Not so the Egyptians.

The traveling Greek philosopher Lucian had some strange stories to tell about animal gods and their worship in Egypt:

The Egyptian temples were big and beautiful, built of expensive stone and decorated with gold and paintings. But if you asked for the name of the god to whom a temple was dedicated you were told that the god was a monkey, an ibis, a ram or cat.

And the Greek geographer Strabo reported from the Fayum:

Near the town of Crocodilopolis [Arsinoë] a crocodile lives in a lake. It is tame to the priests. Named Suchos, it is fed with bread, meat, and wine brought by strangers who come to see the crocodile. My host, a highly regarded man who showed us the holy things there, went with us to the lake. He brought with him a small cake, some fried meat, and a bottle of honey mead. We found the animal lying on shore. The priests approached and opened his jaws. One shoved the cake inside, then the meat, and finally he poured mead down his throat. Satiated, the crocodile jumped into the lake and swam to the other side. Meanwhile another stranger came with similar gifts. The priests took them, walked around the lake, and after they found the crocodile gave him the food in the same manner.

Both descriptions, don't forget, were written by travelers who didn't know what to make of this cult. Presumably, feeding the holy animals was conducted with greater pomp and circumstance.

Early interpretations of the Egyptian animal cult held that what had started out as legend was later transformed into historical tradition. Where people once compared the moon god with an ibis and the goddess Bastet with a cat, they later moved from comparison to identification. But the fact that many animal gods have no equivalent in nature runs counter to their theory. Also, Egyptian religion features many gods not found in other civilizations. Thus Amon was combined with a ram, Sebak with a crocodile, Thoth with the ibis, Bastet with a cat (in that sense there were few pure animal gods). They had double natures characteristic of both.

The Holy Animals

The early Egyptians worshipped nearly all the animals they knew. That included cats and lions, dogs and jackals, monkeys and elephants, hippopotamuses and crocodiles, goats and cattle, frogs and turtles, owls and herons, snakes and fish, beetles and flies.

However, there was a subtle difference in the veneration of individual animals: Some were considered holy; others gods. The holy ones were tended, cared for, and preserved; the others adored. There was always only one Apis bull worshiped as a god, only one divine cat in Bubastis, only one Amon ram in Karnak, only one Suchos crocodile in Crocodilopolis. One animal of each species had to be the highest. But all other members of the species enjoyed better treatment because of this veneration.

This god-animal incorporated the deity of various districts: Apis was the newly won life of Ptah, the Theban ram the reborn Amon, the crocodile the incorporation of the god Sebak.

Anyone who killed a holy animal, even in self-defense, was guilty of sacrilege and faced death. If an animal did have to be slaughtered, rich sacrifices were offered first; the Egyptians believed in animal reincarnation and feared the vengeance of others of the dead beast's species.

Moreover, the Egyptians apparently saw their reincarnated relatives embodied in the animals they worshiped; this is the only rational explanation for their practice of sodomy. Herodotus tells of seeing a woman fornicate in public with a ram. Occasionally, women were brought to the holy Apis bull.

Dr. Alfred Wiedemann, professor at Bonn University, noted in his book *Der Tierkult der alten Ägypter* (The Animal Cult of the Ancient Egyptians) that snails and other small animals were kept in private homes as house gods. They lived in chapel-shaped cages and were given presents and other offerings. Processions in which hymn-singing youths surrounded an Apis bull or some other animal were common and always the center of veneration by the faithful multitude. Professor Wiedemann wrote:

Lavish funeral processions moved down the streets to take the deceased holy animal to his last resting-place. If the animal were held in special veneration, his tomb was a separate building. Thus about 1500 B.C. small chapels were built on terraces above the grave city of Sakkara. . . . The animal was surrounded by gifts and rested in a rock tomb below the chapel.

More often, however, these creatures were not buried in individual graves but in a large tract, such as the Apis grave site of the Memphis Serapeum, where each one was given a cell both as death chamber and home for his immortal soul. Nearby was a common cult room for all tomb inmates. The power of animals buried here was highly regarded. Men of rank—for example, a royal prince, a son of Rameses II—had their last resting-places prepared in their midst in order to partake of their divine protection.

Still, rather than building new animal graves, the Egyptians preferred cheaper mass graves. Natural mountain caves or older tombs which had been plundered of corpses and treasures were, of course, used whenever possible. Hundreds and even thousands of animal corpses were piled up in them. Usually only one species of animal was buried in each site, depending on the prevalent faith in the district—for example the Ibis tombs, plundered centuries ago, in Sakkara; the giant crocodile grave in Monfalut; or a monkey tomb in Thebes. In other areas, however, all dead holy animals were dragged in from near and far and bedded together, irrespective of their species.

The deification of animals in ancient Egypt dates back to an age when stone-age man stood helpless against nature around him. It was a time when he hoped to transfix the animal he wanted to kill by drawing its picture on the wall of his cave; when an animal, in its unpredictability and incomprehensible life-style, seemed a demon.

The Gods Specialize

After Egypt's many districts were consolidated into two empires, there was a surfeit of gods. None of the gods, of course, could simply be "dismissed." Instead, each was assigned a special task. One had to create children, another cared for the dead. One was responsible for farming, another for war. In turn, that allowed the priesthood of individual gods to gather new information from people they dealt with and thus gradually expand their own knowledge. And later, when the pharaoh was able to draw upon the knowledge of all his priests and when his palace became a center of historical knowledge and intellectual achievements, was it any wonder that the people venerated him as god, as all-knowing and all-powerful?

The oldest religious cult emerged from Lower Egypt, where Memphis, Sakkara, and Heliopolis were the religious centers. In Memphis the bald-headed, scepter-swinging god Ptah enjoyed the greatest prestige. He was considered a "founding" god, a creative god, as was Hephaestus in Greek mythology. Later Ptah was fused with the falcon-headed god of death, Sokaris, and, when Osiris was made lord of the underworld, a triple godhead emerged—Ptah-Sokaris-Osiris. Apis, the holy bull, belonged to Ptah.

A bull was also worshiped in the sun temple at Heliopolis, a town called On in Egyptian. His name was Mnevis. The chief god of Heliopolis was Re, the sun god, who was represented as Re-Harachte—with falcon head and sun disk. Harachte, of course, is Horus, the guardian god of the Nile delta and of Lower Egypt.

Horus was first worshiped in Damanhur, the old Hermopolis Parva. After the union of the upper and lower Egyptian empires, he was given yet another fief in Lower Egypt, a town known as Edfu today.

150

According to the historian Diodorus Siculus, Horus, son of Isis, a goddess skilled in medicine, worked as doctor and magician. He was also called "head doctor in the house of Re."

A large shard of clay, an ostracon, now in Strasbourg, carries the following inscription:

> The words of Horus beat back death by keeping him alive, who fights for air.
> The words of Horus make life anew by making the years permanent for those who call on Him.
> The words of Horus put out the fire. His spells heal the feverish.
> The words of Horus save that man, whose fate stands behind him.
> Horus's magic wards off bows by turning the arrows around.
> Horus's magic wards off anger by calming the senses.
> Horus's magic heals the sick.

The text of the next four lines has not been fully preserved, but the emphasis on the power of Horus's words and magic spells is clear.

Hathor, the highest goddess, hailed from Atfih in Upper Egypt, where she was known as "the first of all cows." Her pictures depict a comely woman with a cow's ears and horns. Sometimes the sinking sun is painted between her horns. She was the goddess of the West, where the sun rests above the mountain chains before disappearing among them in order to let the dead enter the underworld.

Hathor's great rival was Mut, embodiment of the maternal spirit. Mut had her stronghold in Thebes, where she was worshiped as goddess of War—she is shown with a lion head—and advanced to wife of the imperial god Amon. Memphis featured the mighty goddess Sachmet, who also wore a lioness head, as befit a goddess of battle who, if need be, could spit fire at the enemy. In paintings Sachmet can easily be confused with Bastet, the cat-headed goddess, although the characters and significance of the two are diametrically opposed. Bastet ("she who comes from the town of Bast") embodied joy and cheer, not war. The many Goddesses and the tasks assigned them are a clear indication that women played a significant role in Egyptian society.

Seth and Horus, the god protectors of Upper and Lower Egypt, occupy a special place in Egyptian religious history. Verse 222 of the pyramid texts (which also contain the coronation rite in Heliopolis) stresses the division: the northern empire for Horus, the south for Seth. Thus Upper Egypt tells the king, "Seth gave you his abodes." And Lower Egypt says, "Horus gave you his thrones." The waterfalls at Elephantine are considered "Seth's downpour," the Nile estuary into the Mediterranean as "Horus's downpour."

At first they were enemies; then—after the unification of the empire—they became brothers, although Horus always held the upper hand.

If Seth were not a god, he might have been called a tragic figure, because of his physical deformity. Seth was shaped like an animal, but not an animal anyone could identify in nature. Archaeologists have picked different animals to embody him: Wiedemann an okapi, Schweinfurth an aardvark (a largely nocturnal anteater), Newberry a wart hog, von Bissing a giraffe, Maspero a jerboa. Presumably he personified some feature of each of them. Seth had red eyes. And red, in contrast to blessed green, was the color of evil.

There still is no adequate explanation as to why Seth wore the head of an ass. Presumably Horus's disciples attempted a crude caricature, but it proved so popular that Seth kept it even after the empire was unified. But the pharaohs generally identified with Horus and only rarely with Seth. And when the pharaohs had their victories recorded in hieroglyphics, it was always done as a falcon on a golden insigne. The falcon was Horus; the gold symbolized the god from Ombos, Seth.

While Seth could count on little affection, Thoth enjoyed a great deal. The ibis-headed Thoth came from the Nile delta and was god of the moon. But because the Egyptians saw the moon and its rhythmic waxing and waning as the personification of order, they considered Thoth the mathematician and scribe of the gods. No one knows why he was sometimes pictured as a baboon.

But Thoth was not without competition as moon god. In Thebes the god Chons took over his chores.

Most of Egypt's gods had such rivals. Even the almighty god of the dead, Osiris, and his wife, Isis, had to dethrone other gods before becoming sole rulers of the underworld. Osiris came from Busiris, as it was known in Greek, where he was first worshiped; presumably he had been a king at the dawn of history whose death inspired a whole mythology. At the beginning of the third millennium, Osiris strengthened his hold on Egypt; first in Memphis, where he absorbed the god Sokaris; later in Abydos, where he replaced the "first in the West" as the death god worshiped as ruler of the underworld.

In his home town of Busiris, Osiris was depicted as a column with a ribbed capital, a symbol which in hieroglyphic writing means "lasting." Death lasts. Osiris's pictures and statues show him as a mummy with green face, because he lived and greened. He wore a pharaoh's crown and held the insignia of power—crosier and fan—in his hands.

Osiris lay below the earth with the whole world on top of him. When he moved, the earth moved. Plants grew from his body and turned him into "new corn." Because water flowed from his feet, he became "new rain." The Nile was the sweat of his hands.

All this helped make Osiris the god of natural order. It was he who emerged as fertile soil from the receding waters of the flooded Nile, who was god of the greening fields and of the autumnal dying, with its promise of renewed life next spring.

Osiris, as god of the dead, had three attendants with the heads of dogs: Anubis, the guardian of the dead, and the two Up-nat brothers, his companions in battle. He was the victim of evil fates. Legend has it that Seth killed him, but that Horus, Osiris's son, avenged his father, whereupon Osiris awoke to new life. The story became a model of caring for the dead. It was a son's duty to provide his father's tomb, cherish his memory, and turn into his worthy successor. Indeed, that model could be followed so slavishly that some dead nobles were dubbed "Osiris," mourned by their mother, "Nut," and their wife, "Isis."

Osiris wore two feathers, insignia of his royal honors, that had been symbols of power of a local god (of the ninth district in Lower Egypt). The "local" was soon merged into Osiris, and, as a result, the district capital was later named House of Osiris. Today it is known as Abu Sir.

Judging the Dead

Those who had departed this life had to face Osiris's judgment of the dead. Osiris sat in the hall of the two goddesses of Justice, surrounded by forty-two knife-wielding demons. They were shadow eaters, flame eyes, or blood eaters. Each represented one of forty-two possible sins. The dead person had to prove he had not committed any of them. If he could, the demons would not attack him.

After his innocence had been established, Horus took the new arrival by the hand and introduced him to his father, Osiris, as a new member of the underworld. Some cautious estimates have been made as to how many members the underworld might have had in ancient Egypt: about 150 to 200 million dead in the time from the Old Kingdom to the New Empire.

Established religion was challenged only once, when, in the thirteenth century B.C., as we have seen, Amenhotep IV abolished polytheism for twenty years, called himself Ikhnaton, and allowed only one god: Aton. How did this major break in the history of Egyptian religion come about?

The idea of "Aton" surfaced first in the Middle Kingdom as the designation for "the star of day." It was said about the royal statues in Amenhotep III's temple in Thebes, "They gleamed more brightly than the sky, their faces radiant like Aton's glowing in the morning." Aton, the star of day, was, of course, the sun, not the heretic King Ikhnaton's invention.

Walther Wolf, who studied the forerunners of Ikhnaton's reformation, has examined the sun hymns with great care. He concluded that words and phrases were less important than the spirit that speaks from these songs.

If reformist ideas had indeed surfaced during Amenhotep II's reign, they would at least have suggested elements of the sun hymn of Amarna—the clearest expression of the new religion. But Wolf found that the old ideas Egyptians had entertained about the sun god since time immemorial still predominated. In these old hymns Aton, Harachte, and Chepre were still juxtaposed; moreover, there were frequent references to the picture of the "sun ape."

How different the hymn to the sun which Horus and Seth, builders under Amenhotep III, carved onto a memorial column! The train of thought is very similar to that in the Aton hymn. At the beginning there is a passage in which old ideas are still strong. Then life awaking at sunrise is described.

Lines five to seven of the Amon hymn read:

When you appear in the morning, the work of day takes shape. When you ride in your majesty the day is short. You sweep through a journey of millions and hundreds of thousands of miles. The time of every day is below you. You wake to rise in the morning. Your rays open the eyes.

Compare a few lines from the Aton hymn:

The earth grows bright when you rise on the mountain of light. When you, as Aton, radiate the day, you drive away darkness. Send down your rays and both lands are filled with joy. They awaken and stand on their feet. You have lifted them up. They clean their limbs and put on their clothes. Their arms worship because you shine. The whole land does its labor.

Aton Was Nothing New

Georg Möller, a Berlin Egyptologist, wrote a monograph dating literary texts from the first half of the New Kingdom. In it, he claims that the hymn to Amon just cited presumably was written during the reign of Amenhotep II or Thutmose IV, but certainly before Amenhotep IV mounted the throne.

Walther Wolf analyzed the hymn like this:

It seems to be a compilation or composite of hymns with differing central figures: Amon-Re of Karnak, Min-Amon, Aton-Chepre of Heliopolis, the Harachte. The god was venerated as king of the gods by celebrating his crown and scepter of his mythological deeds in song, or by honoring the god and his creation. Observations of nature are simple and real and betray a closeness to nature—no surprise to those who know Egyptian tomb paintings—that appears, in this context, new and unusual.

Compare the following verse:

You are the only one, the one who created being, the only one who was alone, when he brought forth all creatures.

So much for the Amon hymn. The Aton hymn praises the creator:

You, only one, there is no other. You have created the earth according to your own heart. You, one and only.

And while Amon is praised as the one who "made herbs for the herds" and the one who "gives air to the chick in the egg," the Aton hymn credits him with "making all cattle give thanks for its fodder," and it is Aton who gives air to the chick "when the chick speaks in the egg."

Obviously, the Aton cult was not a sudden reform initiated by one man. Indeed, some Egyptologists, after studying documents from Amenhotep III's reign, speculated that he might not have been the initiator of the reforms. The theory seems to win visual support from an Egyptian relief, now housed in a Berlin museum, which depicts Amenhotep III offering sacrifices to Aton. Perhaps Ikhnaton was not, after all, the great reformer.

The relief was genuine enough, and there was no mistaking the major characters on it. The riddle was not solved until publication of Heinrich Schäfer's book on Egyptian art in 1963. Schäfer proved that the stone had been "worked over" just years after its creation—and shortly after Amenhotep III's death. In place of some other god, the reformers had chiseled in a picture of the god Aton.

The role Ikhnaton's mother, Teje, played in the Egyptian reformation is still debated. Certainly as Amenhotep III's wife she was pictured more often in monuments and statues than any pharaoh's wife before her, which is surely one indication of her great influence.

Her religious ideas must have influenced Ikhnaton, but we don't know in which direction; there is virtually no mention of Teje in any records during the first crucial years of Ikhnaton's reign when he moved the royal residence to Amarna in order to enhance the Aton cult. Not until the eighth year of Ikhnaton's reign do her pictures reappear—and then in the tomb of her former steward. Apparently she lived as a widow in Medinet Rurab and had not moved to Amarna, where she lived out her days, until then.

A tablet dedicated to Osiris, the old religion's god of the dead, was found in Medinet Rurab and led to speculation that Teje was an adherent of the old faith. But that speculation supposes the tablet to be authentic. It is equally possible that a scribe or priest, devoted to the old religion, faked the relic, for during Ikhnaton's reign Osiris had no standing. There was only one god, Aton, the disk of the sun. The people who had grown up within the old faith did not oppose the reformation but only accepted it unwillingly. The ideas the Heliopolis priesthood had pushed Amenhotep IV to accept were too intellectual and therefore suspect for ordinary people.

But Ikhnaton cared as little for their grumbling as he did about the hostility of the old priesthood. The masses were not asked. They were considered stupid and certainly no match for the pharaoh's power or that of his intellectual palace guard. The priesthood was merely another bureaucracy that could be replaced at will.

Finally, the heretic on the pharaoh's throne left Amon's city, Thebes, to be forgotten in the past. The name of the future was Amarna.

This religious development, however, had a secular base as well. The Egyptians had finally driven out their hated Hyksos rulers and even pursued them into Palestine. As the fourteenth century began, Thutmose III embarked on a course of conquest that took Egyptian soldiers to the banks of the

Tigris and Euphrates. Both tribute and slaves flowed into Egypt from the conquered and subjected peoples. The Egyptian world enlarged and expanded.

New knowledge came from newly discovered lands. The Nile, divine waterway and all-powerful artery of life, was not limited to Egypt alone. *The mountain lands too,* the Aton hymn proclaimed, *were given a Nile in the sky who descended unto them and brought floods to the mountains to enrich their fields.*

Other peoples, too, the Egyptians discovered, had kings and priests. Only the sun was equally powerful everywhere and directed everything.

Amenhotep IV ruled for a little less than twenty years as Ikhnaton. When he died in 1358 B.C., the Aton religion died with him. Tutankhamen moved the pharaoh's residence from Tell el-Amarna back to Thebes—where the old gods ruled once again.

9   Voices from the Eighteenth Dynasty

THE INTERNATIONAL Institute for Psychic Research in London has on file a record made there on May 4, 1936. The record reproduces throaty sounds that are clearly those of a woman. What can be made out of the first scratchings of the 78-rpm record sounds something like *"Iw e tena."*

One might interpret these sounds as being a native African dialect. But if that were the case, the London scientists in 1936 would hardly have indulged in the luxury of recording them. The strange incomprehensible sounds, however, are part of a language that has not been spoken for 2,500 years. *"Iw e tena"* is old Egyptian and means "I am very old." But that is not the really sensational, even incredible, aspect of the record. The most unbelievable part is that both the language and the voice come from the XVIIIth dynasty—spoken during trance by a woman teacher from Blackpool in our own day, but with the thoughts of a woman who lived almost 3,500 years ago. The process is known as xenoglossy, and it has only recently begun to attract scientific attention.

What is xenoglossy? The concept is made up of two Greek words, *xenos*, strange, and *glossa*, speech, tongue. It designates the ability, during dream or trance, to speak sentences in a foreign language which one has never learned. Parapsychologists believe that prerequisites for this ability are spiritual tension or mental stimulation. Since xenoglossy is rare, it has been as yet little researched. The oldest written record of xenoglossy is contained in the history of the apostles (1 Corinthians 12). In the excitement of their mission, the apostles suddenly began to speak in foreign languages. In 1634 nuns in the Ursuline monastery in London are supposed to have spoken Latin, Greek, Turkish, and Spanish while in a trance. And in the middle of the last century Laura Edmonds, an American, gave an interesting example of xenoglossy when she began to speak classical Greek—without knowing what she was doing.

The strange abilities of Ivy B (Mrs. B never revealed her name because of her teaching profession and later assumed the pseudonym "Rosemary") were discovered by accident. At her school she met a music teacher, Dr. Frederic Herbert Wood, who also engaged in parapsychological studies. "At first," Wood wrote in his book *This Egyptian Miracle*, "our common interest was only music. Mrs. B had no idea about parapsychology and was not interested in my research—at least not until that fall evening in 1927 when they sat together and the teacher suddenly began to paint strange letters onto a piece of paper. "It was clear," Wood explained later, "that I had found a so-called 'writing medium.'" Dr. Wood did not realize at the time that Ivy B had reproduced Egyptian words. He only formed that suspicion gradually. Finally he turned to the Oxford Egyptologist Dr. Alfred J. Howard Hulme, who identified the first signs.

Dr. Wood followed Ivy's writings, which never lasted longer than twenty minutes, with a scientist's precision. Then on August 8, 1931, an experiment opened up an entirely new prospect: For the first time Ivy began to utter strange sounds, something like "Ah—yita—zhula." It meant something like "I have heard somebody say something." The sounds were often unclear and hard to identify, so that even Egyptologists had difficulty writing down what was said. But during the course of experiments that stretched over several years, Dr. Wood and Dr. Hulme developed a routine that allowed them to translate the sounds written down during an experiment within a matter of hours.

How is it possible for a woman to reproduce sentences that emerged from the thought processes of someone who died 3,300 years ago?

"I feel these sentences as if they were inaudible language," Ivy B said. "I sense that they are formed in a different part of the brain from normal speech. One can assume it happens somewhere between brain and skull." The words fell more easily from her lips when she thought about nothing than when she concentrated on a question or subject.

She described the process this way: "If someone talks he must first formulate a thought. When the voice speaks through me I think of nothing. My lips move, words are formed; but I just can't say how all this happens." And something else is different from normal speech. "Usually you remember what you say, at least for a short period of time. I can't remember anything I say in a trance. I can neither repeat what I've said, nor can I reproduce its content."

Wood checked her testimony by putting the same question to his medium months and years apart. The answers he received always corresponded to the content of previous answers but were always couched in different words.

Wood also explained that his experiments were often interrupted by outside influences such as airplane noise, radio music, and the rattle of passing automobiles. But Wood contended that such experiments require absolutely calm surroundings in order to avoid any distraction. The experiments, which extended over decades, presuppose complete bodily and mental calm. Before beginning, Wood and Ivy sat opposite one another for two to five minutes, writing. Then Wood jotted down some thoughts or questions while putting the woman into a hypnotic trance which made her able to recognize his unspoken thoughts.

Telika, Fourth Wife of Amenhotep III

It took three years until Wood and Hulme found out whose voice actually spoke from Ivy B. The voice mentioned her name for the first time on December 5, 1931, during a series of twenty-eight Egyptian sentences. Hulme was able to translate every word but one: Ventiu. Six weeks later Mrs. B said another name, Telika, and repeated the name Ventiu. Six months later both names reappeared in a trance conversation. That was something of a puzzle for the Egyptologists, since in the past the voice had called herself Nona, the Egyptian equivalent of "the nameless one."

Only on June 6, 1935, did the voice reveal herself fully. Her real name was Telika. She was born in Babylon, but when she came to Egypt she was given the name Ventiu. She had spoken of herself as Nona, the nameless one, because her name had no place in recorded history.

Egyptologists knew that the Amarna tablet, found in 1886 in the village of Tell el-Amarna, contained among other things the correspondence between Amenhotep III and the king of Babylon, Kadashman En-lil, and that the pharaoh had married Kadashman's sister, but they did not know the queen's name.

Amenhotep III's first wife was Teje, mother of Amenhotep IV, who later became Ikhnaton. The Amarna tablets list three other wives of the pharaoh: the two princesses Giluchipa and Taduchipa as well as the sister of the Babylonian king, Kadashman En-lil, whose name was not recorded. This woman was obviously Telika, the voice. She is mentioned in a letter Kadashman sent to Amenhotep expressing his surprise that the pharaoh now wanted to marry his, Kadashman's, daughter while still married to his sister. "But no one has seen my sister," the Babylonian monarch wrote, "or knows whether she is still alive or dead. You told my messenger as your wives stood before you: 'See your mistress standing here before you!' But my messenger did not recognize her. Was that really my sister?"

The suspicion seems justified that Telika was no longer alive when the Babylonian ambassador arrived, and that Amenhotep wanted to bring his exotic harem back to its original number with Kadashman's daughter. Telika was one of the most hated women at court. Queen Teje was suspicious of her great influence on Amenhotep III. The corrupted

Amon priests feared her sympathy for the then just budding Aton religion, which a few years later was declared by Amenhotep IV to be the official faith.

The influence of the Babylonian queen was not to be underestimated, because, as the pharaoh's wife, she was automatically a temple priestess. Evidently, Telika was highly critical of the machinations of priests and magicians and for that reason alone looked with favor upon the new religion.

From her time as temple priestess Telika reported interesting historical details. She told about the influence of the priests. "I know that the great power of the priests over the people is based on superstition. This superstition allows the priests to dominate the people. The people are afraid of them."

On October 26, 1935, Telika, speaking through Ivy B, confirmed the theory we have propounded in this book. "The high priests use occult sciences such as telepathy. They could tell their own future. Much of their occult knowledge was never written down and only the highest priests knew about those things."

In the temples where the priests indulged their secret practices there was absolute silence. The inner sanctum, where only priests were allowed, was cloaked with heavy curtains. Priests had hair and eyebrows shaved. They were naked except for a loin cloth. Spheric music sounded from long brass instruments and harps to create an oppressive atmosphere during the ceremonies.

Telika also did away with the myth that the pyramids were built at the cost of inhuman cruelty. The trance texts reveal that the Egyptians used various sytems of levers and pulleys with whose help mathematicians and construction workers were able to transport blocks of rock weighing several tons up to the top of the more than hundred-meter-high edifices. Complicated machines weren't needed, but only very precise measurements of the balance of levers and weights. Telika said, "Our wise men in Egypt had knowledge that would be of incalculable value for your world if you could only regain it."

Telika reported that the Egyptians produced electricity from the air but did not use it for illumination, resorting to chemicals instead whose effect was "similar to today's sconces."

On May 30, 1936, Telika reported through her medium, Ivy B:

"I wish I could tell you something about the higher kind of life with which we on the other side have contact. But it is very difficult for me to describe it. We have learned strange things from other beings, but it is as difficult to get in touch with them as it is with you. And yet the souls of the dead can approach anyone more easily than you on earth. Your value judgment is so faulty. The earth is so poorly developed a planet compared to most others. Ability and development of all living beings is at a relatively low stage compared to these higher beings. The state in which you live is like a dew drop in a mighty ocean. Even we are not much more highly developed. You speak of our abilities and our knowledge. I am nothing and except for my paltry skills, know nothing. Sometimes, when I am in the condition you know as meditation, it seems as if my body is penetrated by a blue ray of light from another world. And that develops possibilities of beauty, strength and illumination that dazzle one. The protectors of my life here tell me that these are rays of a higher consciousness to which I would rise once I had lost all contact to the earth for a long enough time. Mankind, in its limited intelligence, cannot bear the fact that it will never have the possibility of understanding the limitless resources of the universe."

During many years of experiments, Dr. Wood was able to squeeze one historical fact from his medium that is of great importance for us—the fact that Telika was murdered. The Amon priests, worried by the mistrust the Babylonian queen bore them, plotted against the pharaoh's wife in order to kill her.

The opportunity came when Telika and Vola, a girl she had adopted, took a boat ride on the Nile. Hired killers came up in another boat and capsized theirs. Telika and Vola drowned. Their bodies were never found.

Wood commented, "After Telika's death reactionary forces eradicated her name from all inscriptions and documents.

That seemed to have been customary at the time. Historians therefore attribute an influence to Teje which in fact belonged to Telika."

Telika even went so far as to offer the possibility of proving her testimony. She had a confidant, a Captain Rama. He uncovered the plot of the priests but could not avenge Telika's death because he himself died on the battlefield. As a war hero, Rama had to be buried with all military honors. But the priests, who hated him, refused him the customary grave gifts, which, in regard to the continued life of the ka, was tantamount to eternal death.

However, Rama's as yet undiscovered tomb will be found one day, Telika contended, and after a sand and stone slide on a mountainside in Upper Egypt. A scroll will be found in the sarcophagus, together with Rama's mummy, which a scribe had secretly hidden there. The papyrus contains a detailed record about Telika's life and death.

Unfortunately the participants in these modern experiments are all dead now. Ivy B died in 1961, Dr. Wood in 1963. But the recordings made during the experiments are still available to modern research. There are even two separate recordings.

The first recording caused such a commotion in scientific circles that Dr. Nadnor Fodor, the director of the Psychic Research Institute, asked Dr. Wood to conduct another such experiment with Ivy B. This experiment too was to be recorded, but in the presence of several scientists.

Wood reported on this second recording in great detail. Dr. Fodor supervised the experiment. It took place at about ten o'clock in the morning in a library with a long table that had a microphone on it. Two studio technicians from W. Day Ltd. had set up their recording equipment in an adjoining room. After Ivy B and Wood had taken their places at the table, Wood asked for a small pad in case Ivy were to begin writing during the experiment. There were no evocative hand motions or any hypnotizing looks. What happened there could most easily be compared to an intensive thought process. Suddenly Dr. Wood bent over toward the microphone and said quietly, "Ready."

That was the signal for the technicians to begin recording. Dr. Wood described what happened next:

"A few moments later 'Rosemary' sighed deeply—the sigh can be clearly heard on the record—and the xenoglossy began in slow, chopped sentences. I have numbered the fragmentary sentences in the sequence in which they are heard on the record, including the pauses. In some cases the meaning of the sentence is understandable, in others one sentence fragment dissolves into the next one or into the one after that."

Dr. Wood's Notes

In order to visualize how complicated and laborious a process the recording and translation of Ivy's old Egyptian sounds really was, we are reproducing Dr. Wood's notes which he transcribed from the second recording. The critic cited in the text is obviously the Oxford Egyptologist Professor Gunn, who insisted that the sounds Ivy B reproduced while in trance has nothing to do with the lost language of ancient Egypt. (Of course he was unable to submit any proof for his contention.) Here is the transcription of the first side of the record:

1135. a[r] nada di hev-en...	We come to record...
1136. ...di geem a[r] oo ent ...	...the language. It is proof ...
1137. ...sa dan: oo neda...	...in order to satisfy the ear. It will show...
1138. ...di[h] eem...	...and hold fast [that]...
1139. ...vee-st a seeleta...	...it really contains a message....
1140. ...Naheemahoon...	...Surely...
1141. ...teeveen di[h] eiran ...	...that has been done before ...
1142. ...a[r] nous...	...from a thing of metal [phonograph]...
1143. ...See ven dihoona...	...that came in order to ease ...
1144. ...donse...	...the difficult thing...

1145. ... Vee nees ta dow dan ...   ... to bring to ear what has been spoken. ...

1146. ... oovekee eena! ...   ... It has not yet succeeded. ...

1147. ... Da zeet! ...   ... This is how it is. ...

1148. ... Da zeet oo nedan! ...   ... This is how it is, as we said. ...

1149. ... Vrong vee-st ...   ... The power makes it possible ...

1150. ... istia, tiya nooda! ...   ... indeed, it is lost! ...

1151. ... Di zeem! ...   ... Help me! ...

1152. ... Kon testa! ...   ... Complete this sentence! ...

1153. ... Doo-a [h]efan eem ...   ... Those in the world of the spirit ...

1154. ... aranta ...   ... inasmuch ...

1155. ... asee gow dan ...   ... they were given what the ear lacks ...

1156. ... di e feran heem ...   ... give me the possibility ...

1157. ... oos ta ...   ... to improve that. ...

1158. ... Aranta di hev-en ...   ... When you see that, we shall come ...

1159. ... deeza khed-en oont! ...   ... and tell our disappointments. ...

1160. ... Aranta ...   ... When you see that ...

1161. ... oo vekee quonta di s ta ...   ... this misfortune will have to be removed. I give this ...

1162. ... a neda ...   ... declaration. ...

1163. ... ar-ef an eftee ...   ... Now ponder ...

1164. ... a zoodan di heenti ...   ... approve and sanction ...

1165. ... vee nee zeest ...   ... and approve what has been written ...

1166. ... a noon ta ...   ... this time ...

1167. ... Asee [h]efan ef ...   ... all this has been elected ...

1168. ... a[r] gua-anta. Di testa! ...   ... to thwart resistance ...

1169. ... Vee nee zoo! ...   ... witnesses that ...

1170. ... Vee nee zoo! ...	... witnesses that ...
1171. ... Di zeem! ...	... Help me ...
1172. ... Di testa, [h]aroonta ef ...	... make a binding declaration. ...
1173. ... Seena [h]esta! ...	... Forget what has been reported. ...
1174. ... Arq antee tema! ...	... Make an end of it. ...
1175. ... a dong! ...	... Give me your hand! ...
1176. ... Zeen eftee! ...	... Look at his judgment. ...
1177. ... oo [h]efan veet ...	... They should destroy ...
1178. ... goon zama ...	... the weak points and prevent ...
1179. ... a vra-ntee ...	... that is continued ...
1180. ... vee f neda ...	... the explanation. ...
1181. ... Zena [h]eiran nee f ...	... Let him hear that ...
1182. ... oo zen-tee oo eiran.	... it may show what happened.

Dr. Wood and Dr. Hulme were pioneers; today experiments of this kind are more frequent. Indeed, the whole area of psychic research has expanded tremendously, not only in numbers of participants but in the degree to which its validity is recognized by the scientific community.

In the 1930s such efforts as Dr. Wood's received short shrift, if they were not dismissed outright. However, because disciplines like xenoglossy are treated today with respect and attention, the possibility of the appearance of another Ivy B increases. In that possibility may lie further answers.

10   The Poisonous Wings of Death

ON NOVEMBER 3, 1962, Dr. Ezzeddin Taha, a physician and biologist at Cairo University, held a press conference—something scientists don't often do, even in Egypt. But the biologist had a sensational announcement to make. He had—or so he claimed—tracked down the cause of the curse of the pharaohs, or at least he had found one cause.

Over an extended period of time he had examined both archaeologists and employees of museums and found that many suffered from a fungus that caused feverish inflammations of the respiratory system. Archaeologists had long observed strange symptoms known as the "Coptic itch," itches which took the form of skin rashes and labored breathing, but heretofore little attention had been paid to such infections. They had been observed only in people who had worked intensively with Egyptian papyri.

At Cairo University's Institute for Microbiology, Taha proved the existence of a series of dangerous disease agents, among them *Aspergillus niger*. Taha believed that this fungus is hardy enough to survive in mummies or grave chambers and pyramids for three or four thousand years.

"This discovery," Dr. Taha declared, "has once and for all destroyed the superstition that explorers who worked in ancient tombs died as a result of some kind of curse. They were victims of morbific agents encountered at work. Some people may still believe that the curse of the pharaohs can be attributed to some supernatural powers, but that belongs to the realm of fairy tales." Antibiotics, he said, could neutralize the pharaohs' curse.

The discoveries he had made under an electronic microscope, Taha stressed, were not the ultimate solution to the puzzle of the curse. It is possible, he admitted, that infections were not the only cause of the deaths of so many scientists. But his discovery did point up the depth and breadth of Egyptian scientific knowledge.

Dr. Ezzeddin Taha's research would surely have led to more concrete results if the scientist himself had not, shortly after his press conference, become a victim of the curse he thought he had demystified.

It happened on the desert road between Suez and Cairo, a black strip of asphalt running straight through the bleak, ochre-colored landscape. There is little traffic on the road. When two cars meet, their drivers wave to each other. Dr. Taha and two of his co-workers were driving to Suez. Then, about 70 kilometers north of Cairo, Taha's car suddenly swerved to the left on the straight road, right into the path of an oncoming car. There was a crash. Taha and his two aides died instantly; those in the other car were badly hurt. Taha's autopsy revealed that he had suffered a circulatory collapse. Had Dr. Taha, who used antibiotics regularly during his research, been on the wrong track after all?

Dangerous Bats

Certainly an infection seems a plausible explanation in any scientific exploration of the curse, and many scientists have pursued the thought.

In October, 1956, the South African geologist Dr. John Wiles climbed into the subterranean grottoes of the Rhodesian mountains. He had no idea he was exposing himself to mortal danger. He was supposed to examine the practical application of bat excrement, similar to guano. Perhaps the many thousands of tons stored there could be used as fertilizer.

In one of the grottoes, about 150 meters underground, Dr. Wiles witnessed a strange spectacle. Suddenly the black roof on the grotto dissolved into a swarm of ten thousand bats who had hung there squeezed close to one another. Wiles had to leave the cave.

A few days later he suffered from indigestion, aching muscles, and high fever. The first medical diagnosis claimed it was pneumonia and pleurisy. But the appropriate-seeming treatment was not effective, and Wiles was taken to Geoffrey Hospital in Port Elizabeth.

When he examined the patient, Dr. Dean, the hospital's director, remembered that American doctors had recently discovered a disease among explorers who had worked in Inca caves in Peru. Dean sent a blood sample of the now critically ill geologist to the United States. The reply confirmed the diagnosis: John Wiles was suffering from the same disease—histoplasmosis, caused by an infectious fungus which grows in bat excrement and other rotting matter.

Antibiotics saved Wiles's life. But Dr. Dean began to wonder if this disease might not also be a cause of the puzzling deaths connected with the pharaohs' tombs.

The Poisonous Worm

While European doctors studied this case, medical historians among them remembered the equally strange appearance of a disease that had ravaged workers engaged in building the St. Gotthard tunnel. It had also been observed in Belgium and France, where it was called *anémie des mineurs* or "miners' anemia." Both tunnel workers and miners shared the same symptoms: faintness and anemia. Indeed, at one time tunnel construction was in serious trouble because so many workers were ill with "tunnel disease," and Swiss hospitals were so jammed that patients had to be shipped to German clinics.

The first indication as to the cause of the illness came when a Swiss doctor discovered hookworm eggs in the feces of one victim. Subsequently, threadworms were found in the excrement of other miners. And extensive examinations of German industrial workers in the Rhineland-Westphalia and Aachen regions revealed the prevalence of anemia.

Two poisonous glands located near the head of the hookworm produce a toxic substance. The poison reaches the host's circulatory system through the intestinal blood vessels and destroys the red corpuscles by dissolving their hemoglobin. These parasites could be another explanation for the curse of the pharaohs. However, they would not account for the many deaths among archaeologists, for although hookworm poison produces desperate exhaustion, no deaths have been reported from it.

Possible Poisons

It is, of course, entirely possible that archaeologists were attacked by parasites during their weeks'-long sojourns underground. But if we assume that the curse of the pharaohs was specifically designed to protect the royal tombs, these matters would not have been left to chance. Poison is a much more realistic theory.

Poison is as old as the history of mankind. The first pharaoh, Menes, grew poisonous plants around 3000 B.C. and had their effects recorded. Unfortunately, these plants have never been classified botanically. But we do know from later ages that opium, hemlock, henbane, arsenic, and monkshood were used. (Aconite was produced from monkshood; just five milligrams are deadly.) Even prussic acid was known—it was used for executions in ancient Greece twenty-five hundred years ago, just as it has been used in the United States in this century. Socrates died by drinking hemlock; the poisonous alkaloid coniine is derived from poison hemlock. Medea killed her rival with death-bringing colchicine. And Mithridates, ruler of Asia Minor, who lived in constant fear that someone would poison him, is said to have swallowed daily a small dose of poison in order to increase his tolerance to it (a tolerance so acquired now being called mithridatism, in his honor).

Cleopatra mixed poisons expertly. In putting together her "witches' brews" she drew upon ancient tradition, which described the poisons' effectiveness in great detail. She regularly tested poisons on slaves, and it is known that Mark Antony feared her art; he ate with Cleopatra only when a taster was present, which the self-confident Cleopatra regarded as an insult. As Pliny tells us in his *History*, Cleopatra cured her lover's distrust with dramatic flair. She took a flower from the garland in her hair, tossed it into Antony's wine cup, and asked him to drink the wine as a sign of his love. Antony saw this as a seductive gesture and put the cup, from which the taster had already drunk, to his lips. But swiftly Cleopatra seized it from the Roman's lips, called over a man brought up from prison, and gave him the cup to drink. The prisoner drank—and fell over dead.

"I poisoned the blossoms," Cleopatra said. "I only wanted to show you that if I wanted to I could kill you despite your taster."

The Greek doctor and pharmacist Dioscorides, who studied Egyptian culture in the first century A.D., concluded in his *Liber de Venenis*, "Poison prophylaxis is difficult because those who work secretly with poisons make sure that even the most experienced are deceived."

The reason we know so little about the preparation of poisons in ancient Egypt makes sense: Toxicology was a secret science of priests and magicians taught only to a select few.

Plants from the Magic Garden

Outside Egypt, on the other hand, the mixing of poisons was a much more widely practiced skill. In the kingdom of Colchis, on the southeastern coast of the Black Sea, the legendary home of Medea and the location of the Golden Fleece, goal of the Argonauts, the kings of mythical times are supposed to have laid out a magical garden surrounded by a wall nine fathoms high and secured with a triple brass gate. In this garden, poison and antidote grew peacefully next to one another. Poison from Colchis was famous down to Roman times. In his *Epodes* Horace turns to Canidia, the mixer of poisons, with these words:

> You, workshop of Colchis poison,
> have always belabored me,
> until I, burned to ashes,
> become a game for bold winds.

Mark Antony, badly defeated by the Parthians in 38 B.C., had to watch helplessly as his beaten troops were decimated by poisons during their retreat through the Middle East; the demoralized soldiers had discovered a narcotic herb that allowed them to forget their sorrows for a time but sooner or later inevitably led to death. Modern toxicologists assume that the plants involved belonged to the Solanaceae family.

When the Romans conquered Sardinia and Corsica in the second century B.C., they found a poison on the island brought there by the Carthaginians. Three hundred years after the Roman conquest, Dioscorides described the "Sardonic herb" that disturbed the senses and deformed the lips into a convulsive (cramped) smile—the well-known sardonic smile.

Knowing the great Egyptian achievements in toxicology, the Roman emperors obtained most of their poisons from the land along the Nile. Caligula, Claudius, Nero, and Caracalla supposedly owned the largest collection of poisons; Caracalla even employed his own magician and poison mixer, Sempronius Rufus.

Even today the African peoples are master poison mixers, especially in the legendary land of Punt. Acocanthera is a genus of plants that proliferate in East Africa. *Acocanthera schimperi*, for example, contains a substance able to paralyze the heart muscle. Sap from the Javanese upas tree, *Antiaris toxicaria*, which is also found in Africa, has the same effect. When the bark is pierced, a highly poisonous, milky liquid flows from the tree and quickly crystallizes. Toxicologists call it antiarin. Experiments have shown that a dose of only 0.000009 gram of antiarin will kill a frog.

In 1859 the British explorer David Livingstone (1813–1873) discovered a poisonous climbing vine above Victoria Falls. The natives derived from it a substance they called kombé, which they used on arrows to kill their foes.

Livingstone also noticed that the natives handled the

seed extract with extreme care. He pointed this out to his botanist, John Kirk, who identified the plant as a *Strophanthus.* Livingstone reported that the poison was strong enough to kill an elephant within twelve hours.

As Bernt Karger-Decker writes in his book *Gifte, Hexensalben, Liebestränke* (Poisons, Witch Brews, and Love Potions), natives in Nigeria used the poison as late as 1885— against representatives of the National Africa Company. Two of its officials complained to a tribal chieftain about the theft of gunpowder from a local factory. During the sometimes heated discussion, an arrow nicked one of the Britons. Subsequently the two managed to escape back to their boat in the Katsina Ala River under a hail of arrows. The Englishman who had been hit first died in the boat. His colleague died excruciatingly several weeks later; he too had been scratched, albeit slightly, by a poisoned arrow during their escape. Karger-Decker explained:

Strophanthus poisoning begins with vomiting and nausea. Next, the heart's impulse delivery system is disrupted. Usually, in normal, not too serious cases, extra systoles appear: every heartbeat is followed by an additional, fairly lengthy, contraction. Sometimes complete heart blockage can occur with a reduction of as much as half the normal number of heartbeats. Generally, however, these symptoms disappear after five to ten days. But in serious cases fibrillation can lead to death. Disruption of equilibrium, hallucinations, and states of confusion are often associated with this condition.

The fourth book of Moses (Numbers 5:18ff) tells of a custom adopted from the ancient Egyptians. If a woman was accused of adultery and refused to admit her guilt, she was taken to the temple. There she was made to drink a poisonous "jealousy" water, a procedure some survived but many did not. A kind of divine judgment, the poisoned water became a lie detector—and generally judge and executioner.

Native African tribes, which still make exceptionally strong poisons, use some prescriptions known to the ancient Egyptians. The toxicologist Dr. Louis Lewin told in his book *Die Gifte in der Weltgeschichte* (Poisons in History) about a poison able to induce cramps—a mixture of euphorbia juice, snake venom, and the poisonous *Haemanthus toxicarius* bulb. Its initial effect is to unbalance the mind; then it paralyzes spine, brain, and breathing center. Professor Lewin wrote:

The durability of this bushman's poison is extraordinary. I have examined poisoned arrows Lichtenstein brought back from South Africa ninety years ago and which have been stored under varying conditions in museums here in Berlin. The poison in the arrows is as potent as if it had been freshly made. I even managed to achieve psychological "states" with it. My latest examination of the bulb itself led to the extraction of an alkaloid, haemanthin, that had the same effect as the plant: the shakes, muscle cramps, as well as great difficulty breathing.

The ancient Egyptians had broad knowledge of poisons, with priests and doctors making the most use of their "magic powers." Poison squirted by a scorpion which lives in North Africa and India can kill a man; symptoms include muscle cramps and paralysis, a weak pulse, and breathing difficulties. The Egyptians knew this. The medical Ebers papyrus warns of the dangers of scorpion bites and recommends honey and hippopotamus excrement as treatment.

Like scorpions, various snakes and spiders have a system of poisonous glands from which deadly poisons can be extracted. Poison from spiders of the genus Lathrodectus, for example, paralyzes the central nervous system and can lead to the formation of blood clots.

Snake and insect poisons are closely related to plant poisons. As the Parisian toxicologist Dr. M. Martiny reported, the shriveling of poisonous glands or the drying up of poisons themselves does not decrease their potency. Not even a marked change in temperature weakens cobra poison; after fifteen-minute exposure to 100-degree-centigrade temperatures, the venom retains full potency. Snake poisons with a protein base, on the other hand, are not as resistant; they lose their effectiveness at 75 to 80 degrees centigrade, as do certain insect poisons. Ultraviolet rays can also neutralize insect poisons, but the pharaohs' tombs, which these rays cannot penetrate, would have made ideal places for storing such poisons and keeping their effectiveness unimpaired.

Modern pharmacology uses many snake and insect poisons as healing drugs. Small doses, therefore, can result in some immunization. Howard Carter spent half his life shut up in the tombs of various pharaohs without succumbing to their curse. Over the years he must have built up bodily resistance against their poisons, for he was sixty-six when he died on March 2, 1939. Still, he suffered his share of pain, complaining frequently during his sojourn in the Valley of the Kings about paralyzing attacks of dizziness and weakness, a sudden rush of blood to his head, hallucinations, and headaches. These are all symptoms that toxicologists such as Martiny attribute to animal poisoning.

Toads are considered ugly and repulsive, yet the ancient Egyptians venerated them as holy animals. Given their highly developed aesthetic sensibilities, that may seem strange. It was not until the 1950s that a Swiss pharmacologist, Professor Kuno Meyer of Basle University, analyzed the poison toads produce in the hump on their ears and found that this gland produces twelve different poisons similar to foxglove in their chemical makeup. Major differences are found in the refinement of chemical structure, but toad poison has the same effect as digitalis. No wonder the Egyptians treated them with respect.

Beetles of Love, and Cactuses That Intoxicate

"Spanish fly," made from dried beetles, has an ancient reputation as a source of poison. The insects, members of the Cantharidae family, are about half an inch long and produce substances with poisonous effects when applied externally. Dried Spanish fly retains up to 50 percent of its toxicity. Skin will blister after Spanish fly powder is applied, while mucous membranes erupt in feverish infection. Ingestion of the powder leads to muscle cramps and mental derangement —effects that spurred its use as an aphrodisiac. *Pastilles à la Richelieu* or *pastilles galantes,* as Spanish fly powder was called in tablet form, were supposed to heighten sexual enjoyment. All too often they merely increased the death rate; an overdose could lead to circulatory paralysis.

Various plants, as we know from South American Indians, produce similar reactions. Peyote, the name of a small, thornless cactus, means "giver of visions." It is a source of trimethoxy-phenyl-ethylamine, better known as mescaline. Peyote also lent its name to an Indian nature religion known as peyotism. Its ceremonial cult included a "peyote meal" designed to allow communication with the "great creative spirit" while in a state of trance.

The danger of many natural poisons tends to be underestimated because of reports about spectacular results modern pharmacology and toxicology have achieved in this area. But in the summer of 1972, when African necklaces made from scarlet and black jequirity beans and the bright red fruits of coral bushes were sold in Germany, the Bavarian criminal court warned, "Those who perspire risk death."

The jequirity contains the toxic protein abrin, and the fruit of the coral bush has a poison similar to curare, which Indians used on their arrows, that can paralyze the body. Since these poisons can be absorbed by natural perspiration, they could also infect sweating archaeologists.

Thus it would not have been necessary for an archaeologist to have oral contact with a poison. Some poisons need only brush or penetrate the skin to become effective. Used to paint artifacts and walls were such powerful poisons as aconite, arsenic, and conium. None of them lost their potency even when dried. Moreover, it is a safe bet that poisonous gases and vapors, in precipitated form, were present in the pharaohs' tombs. The precipitation technique was popular in the Middle Ages as a means of doing away with "unwanted" persons. Soaking a candle wick in arsenic was one of the simplest methods. Light such a candle and the vapors are deadly; they are supposed to have killed Pope Clement VII in 1534 and Emperor Leopold I of Austria in 1705. In the airtight chambers of a pharaoh's tomb, such vapors could precipitate and never disappear. Did poisonous candles burn in the tombs while workmen sealed the entry?

Although there wasn't much variety in the plants grown

in ancient Egypt, the paintings that decorate the tombs made startling and sometimes puzzling use of plants. Min and Amon are usually shown with a small tree some scholars believe is a cypress—probably wrongly, since not a single cypress tree is to be found in all of Thebes.

Some indication as to what Amon's holy plant might be can be found in pictures and texts at Karnak, Medinet Habu, and Edfu; in them the pharaoh hands Amon a lettuce drink. Lettuce, according to the botanists, is the only cultured plant in the Nile delta which secretes milk. This lettuce, which still grows in Upper Egypt, has leaves similar to those of garden lettuce. However, these leaves are not grouped around a central core but along a stalk that can grow one meter high or more.

Lettuce milk, squeezed from the stalk, has been seen as a fertility symbol. That would explain the superstition, still found today, that eating lettuce will help produce many children.

Antibiotics in Ancient Egypt

Both Herodotus and the medical papyri told of the use of "magic plants"; upon botanical analysis these turned out to be onions, garlic, and radishes. Now one can attribute a good deal to these plants, but not usually a medicinal effect. Were their healing attributes only imaginary?

No. There was a good reason why the hundreds of thousands of workers employed in the construction of the great pyramid at Giza were given radishes, onions, and leeks to eat. The major problem in using such huge numbers of workers was not technology but hygiene. An epidemic could spread incredibly quickly and kill thousands in a very short time. During construction of the Khufu pyramid, 185,000 people are supposed to have died.

In order to prevent epidemics of infectious disease, the pyramid workers were given antibiotics—contained in leeks, onions, and radishes. Helmuth M. Böttcher reports in his work *Wunderdrogen* (Wonder Drugs) that in 1947 two scientists isolated from radish seeds a water-soluble substance effective against gram-positive and gram-negative microbes called raphanin. A year later two Swiss scientists proved raphanin's effectiveness against streptococci, staphylococci, pneumococci, and *Bacillus coli*. Similar properties were noted in radish juice, leeks, and onions.

Imhotep Battles Bacteria

It is true that the ancient Egyptians did not know "bacteria" as such—even under some other name. But they understood their physiological effect. Today we know that staphylococci produce pus able to infect skin, kidneys, and bone marrow, while streptococci can cause diphtheria, blood poisoning, and scarlet fever. All these diseases were treated in Egypt with drugs taken from nature's pharmacy. We can assume that pharmacology and toxicology celebrated their first triumphs in the ancient empire—a development which Imhotep, sage to King Djoser whom we have already met, did a great deal to influence.

Imhotep, who was anointed god of healing during his own lifetime, was educated by the Sumerians and surprised the Egyptians with a knowledge of medicine so extensive that people considered it magic. Imhotep's wife, Apopi, suffered from trachoma, an infectious form of conjunctivitis that flourishes in Egypt's dry climate and is widespread even today; it can lead to blindness. Imhotep tried everything he could think of to effect a cure and in the process came up with some highly unusual ideas.

For example, he tore the head and wings from a dung beetle, boiled it in oil, and placed the two halves of the insect on his wife's eyes. This treatment did not help. Experimenting feverishly, he developed a paste made of green slate which he placed on his wife's makeup tray and then spread over her sick eyes. This time there was a cure: the antibacterial salve made the trachoma-stricken eyes fester with pus and break and Apopi could see again.

For the people of the IIId dynasty this was indeed a miracle. Trachoma had usually led to blindness, and Imhotep had prevented that from happening. It was supernatural; he had to be a god. But Imhotep realized something no one else ever had: the existence of tiny "worms," so small they could not be seen with the naked eye—viruses and bacteria able to cause many diseases. He was on the trail of a science developed four thousand years later: bacteriology. It took the invention of the microscope to recognize bacteria and viruses and to combat them.

A Defense Against Grave Robbers

The poison that Egyptians feared most was the "poison of the dead," poisons released during decomposition of the body. Some of the papyri suggest that Egyptian doctors knew cures for "driving out the poison of the dead"—cures of oil and honey or the feces of young girls, cats, donkeys, and pigs. Such medicines are not without their effect: every organism produces antibodies to resist the small amounts of poisonous substances that are absorbed every day. However, it is questionable whether these medicines were able to remove "the slackness of the heart"—after all, cadaver poisons which arise through protein putrefaction are deadly.

That raises the question as to whether poisons can retain their effectiveness and potency for centuries, even millennia, or lose them. There is little doubt that ordinary poisonous substances lose their venom under the impact of light, air, and sun in a matter of years. But stronger poisons can maintain potency for centuries—especially if they are stored in airtight compartments.

The pharaohs' rock tombs and pyramids were ideal breeding grounds for bacteria. Breathing mechanisms are the major differentiation among microorganisms. There are aerobic forms that need oxygen to survive, just as man does, as well as a host of transitional bacteria which develop fairly well with or without oxygen.

Most bacteria are nourished by vegetative and animal substances: fat, carbohydrates, and proteins. The combustion noted on most royal mummies is the result of bacteriological processes. The decomposition of fats, oils, and resins that covered the mummy produced heat which led to a charring of the corpse. Archaeologists wondered for decades why mummies were black. The answer was bacteria.

How long can bacteria live? Can their death-bearing qualities survive the millennia? Is the curse of the pharaohs a biochemical infection of the royal graves, initiated millennia ago?

Chemists and bacteriologists believe this could be one plausible explanation for the curse. There are types of bacteria which, given the right conditions, can survive for centuries. Other bacteria become dangerous only after dying, when they secrete the toxins that threaten man with all kinds of diseases—especially meningitis. And some living bacteria secrete toxins that cause illnesses like diphtheria.

These toxins are "combat material," similar to those the modern armaments industry researches and produces. Plans for chemical and biological warfare are stored in bomb-proof safes of the defensive ministries in East and West. Although most states signed the Hague convention of 1899 and the 1925 Geneva protocols against the use of chemical and biological weapons in case of war, the facts of the matter are different—and grim.

The U.S. Army chemical corps has a research and development division. The British also maintain a research facility for bacteriological warfare. The Soviets and the French are working on chemical and biological weapons, allegedly for purposes of deterrence. After seven thousand years of human development, smart men recalled one fact forgotten in the confusion of technological armament: For centuries more men were killed by epidemics and disease than during wartime combat.

Nerve gas, blood gas, and choking gases are as cheap to produce and as easy to store as stone-age weapons. But their effect is more terrible than the atomic bomb. Biochemical weapons make everything possible: "humane" warfare designed to eliminate an opponent for a time, but also the complete eradication of humanity through genetic destruction. Early in the 1960s the Americans screened a film in NATO circles that showed troops in action while under chemical influence: In the middle of maneuvers the soldiers would throw away their arms, lie down and go to sleep, or run aimlessly about—a harmless way to wage war, a joke almost. But the difference between a joke and death in this kind of warfare is often no more than an atom.

The ancient Egyptians also knew about a kind of nerve poison. During antiquity, Egypt was the world's granary. Ergot, a grain fungus shrouded in mystery for thousands of years, spreads disease and illnesses such as the "cold fire." It begins with strong itching or tingling sensations in the fingers, numbness of the body surface, cramps in various muscle groups, paralysis, and mental derangement.

Although ergot triggered countless epidemics that killed thousands of people—the last great epidemics swept France and the Netherlands in 1828–29 and Germany in 1855–56—science could only master this troublemaker in the twentieth century. Chemical analysis separated out a number of alkaloids including ergosine, ergotinine, and ergonovine. Moreover, other important groups of substances were discovered in ergot: the ergotamines as well as choline and acetylcholine.

The latter are important building blocks for the smooth functioning of the body's command system. One example: A thought is to be translated into muscle action. The thought is transmitted electrically through the nerve fibers to a particular nerve ending. Tiny amounts of acetylcholine are stored there. In response to the corresponding electrical impulse, it flows into the "motor terminal" of certain muscle cells and thus triggers the carrying out of the original order.

Once the brain's command has been executed, the chemical has done its job. But in order to make nerves and muscles immediately receptive for new orders from the brain, the used-up acetylcholine must be removed. A special enzyme does that by splitting the chemical into choline and acetic acid, which are then absorbed into the bloodstream.

It doesn't take much imagination to realize what happens when chemical influence disrupts this command system. If the acetylcholine is not absorbed, the original order that a muscle move is repeated endlessly and results in muscle cramp. Other poisons can close off a muscle's motor terminal and prevent the chemical's entry. In that case some muscles simply don't react at all, no matter how hard the brain tries; finally, the vegetative nervous system, which directs heart-lung activity, quits completely.

It is conceivable that the tombs of the pharaohs were protected by narcotic fungi. Certainly the knowledge that the deadly breath of a guardian demon might touch him on entering a tomb would act as a massive deterrent to any potential grave robber. What did it say on the curse tablet in Tutankhamen's tomb? *Death will slay with his wings whoever disturbs the peace of the pharoh.*

Disruptions of Consciousness

How potent are such poisons? Does one have to swallow powders or potions by the tablespoonful or can they enter the body unnoticed?

Back in 1953 a mysterious accident in the British defense ministry's research facility for chemical and bacteriological warfare showed astonishing parallels to the accidents that victimized Egyptologists. Royal Air Force Lieutenant William Cockayne was sent to the facility in 1952. One evening Cockayne and a chemist went into the laboratory to check out an electrically heated container. A capped bottle with some liquid in it stood in the container. The chemist took out the bottle and said, "This is nerve gas. Even the tiniest amount could kill a man in seconds."

Cockayne reached for the bottle in order to take a closer look at the dangerous poison. He didn't make it. He collapsed, unconscious, to wake up in a clinic, his memory only reaching the point where he had first seen the poisoned bottle.

For sixteen years Cockayne fought to have the British government recognize his right to indemnity. A man formerly brimming with life, he now suffered from deep, periodic depressions. He attempted suicide three times. Dr. Claire Weeks, a psychiatrist, submitted expert testimony to the government that Cockayne had not shown any depressive symptoms before the laboratory accident. A compromise was finally reached: The defense ministry admitted that Cockayne "had suffered minimal exposure to nerve gas."

184

Remember too that many Egyptologists were victims of deep depressions. We have seen that Howard Carter suffered them constantly. Indeed, he several times gave up archaeology, only to return to it. We have also seen that Lord Westbury, the father of Carter's secretary, Richard Bethell, who often accompanied his son to Egypt, jumped out of a window, obviously during a depressive phase. Five years later his widow, too, committed suicide. Carter's friend, Dr. Evelyn White, who participated in the excavation of Tutankhamen's tomb, suffered under such terrible nervous depressions that he refused to allow a doctor to see him, even though he was seriously ill. He told every doctor, "Don't bother. I know what the matter is." Early in 1959 Dr. Zakariaj Ghoneim, chief inspector for the antiquities department of Upper Egypt, committed suicide—after suffering from depressions for many years. These are just a few examples among many.

Devastating poisons such as chlorine, picric acid, or phosgene can be deadly if their fumes are absorbed in high enough concentrations. Their extreme durability make these toxins, when they are used as combat weapons, a problem even in peacetime; corrosion and decay of the poison containers is much more rapid than destruction of the poisons themselves.

Quicksilver was one of the most closely guarded secret poisons in ancient Egypt. Its use in the Old Kingdom is uncertain, but there are documents pinpointing its application as early as the fifteenth century B.C. The highly poisonous "liquid silver" (*hydragyrion* in Greek) occurs in reddish-brown vermilion stone or mercury sulfide. It has long been the alchemists' favorite element. But its unique evaporative quality, even at very low temperatures, makes it a dangerous poison. Quicksilver vapors can damage the nervous system. They are especially dangerous because, unlike the equally poisonous arsenic vapors, they are odorless.

Chessman's Death in the Gas Chamber

Although prussic acid vapors are not completely odorless, they are invisible. At 10 A.M. on May 2, 1960, prisoner No.

66-656 died in San Quentin prison, near San Francisco. His execution had been set nine times and postponed for eight. His name was Caryl Chessman. Judge Charles W. Fricke had sentenced him to death on June 25, 1948, for multiple robbery and rape. Twelve years after the verdict he was finally strapped into a heavy, angular, steel and wood chair in the death chamber. The oval-shaped entry hatch was closed off. Guards pushed a lever, and from a box fastened below the death chair several pellets rolled into a bowl of sulfuric acid. They were cyanide pellets. Hydrocyanic acid, also known as prussic acid, is vaporized during the chemical reaction of cyanide with sulfuric acid. Chessman slumped unconscious after thirty seconds and was dead in three minutes.

Prussic acid is a colorless liquid with a boiling point at 26 degrees centigrade (about 80 degrees Fahrenheit). Death comes from internal choking—when the lungs can no longer absorb new oxygen. It takes only 60 milligrams of prussic acid or 0.3 milligrams per liter of air to kill an adult.

The ancient Egyptians isolated this deadly poison from peach pits. It has been assumed that mummy bandages were drenched in a mixture of prussic acid and volatile oils; at least this provides one explanation for the widespread decomposition of royal mummies. And something else: the tombs were sealed airtight. This presented something of an architectural quandary, since Egyptian theology demanded some opening in the tomb for the ka to come and go as he wished. The shrewd Egyptians solved the dilemma through the use of fake doors which were either painted on walls or built of stone. But why the need for airtight tombs? Did the old Egyptians know that benzaldehyde had a prussic-acid concentration of 2 to 4 percent and that the prussic acid evaporated on contact with oxygen?

There is a third piece of evidence that points to the use of poisonous vapors as a device to protect mummies against thieves. In almost every tomb that grave robbers attacked—and Tutankhamen's is no exception—they drilled a hole about the size of an arm. The opening was too narrow to allow them to fish out any treasures. Clearly it was designed to let poisonous gases seep out. The robbers must have realized that some of their friends had died horribly in other tombs where air had not been allowed to neutralize the poison.

In the early 1950s the United States developed a nerve gas. The formula had been found in captured secret German documents on waging gas warfare. Over the next decade 100,000 rockets were equipped with poison gas warheads. Then, in 1969, something happened to shake the conscience of the world: Several thousand of the warheads, stored in a Utah depot, began leaking. A herd of five thousand sheep was grazing nearby. Within minutes all the sheep were dead. Twenty-four persons became violently ill.

In order to prevent similar incidents in the future, a total of 12,540 warheads stored in army depots at Anniston, Alabama, and Richmond, Kentucky, were encased in 418 concrete blocks weighing five tons each to be dumped into the ocean. But the proposal aroused a storm of protest from politicians and scientists. The army abandoned its plan and reconsidered the disposal problem. Ironically, chemists had by then found a way of neutralizing the nerve gas—if the warheads could be removed safely from their concrete tombs. Since they couldn't be, the "gas in concrete" ended up in the ocean despite all protests.

What Did Horemheb Fear?

The soldier-pharaoh Horemheb may have faced a similar dilemma when he seized the throne and proceeded to destroy every vestige of his predecessor—save his tomb. Though overflowing with gold, it was left untouched. Why? A sense of piety? Surely not. If he feared anything, it would be only the secret powers of the magicians. Certainly it is conceivable that they used poisons or bacterial cultures able to produce poisonous gases to protect the royal tomb.

But this need not have been the only trigger of the curse. Over the centuries, Egyptian priests acquired new knowledge that would have allowed them to change the "protective systems" of the pharaohs' tombs. If "only" poison or bacteria had guarded Tutankhamen's treasures against grave robbers, Horemheb would have sacrificed several hundred soldiers without a moment's hesitation. But since he didn't, we must assume that, at least after Tutankhamen's time (thirteenth century B.C.), a security system was in place whose components were spread among the mummies and grave artifacts so that mere possession of such objects could have deadly consequences.

11 The Radiant Dead

A STRANGE GRAVE in the Idaho Falls cemetery bears the names of three men. Next to the grave stands a shield with the inscription: *Attention, radioactive material.*

The "radioactive material" is the corpses of three men who died horribly on January 3, 1961. It was precisely 9:01 P.M. The experimental reactor SL-1 of the U.S. Army research center at Idaho Falls went "critical." The whole process lasted only 1/20,000 second, but the reactor break made the whole region radioactive. Sirens went off, searchlights rotated. Alarm 1: radiation alarm.

Fifty minutes later the first scouting party, dressed in radiation-resistant suits and equipped with measuring instruments, set off for the reactor center. Meanwhile, earlier fears had been confirmed: Three men were missing, members of the U.S. Army assigned to servicing the SL-1. The first measurements left no doubt: If the three were still in the reactor area, they were dead.

At 10:45 A.M. the men of the rescue squad in their silver-white radiation-proof suits entered the reactor room. Two men lay on the floor. One of them was still alive; he moved as he was being pulled out of the room, but he died before they reached the ambulance.

The second man gave no sign of life, so the men did not take him out for two days, and it was a whole week before the

189

third radiation victim, deep in the reactor center, was brought out. Scientists decided it was too risky to send in a rescue squad. Instead, they used a remote-control crane. As if driven by a ghost, the crane snaked through the automatic door of the reactor building, bumped and rolled into the control room, picked the corpse up with its tongs, and rattled out of the room.

The burial of the three soldiers in Idaho Falls was as unusual as their death. A crane and a concrete truck stood in the cemetery. The coffins in which the dead men lay had been coated with lead and equipped with a shield that said: ATTENTION—HIGH RADIATION LEVELS. After a priest talked briefly, the crane lifted the three huge coffins one at a time and put them into the grave. Then the truck drove up and poured concrete over the coffins.

Radiation accidents like those in Idaho Falls kill about five people a year. Exact numbers are impossible to obtain since such accidents in government-sponsored research facilities are kept secret. Moreover, immediate radiation death occurs only rarely; rather, these deaths are caused by a combination of illnesses that all derive from previous radiation damage.

The Power of Uranium

In 1949 the well-known atomic scientist Professor Luis Bulgarini surprised archaeologists by saying, "I believe that the ancient Egyptians understood the laws of atomic decay. Their priests and wise men were familiar with uranium. It is definitely possible that they used radiation in order to protect their holy places." And, in fact, even in our day rock with uranium content is mined in Middle Egypt.

Is the curse of the pharaohs a lethal belt of death rays? Bulgarini does not exclude that possibility: "The floors of the tombs could have been covered with uranium or the graves could have been finished with radioactive rock. Such radiation could kill a man today or at least damage his health."

It was only in 1896 that the French physicist Henri Becquerel discovered that uranium salts emitted radiation similar to X-rays. A year earlier Wilhelm Conrad Roentgen had proved the existence of this "new type of rays" which, in German-speaking countries at least, bear his name. Roentgen and Becquerel were both Nobel Prize winners. Without wishing to denigrate their achievements, one could ask whether they were not merely "rediscoverers" of something the ancient Egyptians had known and used.

Initially, neither Roentgen nor Becquerel was aware of the importance or the consequences of these discoveries. If the curse of the pharaohs really can, at least in part, be traced back to the impact of radiation, then the Egyptians presided over a greater body of knowledge than the two Nobel Prize winners. For the latter handled radioactive substances at the beginning of this century without any protection whatever, as if they were marvelous toys. In his book *Das Masslose Molekül* (The Extravagant Molecule), for example, Ernst Bäumler reports how Henri Becquerel traveled to London to deliver a scientific lecture, with loose radium in his vest pocket —and suffered serious burns as a result.

There are frightening parallels to the effects of the curse of the pharaohs in an episode from the 1920s. Soon after it was discovered that radioactive substances glow in the dark, a luminous-clock-face industry grew up in New Jersey. Women spent their days putting radiant paint onto clock faces with the help of tiny brushes. In order to put points on the brushes, some workers put the tips in their mouths. It took two years before the first died from feverish inflammations. Only then did physicists and doctors sit up and take notice. More care of on-the-job control removed the danger, but over a ten-year period forty-two women died prematurely, mostly from cancer, as a direct result of radiation exposure.

Remember that many Egyptian scientists and explorers died without anyone being able to fix a precise cause of death. Several archaeologists complained about excessive fatigue. Some showed clear signs of brain damage after working in Egypt, while still others suffered no damage at all.

What is the effect of radiation on the human organism? For how long can radioactive material give off dangerous death rays?

The Swiss radiation specialist Dr. Jacob Eugster, of the University of Bern, has shown that radioactive decomposition of the nucleus does not take place at a constant pace but is subject to outside influence. To prove his thesis he carried out a highly unusual experiment. He divided a radioactive substance and exposed one half to ultraviolet rays on the top of the Jungfrau while putting the rest in the Simplon rail tunnel. He found that the uranium in the tunnel decomposed much more slowly than that on the mountaintop. In other words, materials remain radioactive much longer underground.

Relatively small amounts of radiation can cause serious damage to health. And unlike chemical poisons, radiation cannot be neutralized. Radioactive substances cannot be changed into something else, nor can they be removed. Once the human organism has absorbed them, they stay there. New exposure merely adds to the amount "in storage."

Radiation energy is used up in the form of chemical reactions. The body's cell structure can be destroyed within a fraction of a second. In cases of less intensive exposure, many different cells are attacked at random. Biological consequences worsen in direct relation to the importance of the affected cell substance to the life of the cell and, in turn, the cell's importance to the viability of the entire organism. Radiation damage to cells whose function is duplicated by others can be safely ignored. But destruction of a unique cell component is serious, especially if the cells regulate body metabolism or are carriers of specific hereditary characteristics.

Leukemia and embryo malformation are the most common forms of radiation damage. It does not matter how much radiation the body absorbs; even small amounts can cause leukemia, for once the radioactive elements are in the body, the bone marrow, the most important blood-forming organ, is exposed for many years while white blood cells multiply unchecked. And for the most part leukemia is still incurable, so that death is only a matter of time.

Death from radiation is horrendous. Its effects may be slow and hardly noticeable to outsiders. There have been many such cases in recent years. A closer look at two of them suggests interesting comparisons with the deaths of some archaeologists.

On March 1, 1954, the Japanese fishing boat *Lucky Dragon* was caught in a rain of radioactive ash triggered by a U.S. H-bomb explosion in the Marshall Islands. The test had tragic consequences. All twenty-two crew members suffered radiation damage. One of them, the forty-year-old fisherman Kubojama, died six months after the radiation disaster.

According to his physician, death was directly attributable to radioactivity. The immediate cause of death, the doctor said, was circulatory collapse, the result of radioactive liver damage. Kubojama's liver had shrunk to a fraction of its normal size, weighing only 820 grams instead of 2,200. The doctor believed that this liver shrinkage led to jaundice, which in turn affected heart and kidneys. Bleeding in the kidneys followed, and the pancreas was also affected.

Kubojama's wife, Suzu, said that her husband's last words were, "I'm so tired. It hurts a lot. . . ."

We have seen that most Egyptologists, too, complained of great fatigue shortly before they died. Since the "mysterious illness" which was often listed as cause of death did not demonstrate any readily identifiable external symptoms, the possibility of radiation sickness cannot be excluded. The fact that the mystery disease's effect varied greatly is additional evidence for the radiation theory. Some scholars suffered from physiological changes soon after they began working in the tombs or with the mummies. In others these effects did not show up for months or years. Some died quickly and unexpectedly; others suffered brain damage. And finally there were men who took part in excavations and were never hit by the curse of the pharaohs in any form.

Such varied reaction to radiation damage is not unusual. More than twenty years after the atom bombing of Hiroshima and Nagasaki in August, 1945, the Japanese Ministry of Health published a commemorative volume which revealed how different the impact of radiation had been on the population. Through 1964, about 200 people died every year from the effects of radiation. And each year 150 persons showed symptoms of radiation damage for the first time since their exposure to the bomb.

The example of a then twenty-year-old bus conductor, Kimiko Matsuda, is instructive. She seemed perfectly healthy after the catastrophe but suddenly began complaining of exhaustion. Seven days later she was dead. Kimiko's mother and her two sisters had suffered such heavy radiation damage that they were taken to a hospital days after the attack and died shortly thereafter. Kimiko's father lived eighteen years, until 1963. Her brother, six years older than she, is still alive and in reasonably good health. Yet when the bomb fell the whole Matsuda family was together, in the same house.

Any comparison between radiation following an atomic explosion and the radioactive rays that may be in Egyptian tombs and mummies, is, of course, exaggerated. Still it does make the point that radiation can have very different effects on different people—and it should be noted that damage caused by lengthy exposure to weak radiation can produce the same results as a higher but shorter dosage.

A small but constant exposure to radioactive material can result in genetic change. It can also cause cancer. A report of the British Council for Medical Research, for example, states that "it seems that any amount of radioactive strontium, absorbed through the bones, makes cancer formation more probable, perhaps by reducing the time-span until a cancer forms, and that the incidence of cancer increases in proportion to the radioactive dosage."

Strontium is an alkaline metal with an atomic weight of 87.62. After a nuclear explosion, a heavy radioactive isotope called strontium 90 is present in the fallout and is eventually absorbed in such basic foods as meat, milk, and eggs (through the chain of life mechanism), to be deposited in the bones of human beings and animals. Blood formation is thus exposed to steady radiation.

Strontium 90 has a half-life of twenty-eight years, the time required for the radioactive decay of one half its mass. This fact raises the same question about radioactive materials as about poisons and bacteria: Can such substances maintain their dangerous potential for several thousand years, and, if so, is their radiation strong enough to kill?

The answer depends on the half-life of the various elements. First, a definition: Half-life is the speed of atomic change, the time it takes half an atomic nucleus to decay. After two half-life periods, one quarter of the element will still remain. Half-lives vary sharply: one hour for a chlorine isotope, 2.6 years for a sodium isotope, 12.8 years for tritium (a radioactive isotope of hydrogen), 1,580 years for radium, and 5,730 years for carbon 14. A radioactive isotope, with an atomic weight of 230, formed by the decay of thorium, has a half-life of 1 million years. The half-life of a beryllium isotope is 2.7 million years, while that of uranium 238 is estimated at 7.5 billion years.

Isotopes of the same element differ from one another in the number of neutrons in their nuclei. Most elements are not uniform substances but are mixtures of isotopes, a phenomenon known as isotopy. The isotopy of lead (atomic weight 207.2) is one of the most interesting, as the decay of uranium and thorium eventually produces different isotopes of lead— over the course of billions of years. According to the laws of atomic decay, a thousand kilograms of uranium produces one gram of stable lead in 10,000 years.

A barely visible result thus presupposes enormous expenditures of energy. If radioactive materials were stored in the royal tombs, they did not have to be placed behind or under huge masses of stone or walls of metal. Given the high level of Egyptian science, it is quite plausible to suspect that the Egyptians knew about the process which the Joliot-Curies discovered in 1934: Particle bombardment of the atomic nucleus can produce artificial radiation in elements that are not normally radioactive.

If we allow this hypothesis to stand, perhaps some of

a mummy's many amulets, as well as those artifacts with no known symbolic or functional purpose, contained deadly radioactive elements, designed to carry out the death formulas and curses the gods could not fulfill. The deaths of many explorers and archaeologists could then be explained, and perhaps even the most spectacular ship catastrophe of our century.

The Mummy on the Titanic

The *Titanic* collided with an iceberg on April 14, 1912, on her maiden voyage from Southampton to New York, and sank with a loss of fifteen hundred people. It was considered the most beautiful, the biggest, and the fastest ship in the world. It was also held to be unsinkable.

The skipper of the *Titanic*, Captain Edward J. Smith, played a mysterious and not yet fully explained role in this catastrophe. Smith was a first-rate, experienced seaman—otherwise he would never have been named to his post. But on that April day he acted strangely. It began with the course he steered, the ship's unusually high speed, and his singular reaction to asking for help, and ended with a rescue plan announced only at the last minute.

On board the *Titanic* were 2,200 passengers, forty tons of potatoes, 12,000 bottles of mineral water, 7,000 sacks of coffee, 35,000 eggs—and an Egyptian mummy that Lord Canterville wanted to take from England to New York.

The mummy was the carefully prepared body of a prophetess who had enjoyed a great vogue during the reign of Amenhotep IV, the heretic pharaoh who took the name of Ikhnaton. Her grave had been found in Tell el-Amarna. A small temple had been built for this prophetess, the "Temple of the Eyes."

The female mummy had been equipped with the usual amulets and artifacts. An amulet with the figure of Osiris and the inscription *Awake from the swoon in which you sleep and a glance of your eyes will triumph over everything that is done against you* had been placed beneath her head. Was this a hint that the remains of the prophetess enjoyed special protection?

The mummy was encased in a wooden crate and, because of its great value, had not been placed in the hold of the *Titanic* but behind the command bridge. Many scientists who handled mummies showed clear signs of mental derangement. Did Captain Smith, too, look into those fatal radiant eyes? Could he, too, have been the curse's victim?

The Underground Passages of Umm Garayat

They did not have bulldozers, only muscles, yet their achievements were tremendous: The ancient Egyptians took from the earth whatever it was willing to give up, gold above all else. Since gold and uranium are found in the same rock, there is little doubt that they also mined uranium. And uranium is still mined in Egypt today, as we have already seen.

Several papyri tell us about the gold mines of antiquity. There are several mines in the Umm Garayat region, about 60 kilometers east of the Nile. Mining engineers estimate that 100,000 tons of rock were brought out from there during antiquity.

A stone inscription was found near the village of Kaban which reports on an unsuccessful effort to dig a well during the reign of Rameses II. In it, the area is referred to as the "Valley of the Gold Mines." And a papyrus now in Turin also mentions the area, saying, "The mountains from which gold is taken are marked in red." Pharaoh Seti I is supposed to have mined gold there around 1300 B.C.

It is true that neither in any papyrus nor on any wall inscription are uranium and thorium mentioned or concepts that could be interpreted as referring to them. But that doesn't prove the Egyptians didn't know these two elements. They could have used their power without knowing its source.

One ton of earth contains an average of 70 grams of copper and 17 grams of lead but only 0.002 gram of gold. The Egyptians who dug up tons of gold for their tombs, are sure to have encountered thorium and uranium, since an average ton of earth crust contains 11 grams of thorium and 4 grams of uranium.

Gold and uranium are often found in the same mines because both elements frequently occur in granite and gneiss regions. The famous gold ore of Witwatersrand in South Africa, for example, the richest in the world, not only contains the incredibly high quantity of 6 to 10 grams of gold per ton of rock but uranium and thorium as well. Several Witwatersrand mines recently even switched production from gold to uranium.

The Egyptians mined gold even before building the great pyramids. The archaeologist J. E. Quibell, who discovered some prehistoric graves near the village of El Kab, found a bar of gold in one of them. A Babylonian king sent stone tablets to both Amenhotep III and Amenhotep IV on which he asked each pharaoh for twenty talents of gold to build a new temple. He pointed out that his father had received gold from the pharaohs, as had the king of Cappadocia. Clearly there was gold aplenty.

Around 1900 several mining companies examined old Egyptian mines to see if renewed activity might be worthwhile. Not unlike the American gold rush, a total of thirty-three expeditions marched through the Egyptian and Nubian deserts in order to see what the Egyptians had left behind. It was decided that the mines had been thoroughly exploited. Nevertheless twenty-five companies, mostly British, obtained new mining concessions from the Egyptian government.

The most important of these companies was the Egyptian Mines Exploration Company, whose concession stretched from the 25th to the 27th degree latitude along the Red Sea. In February, 1903, in the area around Umm Russ, chief engineer C. J. Alford came upon quartz veins that contained gold and uranium. The ancient seams branched across an area of six square kilometers. Alford also found hundreds of decayed stone huts which had housed miners.

Egyptian Sudan Minerals prospected to the south of the Egyptian Mines Exploration Company. Their search extended all the way into Nubia, an area where, according to Diodorus Siculus and Agatharchides, diggings had been made in the age of Ptolemy. The mining company had set up its headquarters in the region laced with shafts and ditches, known today as Derekib.

Gold-veined rock was still found there. At the end of one such tunnel the explorers came on a wall of heavy stones with weathered hieroglyphics on it. The mining engineers wrote in their report that they found this "most strange." But since they could find no explanation for their discovery, they closed up the gallery and a nearby vertical shaft.

An indication that more happened in the Egyptian mines than we realize comes in a Nile Valley Company's digging report. The firm had a concession to the west of that of Egyptian Sudan Minerals. Umm Garayat, where mines were protected by watch towers whose remains are still visible, was part of that concession.

Wadi Ungat lies to the southeast of Umm Garayat. Nile Valley Company engineers discovered hieroglyphics there too which no one has been able to decipher. So far, archaeologists have only been able to identify the author. The last line says: *Amenhotep, the scribe.*

What did a scribe do in a mine? What could have moved him to scratch hieroglyphics into the underground rock? What persuaded the ancient Egyptians to wall up mine galleries and put inscriptions on them?

The current stand of Egyptology does not allow a clear answer. But although we still lack final proof that the Egyptians were acquainted with the effects of radioactivity and radiation, there is no proof either that they did not make use of such knowledge.

12   Death and Life from the Stars

At two thirty in the morning a fire truck raced through the Icelandic town of Vestmannaeyjar, on the offshore island of Heimaey. It was the night of January 23, 1973. A caller had told the fire department, "A house is in flames in the east of town." Four minutes later the firemen were back but their sirens continued to wail. The reported fire could not be put out; it was a volcanic eruption.

The volcano Helgafell, the "holy mountain," on the little sixteen-square-kilometer island off the southern coast of Iceland, had not shown any sign of life for 7,000 years. But on that fateful January 23, 1973, a small side crater erupted without warning and tore a 1.5-kilometer-long fissure into the earth and spat 100 cubic meters of lava a second into the air.

Glowing torrents of lava flowed into the sea. Houses burned. Cars were buried. The sea boiled in the Vestmannaeyjar harbor. Happily, the wind stood favorably and for the first day kept the fire cloud from the town. Although some inhabitants lived close to the crater, no one died.

Scientists are going to concern themselves with that 1973 eruption in several thousand or even hundreds of thousands of years—for a very special reason.

The lava a volcano throws into the sky is made up of particles containing iron. The earth's magnetic field directs these particles in their flight. Like innumerable small compass needles, all fly in the same direction. The congealed lava, which finally turns into basalt, will show hundreds of thousands of years hence the exact magnetic field of the earth in 1973.

Should, for some reason or other, the date of this volcanic eruption ever be forgotten, it would be possible to calculate the time merely by the direction of the basalt, because the earth's magnetic field is subject to constant change. We know today that 700,000 years ago the magnetic north pole was located where the geographic South Pole is today and that 200,000 years before that it was in the same place as today. During the 76 million years of the earth's history, 171 magnetic-pole reversals have taken place.

These polar changes trigger changes in climate, earthquakes, and volcanic eruptions. But, most importantly, they bring about changes in the cosmic energy balance. And that can have deadly results. Magnetic storms or sudden changes in the geographic magnetic fields of the earth, such as those that have been recorded during heavy sunspot activity, give some idea of the enormous impact that polar changes can have.

The differing interias of various liquid and solid substances in the inner earth create its magnetic field. The hard core of our planet is covered with liquid layers which, in turn, are enclosed in a denser mantle. Since according to the law of gravity these various layers are exposed to differing speeds of rotation, electric currents and magnetic fields are created, just as they are in a dynamo. Such a current flows around the equator. During a polar reversal the "north" magnetic pole flips to the southern hemisphere, while the "south" magnetic pole flips to the north.

The geographic and magnetic north poles do not coincide even today. The magnetic north pole wanders constantly. During the tertiary period it could be found at 70 degrees northern latitude and 60 degrees western longitude; 350 million years ago it was at 30 degrees northern latitude and 45 degrees western longitude.

For more than a hundred years scientists have registered the steady weakening of the earth's magnetic field. Recent calculations indicate that, if this development persists, the earth's magnetic field will have reached zero in two thousand years. In a continuation of this process, it will then rebuild itself in the opposite direction. If and how organisms would survive this polar reversal remains a scientific puzzle. In any case, people will have to be concerned about scientific problems hardly anyone takes seriously today—or, should we say, that no one takes seriously any longer?

The physical strength of a magnetic field can be determined by simple measurements. The earth's horizontal magnetic field has a field force of 0.1 gauss. Sunspots can reach a field force of 2,000 to 4,000 gauss. In comparison, the lead-in wire to an electric bulb has a field force of 0.2 gauss.

The earth's magnetic field is duplicated in all objects that contain iron. Iron hammers used in the northern hemisphere build a magnetic south pole on their hammering side. A magnetic north pole forms on the handle of a umbrella when it is turned toward the earth. Forces are at work here to which science pays little heed because they don't seem to have much practical application. But the ancient Egyptians with their exact observation of the heavens were on the trail of phenomena which we are only now beginning to take seriously again.

Why did the Egyptians, who loved and venerated their dead so much that they kept their mummified ancestors standing vertically in their living rooms, often for many years, bury their pharaohs far removed from any human habitation in huge cities of the dead? Thebes located its city of the dead in the Valley of the Kings, Memphis in the grave field of Sakkara and the pyramids of Giza. Could it be that these regions are particularly susceptible to cosmic influences?

Our whole planetary system is subject to an electromagnetic and radioactive correlation, to which all organic life is subject. The magnetic field, for example, catches cosmic radiation. That's why electromagnetic radiation particles can't move freely and in a straight line but are forced into spiral paths which run along the magnetic field line.

The earth's radiation zones, named the Van Allen belts

for their discoverer, are made up of high-energy particles of cosmic radiation which are subject to the earth's magnetic field. And this whole complicated, interlocking system is very easy to disrupt.

The Fateful Spots of Re

If the Egyptians considered anything holy, it was the sun. And if their scientific interest was concentrated on any one thing, it was the sun. From the earliest times, Re, the sun, was the highest god and, later, the planet most worthy of exploration.

Babylonian cuneiform texts tell of precise observations of the sun, the decrease and increase of light, and about the spots observed on the sun's surface. But then, it seems, these strange sunspots were again forgotten. The Chinese took an interest in them in the thirteenth century A.D., and they also aroused Galileo's scientific curiosity. In the middle of the last century German astronomers discovered that sunspot activity reaches a peak every eleven years.

Today we know that sunspots have a strong influence on organic and cosmic activity on earth. Major natural disasters are connected to maximal sunspot activity.

On August 27, 1883, the volcano Krakatau erupted in the Sunda Strait, killing 80,000. At the time, sunspot activity was at its height. Major earthquakes shook San Francisco and Messina in 1906 and 1908 respectively, during intense sunspot activity. In September, 1926, a tornado ravaged large sections of Florida, a cyclone struck Jamaica, cloudbursts lashed Nebraska. Sunspot activity was again at its height.

What are sunspots? A burning light bulb held in front of a glowing piece of steel appears to the eye as a dark spot. The dark spots on the sun disk are not cold or congealed masses, either; they merely have a much lower temperature than their surroundings.

The reason for these drastic temperature changes can be found in the sun's magnetic field. It changes direction and force more frequently than the earth's. Resulting differences in field force can be a thousandfold.

Just as they do in the earth's magnetic field, electric field currents in the sun's magnetic field lead to changes in temperature. Sunspots lower the temperature of the sun's surface from 6,000 degrees centigrade to 4,000–5,000 degrees. However, sunspots are limited to an area that runs from 30 degrees north to 30 degrees south of the sun's equator. They make up little more than 1 percent of the sun's surface. Nevertheless, their impact is enormous.

For the variations in the sun's magnetic field are transmitted to the interplanetary magnetic field of the earth with a delay of four and a half days. In other words, a field line connection exists between sun and earth.

Two astrophysicists, NASA's Dr. Norman F. Ness and the University of California's Dr. John M. Wilcox, made the first precise measurements in 1964 when they analyzed the magnetographic recordings made at the Mount Wilson Observatory together with data the research satellite IPM-1 had radioed back from space.

Sun flares, eruptions of the gaseous material above the sun, are closely connected to sunspot activity. They result in higher emissions of radiation and ultraviolet and X rays. An ionized gas cloud reaches earth but is stopped by our planet's magnetic field. The resultant field fluctuations can reach a thousand times their normal force.

An impressive demonstration of these astrophysical phenomena was given on February 8, 1958. That day radio astronomers at the Harvard radio observatory in Texas reported "suspicious noises" coming from space. Astronomers at Sacramento Peak in New Mexico registered unusually high sunspot activity. A radio telescope in Honolulu located the subsequent flares.

Twenty-four hours later all hell broke loose on earth. Polar lights glowed in the night sky. Transcontinental radio transmission was disrupted. Almost a hundred airplanes flying across the Atlantic lost all radio contact. The underwater telephone cable between Scotland and Newfoundland suddenly registered a voltage of 2,000 volts. Toronto's power system collapsed. Events 150 million kilometers away were responsible.

The Power of the Moon

A growing number of physicists and doctors now believe that the influence of sun and moon on organic growth and on man's susceptibility to disease should not be underestimated. Thus the annual rings on trees appear to show the same eleven-year cycle sunspots do. Bamboo cut during a new moon is more durable than that felled when the moon is full; the former lasts ten to twelve years, the latter only seven to eight. The Romans cut the wood they needed to build ships and bridges when the moon declined. The practice, we have learned in the meantime, is not based on obscure superstition but on the experience of biological fact: As the moon increases, juices rise in the wood and the sugar in them attracts wood-eating insects. As a result the wood tends to rot more easily. When the moon declines, the sugar turns into starch and consequently wood cut at that time does not rot as quickly.

The influence of the moon is the subject of many popular sayings, especially among farmers. Thus it is best to sow as the moon grows fuller, and to harvest during its decline. Pain is more intense during an increasing moon, while snake venom is less potent when the moon shrinks.

Fact and fancy are surely woven together in these sayings. Yet biologists believe the moon does influence important life processes, especially among sea creatures: Some snails and shellfish lay their eggs in accordance with the moon's direction.

Until about two hundred years ago the influence of the moon on the rhythm of the tides was pure speculation. Conventional science accepted the moon-caused 372-minute interval only early in the nineteenth century. Today we even assume that the attraction of the moon can lift the earth crust by 25 centimeters. Harvard physicists determined that the distance between the United States and Europe varies on some days by as much as twenty meters due to the rising and falling of the earth's surface.

> When the constellation of the Pleiades, the
> daughters of Atlas, rises, then begin the
> harvest, but plow when they descend.

Forty nights and days do these stay hidden,
but when in the course of the year they reappear,
then begin to sharpen your sickle for new harvest.

These are verses from the Greek poet Hesiod's *Works and Days,* which gave harvest advice based on the stars. In the light of modern astronomy they are inexact, for between the evening descent and morning rise of the Pleiades lie forty nights and thirty-nine days. But Hesiod (8th century B.C.) was not a scientist; he could report only his own experiences.

Bombardment from Space

What we commonly call "sun" or "light" is in reality a physical process with cause and effect. There is little point in talking about the uncertainties of its creation, but the effect of sunlight is of extraordinary interest to this discussion.

The sun bombards the biosphere, the earth's living space, in amounts that would be fatal to man were it not for the earth's magnetic field.

Ultraviolet rays are the best-known form of radiation. They boost resistance to disease, encourage vitamin D formation, help heal skin and bone tuberculosis, and reduce those bodies in the skin which stabilize vitamins A, B-2, C, D, and E, while their increase or decrease demonstrably has a direct effect on the vegetative nervous system. In short, ultraviolet radiation can profoundly influence human physiology.

The atmosphere can hold off shortwave rays so effectively that cosmic ultrarays, for example (which should not be confused with ultraviolet rays), lose as much of their force on hitting the atmosphere as they would by slamming into a 90-centimeter-thick sheet of lead or a ten-meter-wide wall of water. These cosmic ultrarays are made up of electrons, mesons, protons, neutrons, and high-energy photons. Neutrons and photons penetrate the atmosphere, while electrons and protons are trapped by the magnetic field.

That explains why astrophysicists talk about primary radiation and secondary rays. Primary rays are those which have not been changed by the atmosphere. Secondary rays, which can penetrate deeply into the earth, have little in common with primary radiation.

Eighty percent of the primary ultrarays are protons, most of the rest alpha particles. Proton energy is enormous. It can range from a billion electron volts to several trillion.

Cosmic radiation has been used in archaeology. Professor Luis W. Alvarez, a Nobel-Prize-winning physicist and amateur Egyptologist, decided in 1965 to see if cosmic radiation could be used for exploration of the Khafre pyramid near Giza.

Ever since Giovanni Belzoni crawled into this, the second largest pyramid, in 1818 and found a single empty grave chamber, Egyptologists have wondered if there was not another as yet undiscovered chamber. The passages inside the pyramid are unusually simple in design, quite unlike the angular corridors of the other great pyramids, which all have two chambers instead of one.

Alvarez set to work on a seemingly impossible task: finding a room 15 or 20 meters square, hidden somewhere inside 4.4 million tons of rock.

In the past archaeologists had relied on prior experience in order to solve similar riddles or had drilled or dug pretty much at random. But neither method would help here. Experience could be no guide and extensive drillings were too dangerous to risk, lest they damage the pyramid's structure.

Nuclear Research in a Pryamid

Luis Alvarez based his approach on the following (as it would turn out, correct) hypothesis: Cosmic ultrarays are pulverized in the upper atmosphere. About 80 percent of this energy hits the earth as medium-heavy mesons—particles able to penetrate anything, including the pyramids. These particles can be measured. If appropriate measuring instruments were placed below the pyramid and at various angles in it, radiation levels should be higher whenever particles pass through a hollow chamber, since air does not slow the particles as much as rock does.

The obvious and best place to install such equipment

was in the only room that had as yet been found in the pyramid—the Belzoni chamber, named for the man who had rediscovered it. The chamber is located 130 meters below the pyramid peak and at its exact center.

The installation of thirty tons of complex telemetric equipment began in the spring of 1967. It was quite a trick: The pyramidal passages were only 120 centimeters wide, so the apparatus had to be taken apart first and put together again inside the pyramid.

The work load was shared by the Egyptian pyramid specialist Dr. Ahmed Fakhry; Dr. Fathi el Bedewi, a Cairo University nuclear physicist; and Alvarez and his team from the University of California's Lawrence Radiation Laboratory. After three months of installation work, measurements were set to begin—but then the Six-Day War broke out and the project was delayed.

Finally, in the spring of 1968, Alvarez began measurements he had taken three years to prepare. The spark chamber he set up inside the pyramid worked like this: Aluminum plates stacked on top of one another were put into a gas-filled chamber under high voltages. When a particle penetrated the pyramid and struck one of the plates, a spark jumped to the next one. The impulse was registered on a magnetic tape.

According to Professor Alvarez's calculations, particles loaded with energy below a level of 55 billion electron volts should be absorbed by the pyramid's rocks and therefore not arrive in the grave chamber at the bottom. The spark chambers were designed to record only particles which registered a load of 10 billion electron volts of energy—after having passed through the pyramid.

First results astonished the observers. The number of particles that reached the grave chamber was much larger than anticipated. Measurements were carried out at an angle distance of 3 degrees, and an average of 84 particle impacts per minute was measured. The surveyed area stretched over a cone standing on end at an angle of 70 degrees. That covered about a fifth of the pyramid's space.

The measurements took months. An 1130 IBM computer

at Cairo University analyzed the magnetically stored data. Transferred onto a rotogravure screen, the data clearly showed the lime lining at the top of the pyramid. A dark shadow that seemed to point toward a hollow space, and caused some excitement among archaeologists, turned out to be a reflection from the measuring equipment. Analysis of the magnetic tape data finally convinced Alvarez that Pharaoh Khafre had indeed built only a single tomb chamber into his pyramid.

Clearly, there is more energy between heaven and earth than an earlier science had supposed. These energies could prove a blessing for mankind, if men learn how to control them. But they could also bring death and destruction.

And yet when this energy reaches the earth it has already lost most of its strength. The transformed secondary rays have much greater impact than the primary rays. Particles can penetrate several thousand meters into the earth.

In recent years atomic physicists and archaeologists have, on occasion, worked closely together, especially in determining an object's age with the help of radioactive carbon. Cosmic radiation produces radioactive carbon, C-14, from the nitrogen in the upper atmosphere. The principle is similar to that used in atomic reactors. In time this carbon burns into carbonic acid and mixes with the normal carbonic acid in the atmosphere.

Willard F. Libby, a noted U.S. chemist, made use of this natural process to develop an interesting "aging" method for which he won a Nobel prize. Every organism, be it man, animal, or plant, has in its carbon traces of radioactive carbon corresponding precisely to amounts present in atmospheric carbonic acid, the "mother" substance of organic carbon.

Radiocarbon decay and new C-14 formation through cosmic radiation keep each other in near balance. When an organism dies, supplies of new carbon stop. Putrefaction and decomposition generally put the dead organism back into the natural cycle: Dust is absorbed into plants, plants are eaten by animals, animals either die or are eaten by men.

But if a dead organism does not rejoin that cycle and survives intact for centuries or perhaps millennia, it becomes subject to radiocarbon decay. Its C-14 content decreases steadily. Scientists have found that over 5,730 years half the C-14 atoms have changed back to nitrogen (C-14 half-life).

This method of determining age is accurate only if the concentration of carbon dioxide in the atmosphere has remained constant over the millennia. (Measurements made after nuclear explosions have showed substantial sectional fluctuations in C-14 content, but these differences in concentration disappeared within a matter of weeks.)

The Crazy Measurements

Results American scientists achieved determining the age of grave gifts in the pharaohs' tombs are nothing less than sensational. It seemed as if all the equipment had gone crazy. Mummies were suddenly five hundred years older than the appropriate sarcophagus. Grains were older than the containers in which they were found. Either the whole system of measuring age was faulty or the Egyptians did indeed understand how to influence radioactive decay.

If such phenomena are observed in, of all places, the graves of Egyptian kings, wouldn't it make sense to assume that it was done to protect the mummies? In determining ages up to 5,000 years, scientists generally accept an uncertainty factor of plus or minus 40 to 70 years. Larger deviations, they believe, must have other causes, probably very good ones.

Early in the 1950s, for example, physicists analyzed bushes growing in the green strip on the autobahn between Heidelberg and Mannheim. The result was something of a shock: According to the measurements the bushes were five hundred years old. Was carbon-dating based on faulty premises after all?

On the contrary, the method's basic validity is demonstrated by this example. The bushes were a special case. They grew among highly concentrated auto-emission gases (carbon dioxide without C-14). The normal C-14 content was thinned out by "dead" carbon. As a result, living wood checked out at age five hundred.

We may conclude that deviations from the standard C-14 carbon content are caused by outside influences. A study of these influences on the pharaohs' tombs would seem worth the attention of both physicists and archaeologists. Indeed, such study could well bring us closer to unlocking the secrets behind the curse of the pharaohs.

13 The Secrets of the Pyramids

SOVIET PRIME MINISTER Nikita Khrushchev toured Egypt for sixteen days during May, 1964. He made the trip because the first section of the Aswan Dam, built with Russian help, had been completed.

Shortly before returning home, Khrushchev stopped at the world-famous Mena House Hotel. Built in 1869 at the foot of the high plateau with the great Giza pyramids on it, the hotel has had kings and heads of state from all over the world as guests. The 1943 allied summit meeting among Churchill, Roosevelt, and Chiang Kai-shek took place here. (The British and Chinese leaders visited the Khufu pyramid; FDR declined with thanks.)

The day after Khrushchev's arrival he was slated to visit the pyramid when a cable arrived from Moscow. The KGB wired, STRONGLY ADVISE AGAINST ENTERING THE PYRAMID. Khrushchev obeyed. An official explanation was never issued. What did the Russian secret police fear?

For more than a century scientists all over the world have pondered the phenomenon of the pyramids, the only remaining fully intact wonder of the world. The first precise measurements were made toward the end of the nineteenth century; ever since, the possibility that these curious and monumental buildings had been erected in this place, and in this architectural style, by chance has been discounted.

Snefru was the first pharaoh who wanted to build himself

a real pyramid. But the structure begun near Medum was never completed because Snefru moved his residence farther north. He had a second pyramid built in Dahshur, north of Sakkara. It was ninety-seven meters high. Snefru's successors, Khufu and Khafre, built their pyramids near Giza: Dedf-re built near Abu Roash, Menkure again in Giza. During the Vth dynasty the pyramids of Sahure were constructed, and during the VIth the pharaohs built near Abu Sir. There are sixty-nine major pyramids in Egypt today. Were these buildings only tombstones, or is an impenetrable secret hidden behind their unique architecture?

The well-known Egyptologist Richard Lepsius believed that each pharaoh laid the cornerstone for his tomb at the beginning of his reign and then proceeded to enlarge it, a process akin to the formation of annual rings on a tree. But as has happened so often in the past, new research has made that theory obsolete. Construction of a pyramid was carefully thought out before the first stone was laid; this conclusion is unchanged despite indications of revisions of building plans during construction.

The design of the Khufu pyramid, for example, was changed three times during the twenty years it took to build. But the geographic direction remained constant. The first measurements with reasonably sophisticated equipment were undertaken by the Egyptian government in 1925. The results stupefied the experts and had to be repeated: The largest deviation from the four major compass points amounted to ½₂ of a degree, and that on the east side of the north-south pyramidal axis.

The ancient Egyptians allegedly did not have the compass. No one has yet come up with an explanation as to how 1.3 million granite blocks that weighed up to 16 tons each could be placed next to—and on top of—each other so precisely that deviations on the 230-meter-long "blueprint" basal lines totaled no more than fractions of millimeters and with mortarless seaming in so tight a fit, since even a centimeter-wide crack is invisible, given a pyramid's enormous dimensions. It is worth noting, too, that a cover of Tura limestone had been placed over the still existing basic structure. No, there has to be another explanation as to why they were built to such precise measure.

When a Pharaoh Measured

The basic measuring unit was the Egyptian ell, made up of seven hands (one hand equals four fingers). A finger corresponds to 1.9 centimeters, a hand to 7.5 centimeters, and an ell to 52.5 centimeters. Measurements were taken with ell sticks, some of which survive, and with measuring ropes.

Both measuring instruments are puzzling; stringing hundreds of ell sticks together risks a high error quotient, just as does the use of long measuring ropes, which are exposed to fluctuations in temperature and humidity and may contract and expand. How could the Egyptians manage their precise measurements with such inadequate tools?

We know how they achieved their angle accuracy in building the pyramids. The Rhind papyrus, now in the British Museum in London, contains examples on how to measure which clearly demonstrate that some trigonometric functions were known as early as 2000 B.C. The papyrus also features several math "homework" questions based on pyramid construction from which it is easy to deduce that the Egyptians did not know how to measure angles until at least the Middle Kingdom. The gradation of a pyramid slope is not expressed in degrees but in units of length—by citing the displacement difference between the top and bottom stones. A pyramid angle of 5-¼ hands, therefore, means that the second row of stones has been set back 5-¼ hands, or 39.4 centimeters, from the first. The Egyptians only used single fractions such as ¼, ⅙, or ¹⁄₂₅. However, subtraction of these single fractions from whole numbers resulted in other fractions, for example, $2 - ¼$ = 1-¾; or $2 - ⅙ = 1-⅚$.

Study the pyramid calculations in the Rhind papyrus and one thing stands out: The floor plan and the height of the pyramids are given in whole numbers while the slope gradations are sometimes expressed in complicated fractions. For example, problem No. 56 in the 3,700-year-old document gives the pyramid length as 360 ells, its height as 250 ells, then asks for the calculation of the gradation slope, which can be figured out by using 5-½₅ hands (equals 54° 15′). Since length and height are also given in whole numbers in other math examples, there is little doubt that the Egyptian pyramids—except for the very first ones—were not accidental forms but geometric bodies carefully measured and laid out before they were built.

But how was this particular form developed? The pyramid shape does not conform to the Egyptian ideal of beauty. Only two surfaces are visible at one time. Moreover, their perspective distortion tends to confuse. Nor by any stretch of the imagination could it have been a question of choosing that particular form in order to cut back the amount of building material used. That leaves two theories: The shape was designed to be either symbolic or functional.

It is too glib to call the pyramids staircases to heaven. The results of too much research would have to be based on mere chance to make that explanation plausible.

All planes on an Egyptian pyramid can be seen at the same time only from the air. Therefore, the sun, light, radiation, or other cosmic forces seem to have played a role in their construction. The British scholar Dr. Brown Landone, who studied pyramid architecture for twenty-two years, proved that the sun has a definite relationship to the pyramids. The foundation line of the Khufu pyramid is 365.24 ells long—precisely the number of days in our (sun) year. A game with numbers? An accident?

Looking back to the origins of astronomy, it is clear that the sun and the moon prompted the development of astrology with their alternating appearance in the heavens and their visible influence on events here on earth. If the sun were able to open the calyx of a flower in the morning and the moon to close it at night, surely the hand of divine providence was able to determine the actions of men as well.

Sun and moon were the first planets to give the Egyptians a system. After systematic observation of the night sky they were able to add five other planets that moved like the sun and the moon and changed brightness and color. According to current planetary nomenclature these were Saturn, Mars, Mercury, Venus, and Jupiter. Thus seven planets were the first gods—and the source of the holy number 7.

The Observatory

The well-known British astronomer Richard A. Proctor, who spent years researching the Khufu pyramid, said in his book, *The Great Pyramid,* "If we realize that at the time of Pharaoh Cheops [Khufu] astronomy was really nothing more than astrology and astrology a very important part of religion, we get a sense as to why the Egyptians piled up such enormous masses of rock."

Proctor believed that before Khufu's reign the pyramid was actually an enormous high plateau that reached up to what is today the king's chamber in the pyramid, at the fiftieth stone row, and that this plateau was used for astronomical observation. As absurd as the theory may seem at first glance, there's little doubt that astronomy played its part in the way pyramids were built. One entry to the royal chamber in the Khufu pyramid, for example, provides the sighting of certain stars at fixed times. Is that fact really only an accident?

Duncan Macnaughton, another pyramid scholar, went farther: He believed the entries to the pyramids were specifically designed for the observation of Sirius and that the star could even be seen during the daytime when its trajectory moved between 26° 18′ and 28° 18′ on the southern sky, with the long dark tunnels acting as a kind of "telescope." We have seen that, for the Egyptians, Sirius (or Sothis) was the most important star, since its appearance announced the advent of the new year and of the Nile floods.

Sirius' first heliacal rising of the year, when the star becomes visible before sunrise, signaled the imminent beginning of the Nile floods. The Dutch scholar B. L. van der Waerden, who concerned himself with the origins of astronomy, contended that before Egypt introduced a solar year

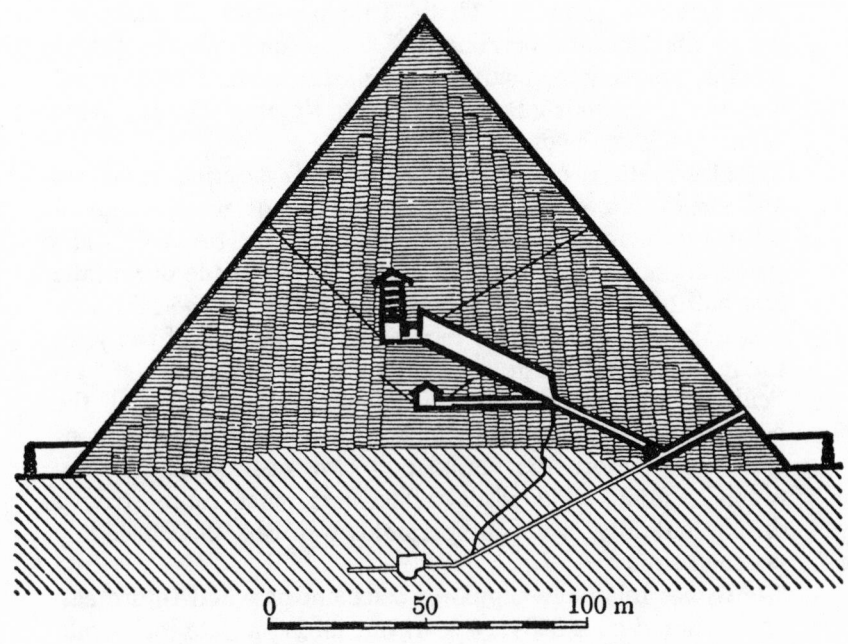

A wonder of the world and a geometric puzzle: The 146-meter-tall Khufu (or Cheops) pyramid of Giza with its three grave chambers. The function of the "grand gallery" in the middle still remains unexplained.

with 365 days, its year was divided into a cycle of three seasons that began with the floods, "inundation," and included "sowing" and "reaping." This cyclical year was replaced by a solar year of twelve months with thirty days each and five intercalary days for a total of 365 days. But since the full solar year is six hours longer than 365 days and thus lags behind the sun clock a full day every four years, the start of the Egyptian new year wandered through all the seasons as the centuries and millennia passed by.

The seasons were divided into three four-month periods.

The first four months (Thoth, Paophi, Athyr, Choiak) are called the "months of flooding," the second quartet (Tobi, Mechir, Phamenoth, Pharmuthi) are the "months of growth," and the third four (Pachons, Payni, Epiphi, Mesore) were called the "months of heat."

Observations on the Khufu pyramid's position as to sun and shade demonstrated that the Egyptians were aware of other astronomical orientation points during the year. The pyramid's northern triangle lies totally in the shade during the first half of the year, but when the sun rises in the northeast and sinks in the northwest during the second half of the year, sunlight also falls on the north side of the pyramid. Of particular interest are the two transitional periods when half the north side is in the shade and half in the sun. This happens two weeks before the vernal and two weeks after the autumnal equinox. The visual effect was much more striking during antiquity, when the pyramids were sheathed in highly polished stone.

It was relatively simple to calculate past and future calendars based on a 365-day year. But setting a date for certain religious holidays that had to fall in a specific season was much more troublesome without intercalation. The priests finally resolved the problem by setting the dates anew each year.

The Egyptian solar calendar remained in force until the age of Augustus (63 B.C. to A.D. 14), the first Roman emperor, when a sixth intercalary day every four years was introduced in Alexandria—the birth of the Alexandrian calendar. But, as is suggested by the writings of the most important astronomer of antiquity, Ptolemy (about A.D. 140 in Alexandria), and by Egyptian planetary tables dating back to the Roman emperors, both calendars were used simultaneously for several centuries.

Actually, the Egyptian calendar was corrected almost two centuries before Augustus. Astronomers, priests, and politicians active in the town of Canopus, northeast of Alexandria and famed for its oracle and the Serapis temple, decided in 238 B.C. to add six hours to their year. But the edict of Canopus was not put into practice until the Augustan age.

Initially astronomy was not a subject for scientific research but a pragmatic orientation aid in the unpredictable flow of time. Where else but in the sky could one look to recognize constants, systems, and periods? And isn't it in fact a miracle that a star, observed for months, suddenly disappears, only to reappear seventy days later?

The Greek poet Hesiod was a disciple of the ancient Egyptian teachings. In *Works and Days* he described the phases of the fixed stars and the planets. He wrote about the end of winter, "When, sixty days after the sun has turned, Zeus ends the days of winter, then Arcturus' star will leave the holy flood of Oceanus behind him and first rise in radiant glory from the twilight."

Initial observations of the stars were recorded in the world's first calendar. The oldest Egyptian calendars date from the twentieth century B.C. and, strangely enough, were inscribed on the inside of coffin lids. The faith in rebirth was so strong that the graves were equipped not only with food and artifacts but with a calendar as well.

In these calendars there are clear references to time stars and star formations. They show that the old Egyptians recognized thirty-six groups of stars. The apparent circle in which the sun seems to move, the ecliptic or zodiac, is subdivided into thirty-six parts. Begun as a measurement of time, astronomy became the astrology of the priests and magicians. Many temples and tombs contain pictures interpreting the stars; for example, in the temples of Edfu, Esneh, and Dendera, and in the graves of Rameses II, Seti I, and Senmut, Hatshepsut's chancellor.

While astrology still exists, pyramidology, the science of exploring the pyramids, has been forgotten, although both went hand in hand for many centuries. There is, of course, a simple explanation: Astrology can be and is practiced in nearly all the nations of the world, while pyramid research is only possible in Egypt. It is, after all, the only place that has pyramids—except for Mexico, where the geometric construction is quite different. Transillumination of the pyramids with the help of modern measuring equipment, as well as para-scientific research, only began in the second half of the last century.

Sense and Purpose of Geometric Construction

The symbolic geometry of the great pyramid first aroused the interest of scholars from around the globe: its ground plan is a square, the elevation a triangle. The triangle, a symbol of divinity (Osiris, Isis, Horus, or holy trinity), stands above the square, symbol of material things. Since the Egyptians saw the death cult as the highest form of duty and of intellectual contemplation, the symbolic import of its construction cannot be ignored.

But a much more likely explanation for the pyramid's unique shape is that it was designed as functional architecture to reflect the scientific knowledge priests and magicians possessed and thus subject the pharaoh buried there to very definite influences. The Greek philosopher Plotinus (A.D. 205–270), a neoplatonic mystic who reported on the existence of secret cults in ancient Egypt, considered this theory, without, however, being able to furnish any details. He justified this lack of knowledge by contending that "it is a law among these secret cults not to betray a secret to the noninitiated." And any infraction of this commandment was punishable by death—for both the betrayer and the recipient of unauthorized information. A. P. Sinnett, a British scholar, has written widely about initiation ceremonies into these mystic cults.

Novices were subjected to gruelling tests of their steadfastness, courage, and intelligence. Drugs and beatings backed up psychological pressure suggesting that the novice was falling down an abyss or was being crushed by rocks; that he walked across a high swaying bridge or through a wall of fire; that he was drowning or being attacked by wild animals.

Such initiation ceremonies are depicted in the great temple of Philae. Unlike the generally very naturalistic Egyptian reliefs, this one is executed in symbolic terms, quite understandably so, given the secrecy of the cult.

In his book *The Great Pyramid in Fact and in Theory,*
William Kingsland speculated that these ceremonies may
have been held in some of the many side chambers of the
pyramids. Some of the Books of the Dead contain hints that
they might have been, mentioning the terrifying, hostile
forces the dead must face before they are allowed to enter
the realm of Osiris.

Mental Imbalance in the Royal Chamber

Could the pyramids really have been misused for cultic ceremony? Quite probably. Certainly there is plenty of evidence to support the thesis and virtually none to oppose it.
For the pharaoh was always an "initiate," or insider. And
since the burial and care of the dead was a matter for priests
and magicians, it would not have been unusual to hold mystic
rites inside the huge monuments to the dead. The question
remains, however, as to whether the rites were really conducted under the influence of drugs and of beatings, as has
been suggested.

As we have already seen, the pyramid shape does influence the dehydration and conservation of dead bodies.
Animal experiments and tests with dead organs have proved
that organisms remain preserved in a pyramid in some inexplicable way. Of course, these relatively recent discoveries
should surprise no one, given the effort the Egyptians expended on body conservation. It is also interesting to note
that really complicated mummification of the dead began
only after pyramids were no longer being built. Until then,
simple embalming sufficed.

A second observation is equally inexplicable: A pro-
longed stay in a pyramid can adversely influence mental
balance. Was that the reason why the Russian secret police
warned Khrushchev against entering the Khufu pyramid?

The Englishman Paul Brunton, neither an Egyptologist
nor a parapsychologist, examined that phenomenon more
closely. He had himself locked into the king's chamber in the
Khufu pyramid for a whole night, a project whose major
difficulty consisted in obtaining permission to do so from Cairo

authorities. Finally, Cairo's police chief relented and allowed Brunton to spend a night in the pyramid.

Brunton spent his first hours in the great gallery, the narrow but high diagonal passage that leads into the royal chamber. Then he sat down in a corner of the chamber. Suddenly he felt as if he could no longer think clearly. He closed his eyes and suffered from visions:

Fear, fright and terror persistently showed me their terrible faces. Without my wanting them to, my hands were clamped together like a vise. . . . My eyes were closed but these grey, gliding, fog-shrouded shapes pushed themselves into the field of my vision. And always there was this unrelenting hostility. . . . A circle of hostile creatures surrounded me, huge, elemental creations, frightening figures of terror from the underworld, grotesque shapes, madmen, hulking and devilish apparitions passed around me, they were tremendously disgusting.

The explorer, who had experienced many adventures during his lifetime, was close to a nervous collapse. He felt his muscles stiffen so he could no longer move. It was as if some sinister force were working on his five senses. He was taken out the next morning, completely listless.

Emotional factors, of course, may have played a role here, even for an adventurer like Paul Brunton. After all, who would enjoy spending a solitary night in the grave chamber of the Khufu pyramid! But there are enough witnesses to attest to similar phenomena during the day and in the presence of many people.

The last time I visited the Khufu pyramid in 1972 I met members of a German travel tour who were being taken through the pyramid by Egyptian guides. A Spanish lady who had attached herself to the tour suddenly began to scream at the upper end of the great gallery. She collapsed onto the footbridge and could not move. With great difficulty, she was taken through the barely one-meter-high bottom exit of the gallery. Once outside her cramps let up. I asked the woman if she could explain the incident or if anything similar had ever happened to her before. But she was quite perplexed. "It was as if something had suddenly hit me," she said. Later the guide told me that such "attacks" happened quite often.

H. V. Morton, author of the book *Through Lands of the Bible*, described how he fell victim of these strange forces during a visit to the Khufu pyramid. Morton, who had also taken a group tour, was suddenly afflicted by a sense of panic while in the royal chamber. He felt faint and, as he himself described it, crawled out on all fours.

Death of Two Pyramid Explorers

Two archaeologists who spent years in the pyramids died so suddenly that even skeptics have now connected their deaths to their explorations. The well-known British Egyptologist Sir W. M. Flinders Petrie, who was better versed in pyramid theories than just about anybody else, died unexpectedly and inexplicably in Jerusalem on July 28, 1942, on his way home from Cairo.

Petrie had barely survived the death of his colleague, Professor George A. Reisner. The American archaeologist had made important finds in the twenties and thirties. Among other things, Reisner discovered the magnificently equipped tomb of Khufu's mother, Hetephere, located somewhat to the east of the pyramid. He also made radio history in 1939 with the first broadcast from inside the pyramid's royal chamber. His death in the spring of 1942 was no less sensational than his broadcast. Reisner collapsed inside the pyramid and lay there as if paralyzed. He had to be dragged out into the open through the narrow passageway. Then he was taken to the excavators' camp, where the archaeologists kept their equipment. He died there without regaining consciousness.

Since these mysterious 1942 deaths many scientists have studied the physical significance of the pyramids. Physicists are sober people. In searching for the secrets of the pyramids they forgot all about historical tradition and symbolic geometry and searched instead for the possible function of the form. The problem at issue was this: Does the shape of the pyramid attract an accumulation of cosmic radiation, magnetic

223

oscillation, or unknown energy waves? Does the pyramid shape act like a condenser, or a lens, for some forms of energy? Did the priests and mystery cults know secret methods for freeing powerful energies?

One of the mistakes we make most frequently today is to believe that everything has been discovered. Every war teaches us better. Friedrich Engels believed in 1878, for example, that the Franco-Prussian War had demonstrated the peak of technological warfare, since from that day on any army could be hit from a distance by huge cannon. Today we merely smile at such naïvete.

When the first atom bombs fell on Hiroshima and Nagasaki, U.S. Air Force chief General Carl Spaatz sent a cable to the Pentagon that began, THAT ATOMIC BOMB DISPOSES OF ALL HIGH GROUND. Since then dynamite has become obsolete in waging potential war, and even atomic energy is no longer the ultimate modern technique of destruction. Death rays are the latest discovery, what the experts call laser beams—light amplification by stimulated emission of radiation.

All these are forms of energy which war, "the father of all things," to quote Heraclitus, has given us. And if we subject them to a physicist's examination, we must admit that the principle of using this energy is really much simpler than, say, electricity. What complex methods and equipment are needed to produce electric power! On the other hand, laser beams, which can be used to do almost anything today, from digging tunnels to performing eye operations, are really nothing more than a reinforcement of light. In the so-called laser guns a light ray is intensified through forced emissions of "stimulated" atoms and molecules, and a light is created ten million times "cleaner" and much brighter than sunlight.

Laser Research Without Secrets

When a Hughes Company research team in Malibu carried out the first successful laser test in 1960, the event was celebrated as a scientific sensation. The new magic word, laser, appeared everywhere: in the newspapers, on television, in the universities and research laboratories, at meetings and congresses.

Now let's assume that Dr. Theodore Maiman, the head of the Malibu research project, brainwashed all his co-workers, condemned them to absolute silence about their discovery, threatened death to any physicists who betrayed the secret, and locked his colleagues into their institute for life—in that case Dr. Maiman and his team could have experimented for decades in order to find new applications for this form of energy. And at some point, after many years, when these crazy physicists would be known only from hearsay, someone might have found a spiral-shaped silver glass tube with a ruby-colored staff inside, a curious relic, inexplicable in its lack of function. No one would hit upon the idea that these spirals were the core of a laser gun. Of course, other forms of energy would have been discovered in the meantime, but the Malibu scientists would have taken the laser secret to their graves with them.

That this is an absurd idea is not so much a matter of the events themselves but of the assumptions that underlie them. There is no brainwashing, no threats of death, no group of incarcerated physicists in Malibu. But all these missing ingredients existed in ancient Egypt, where magicians ruled a totally obedient people, obedient because what the magicians accomplished simply exceeded the imaginative power of simple folk. We tend too often today to underestimate the scientific potential of this, the most intelligent people in the history of civilization.

The Cairo physicist Dr. Amr Gohed, who in 1969 carried out the computer analysis of Professor Luis Avarez's radiation experiments in the Khufu pyramid, said about cosmic radiation inside the thirty-five-hundred-year-old structure, "What happens inside the pyramids contradicts every known law of science and electronics."

Dr. Gohed was talking about the analysis of the magnetic tapes on which the radiation impact inside the royal chamber had been recorded. The impulses could be reproduced both visually and acoustically. Photometric strips clearly

Radiation condenser or laser gun? Archaeologists discovered this sketch of an optical instrument in ancient Meroë.

showed line structures, symbols, and geometric forms. But that was not what perplexed the physicist. It was rather the fact that the symbolism and geometry changed from day to day—despite identical working conditions and use of the same measuring instruments. As Dr. Gohed told the *New York Times,* "Either there is a major error in the pyramid's geometry which influenced our measurements, or we are dealing with a mystery that lies beyond rational explanation—call it what you will, the occult, the curse of the pharaohs, witchcraft or magic. In any case, there is a force at work inside the pyramids that contradicts all scientific laws."

Neither astrophysics nor parapsychology are yet in a position to say what kind of energy is at issue. Is it psychotronic energy, material radiation, or some form of known energy no one has thought of because it is simply not expected in that place?

X-Ray Flashes from Space

Sometimes science makes accidental discoveries that give us an inkling of the still-hidden secrets of astrophysics. Munich's *Süddeutsche Zeitung* ran the following report on March 9, 1973:

X-RAY FLASHES FROM HERCULES—A PULSE IN A DOUBLE STAR SYSTEM CAUSES STRANGE EFFECTS. Every 1.23783 seconds an X-ray flash reaches earth from the star formation Hercules. This is the result of observations made by the Uhuru satellite, which equipped with the most sophisticated X-ray detection equipment, is currently scanning space above the earth's atmosphere in search of new X-ray sources. The satellite has now found so many X-ray sources that X rays simply aren't a space rarity anymore.

The pulses, energy sources in space that give off brief impulses, are not an astrophysical novelty. What is new is the kind of energy—X rays—and the fact that these pulses stop their activity after 1.7 days for four hours. But it only seems that way. As recent research done at the Wise Observatory in Tel Aviv has demonstrated, X-ray flashes are screened from earth only every 1.7 days by a planet in the Hercules star formation, discovered in 1936 and dubbed HZ Hercules. Since HZ Hercules changes its brightness every 1.7 days, one can readily conjecture that HZ Hercules and the hitherto unknown X-ray source are two stars, one of which circles around the other every 1.7 days.

This is not to suggest that the ancient Egyptians gazed into space through huge mirror telescopes looking for new stars. But it is certainly likely that they made observations and analyzed organic reactions or that they at least tried to arrange them into a system. And one more point: They had available an enormous amount of time for their research. There are more years between the construction of the Khufu pyramid and Tutankhamen's death than between the birth of Christ and the discovery of America.

Class pride in ancient Egypt was not only highly developed among the pharaoh families—so developed that male descendants were given the same name through the centuries—but also was deeply rooted in the consciousness of priests and magicians. Researching just a single problem could stretch over several generations. A father would pass the problem—and the experiences he had gained trying to solve it—on to his son, the master to his pupil. The science of the ancient Egyptians was less research science than the science of experience. The architecture of the pyramids is the best proof. Decades were spent experimenting. The various construction phases show this clearly. Who could doubt that the shape and the site of the pyramids were selected on the basis of relevant experience?

Some Closing Thoughts

This book is not an attempt to prove triumphantly that the curse of the pharaohs exists. Rather it is meant as an investigation first into known facts and second into possible avenues of explanation for those facts. Did the ancient Egyptians deliberately turn their pharaohs' tombs into death traps? How? By leaving behind poisons with incredibly long potency? By using radioactive materials? By harnessing cosmic ultra-radiant energy? The curse of the pharaohs remains a phenomenon that has as yet no final explanation, a phenomenon with its roots deep in ancient Egypt, that civilization which still reaches across the centuries to tantalize, confound, and humble the arrogance of contemporary science with its secrets of the pyramids and the people who built them.

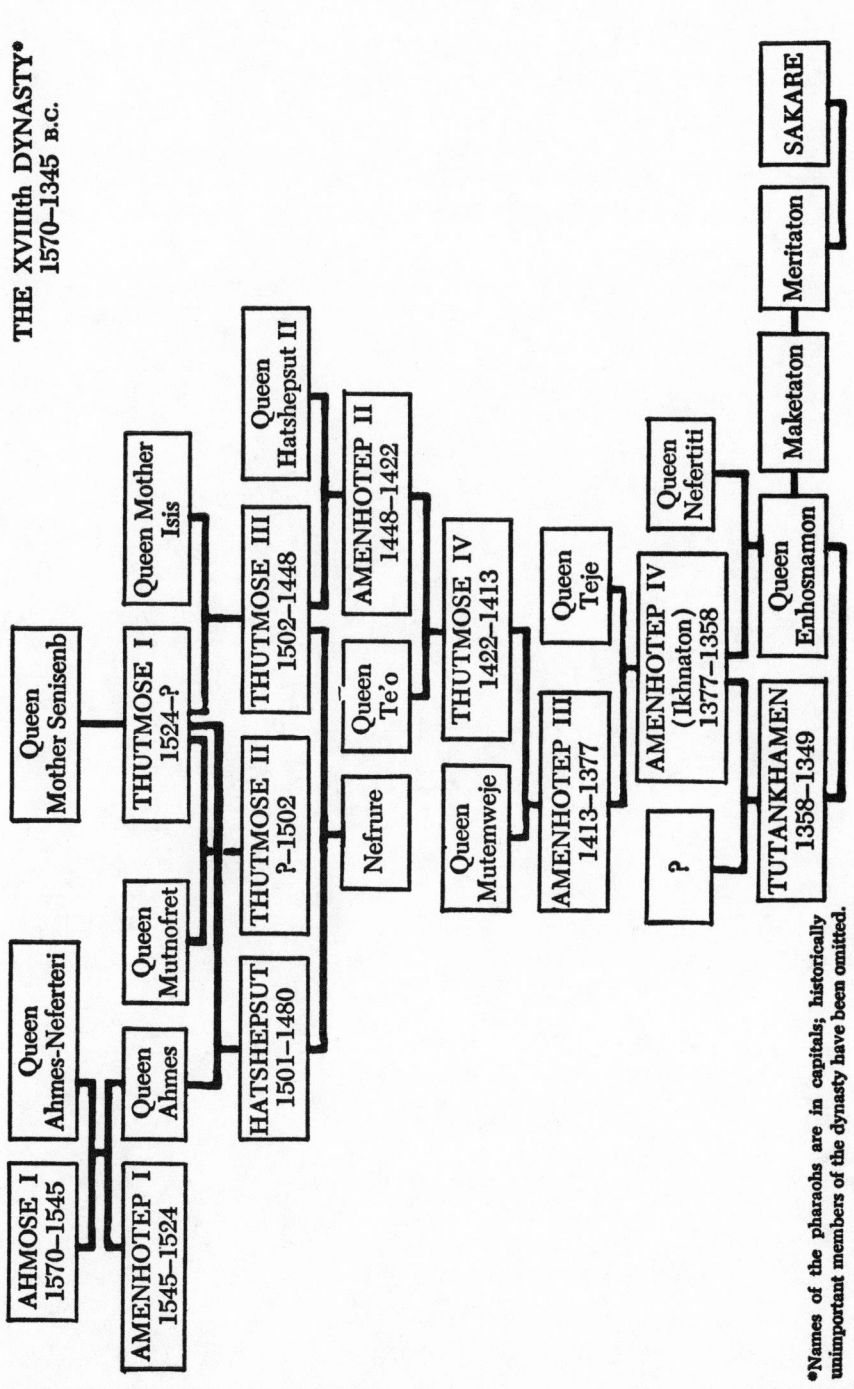

THE XVIIIth DYNASTY*
1570–1345 B.C.

AHMOSE I
1570–1545

AMENHOTEP I
1545–1524

Queen
Ahmes-Neferteri

Queen
Ahmes

Queen
Mutnofret

Queen
Mother Senisenb

THUTMOSE I
1524–?

Queen Mother
Isis

HATSHEPSUT
1501–1480

THUTMOSE II
?–1502

THUTMOSE III
1502–1448

Queen
Hatshepsut II

Nefrure

Queen
Te'o

AMENHOTEP II
1448–1422

Queen
Mutemweje

THUTMOSE IV
1422–1413

Queen
Teje

AMENHOTEP III
1413–1377

?

AMENHOTEP IV
(Ikhnaton)
1377–1358

Queen
Nefertiti

TUTANKHAMEN
1358–1349

Queen
Enhosnamon

Maketaton

Meritaton

SAKARE

*Names of the pharaohs are in capitals; historically
unimportant members of the dynasty have been omitted.

Chronology

THE OLD KINGDOM (*2850–2050* B.C.)

Ist and IId Dynasties	Royal graves near Abydos: King Menes	2850–2700 B.C.
IIId Dynasty	Step pyramids of King Zoser in Sakkara	2700–2600 B.C.
IVth Dynasty	Pyramids of Giza: Khufu, Khafre, Menkure	2600–2500 B.C.
Vth Dynasty	Pyramids of Abu Sir: Sahure, Neferirkare Niyuserre	2500–2350 B.C.
VIth Dynasty	Pyramids of Sakkara: Teti, Pepi I, and II	2350–2200 B.C.
VIIth to Xth Dynasties	The Heracleopolitans	2200–2050 B.C.

THE MIDDLE KINGDOM (*2050–1570* B.C.)

XIth Dynasty	Mentuhotep (Intef) of Thebes	2050–1991 B.C.
XIIth Dynasty	Amenemhet I–IV and Sesostris I–III	1991–1792 B.C.
XIIIth Dynasty	Collapse of the Empire	1778–1700 B.C.

| XIVth to XVIth Dynasties | Invasion of the Hyksos | 1700–1610 B.C. |

THE NEW KINGDOM (1610–712 B.C.)

XVIIth Dynasty	Driving out of the Hyksos Seqenenre and Kamose	1610–1570 B.C.
XVIIIth Dynasty	Ahmose I	1570–1545 B.C.
	Amenhotep I	1545–1524 B.C.
	Thutmose I and II	1524–1502 B.C.
	Queen Hatshepsut	1501–1480 B.C.
	Thutmose III	1502–1448 B.C.
	Amenhotep II	1448–1422 B.C.
	Thutmose IV	1422–1413 B.C.
	Amenhotep III	1413–1377 B.C.
	Ikhnaton (Amenhotep IV)	1377–1358 B.C.
	Tutankhamen	1358–1349 B.C.
	Ay	1349–1345 B.C.
XIXth and XXth Dynasties	Horemheb, Rameses I to IX, Seti I and II	1345–1085 B.C.
XXIst to XXIVth Dynasties	Kings of Tanis, loss of Nubia, the Lybian kings, Sheshonk I	1085–712 B.C.

THE LATE PERIOD (712–332 B.C.)

XXVth Dynasty	The rule of Ethiopia	
XXVIth Dynasty	Psamtik I and II	712–633 B.C.
	Cambyses of Persia conquers Egypt	663–525 B.C.
XXVIIth Dynasty	The rule of the Persians	525–332 B.C.
XXVIIIth to XXXth Dynasties	Kings of Sais, Mendes, Sebennytos	404–341 B.C.
	Alexander the Great	332 B.C.

Notes

CHAPTER 1: THE CURSE

1. Winifred Burghclere, in her Introduction to *The Tomb of Tut-ankh-Amen* by Howard Carter and A. C. Mace (New York: Cooper Square Publishers, 1963), vol. I, pp. 25–27.
2. Charles Breasted, *Pioneer to the Past: The Story of James Henry Breasted, Archaeologist* (New York: Charles Scribner's Sons, 1943), p. 330.
3. Carter and Mace, *The Tomb of Tut-ankh-Amen* (1963 ed.), vol. I, pp. 95–96.
4. Ibid., p. 99.
5. Ibid., p. 126.
6. Ibid., p. 178.
7. Ibid., pp. 180–81.
8. Ibid., p. 182.
9. Ibid., p. 183.
10. Ibid.
11. Ibid., p. 39.

CHAPTER 3: SUICIDE FOR THE ADVANCEMENT OF SCIENCE

1. Walter Bryan Emery in the *Illustrated London News*, March 6, 1956.
2. Giovanni B. Belzoni, quoted in M. Willson Disher, *Pharaoh's Fool* (London: William Heinemann Ltd., 1957), pp. 97–98.
3. Charles Breasted, *Pioneer to the Past*, p. 357.
4. Ibid., p. 359.
5. Ibid., pp. 359–60.
6. Ibid., pp. 412–13.

CHAPTER 4: GRAVES AND GANGSTERS

1. The town register of the west side of the city of Seti I's temple, up to the settlement of Mainnehes. Papyrus 10 068, British Museum.
2. Quoted in M. Willson Disher, *Pharaoh's Fool*, pp. 96–97.
3. Ibid., p. 97.
4. Charles Breasted, *Pioneer to the Past*, pp. 74–75.
5. Ibid., p. 76.
6. Ibid., pp. 161–62.

CHAPTER 5: AUTOPSY OF A PHARAOH

1. Howard Carter and A. C. Mace, *The Tomb of Tut-ankh-Amen* (1963 ed.), vol. II, pp. 106–7.
2. Ibid., pp. 144–45.
3. Ibid., pp. 107–8.
4. Ibid., pp. 129–30.
5. Ibid., pp. 131–32.
6. Ibid., p. 156.
7. Ibid., p. 157.
8. Ibid., pp. 156–57.
9. Ibid., pp. 158–59.
10. Ibid., p. 159.
11. Ibid., p. 155.
12. Ibid., p. 110.
13. Ibid., p. 113.
14. Ibid., pp. 152–53, 155.
15. Ibid., p. 153.

CHAPTER 7: ON THE ROAD TO IMMORTALITY

1. Berlin papyrus 12 412, XIXth dynasty, 1345–1200 B.C.

Bibliography

Andreas, Peter. *Was niemand glauben will: Abenteuer im Reich der Parapsychologie.* Berlin, 1967.

Ankel, Cornelius, and Rolf Gundlach. *Archäologische Datenverarbeitung.* Berlin, 1969.

Bächthold-Stäubli, Bechthold. *Handwörterbuch des deutschen Aberglaubens.* Berlin, 1927.

Barta, Winfried. *Aufbau und Bedeutung der altägyptischen Opferformel.* Glückstadt, 1968.

————. *Das Gespräch eines Mannes mit seinem Ba.* Berlin, 1969.

Bäumler, Ernst. *Das masslose Molekül: Bilanz der internationalen Krebsforschung.* Düsseldorf, n.d.

Beckerath, Jürgen von. *Geschichte des Alten Ägypten.* Munich, 1971.

Bellorini, Egidio. *G. B. Belzoni.* Turin, 1930.

Belzoni, Giovanni B. *Narrative of the Operations and Recent Discoveries . . . in Egypt and Nubia. . . .* London, 1820.

Bender, Hans. *Parapsychologie: Entwicklung, Ergebnisse, Probleme.* Darmstadt, 1966.

————. *Parapsychologie: Ihre Ergebnisse und Probleme.* Bremen, 1954.

Bindel, Ernst. *Ägyptische Pyramiden.* Stuttgart, 1957.

Boessneck, Joachim. *Archäologisch-Biologische Zusammenarbeit.* Wiesbaden, 1969.

Böttcher, Helmuth. *Wunderdrogen.* Cologne, 1959.

235

Borchardt, Ludwig. *Beiträge zur ägyptischen Bauforschung und Altertumskunde.* Cairo, 1938.

————. *Die Pyramiden.* Berlin, 1911.

————. *Gegen die Zahlenmystik an der Grossen Pyramide bei Gise.* Berlin, 1922.

Bozzano, Ernesto. *Übersinnliche Erscheinungen bei Naturvölkern.* Bern, 1948.

Breasted, Charles. *Pioneer to the Past: The Story of James Henry Breasted, Archaeologist.* New York, 1943.

Breasted, James H. *Ancient Records of Egypt,* vols. 1–4. Chicago, 1906–1907.

————. *The Dawn of Conscience.* New York, 1933.

————. *A History of Egypt.* New York, 1909.

Brugsch, Heinrich. *Die Ägyptologie.* Leipzig, 1891.

————. *Die Geschichte Ägyptens.* Leipzig, 1877.

————. *Inscriptio Rosettana.* Berlin, 1851.

————. *Steininschrift und Bibelwort.* Berlin, 1891.

Brunton, Paul. *Search in Secret Egypt.* New York, 1936.

Budge, E. A. W. *Book of the Dead.* London, 1928.

————. *Papyrus of Ani.* London, 1913.

Büscher, Gustav. *Strahlen und Strahlenwunder.* N.p., n.d.

Carter, Howard. *The Tomb of Tut-ankh-Amen,* vols. 1–3. London, 1923–1933.

———— and the Earl of Carnarvon. *Five Years' Explorations at Thebes, 1907–1911.* London, 1912.

Ceram, C. W. *Götter, Gräber und Gelehrte.* Hamburg, 1949.

Champollion, Jean-François. *L'Egypte sous les Pharaons.* Paris, 1814.

————. *Lettre à M. Dacier, relative à l'alphabet des hiéroglyphes phonétiques.* Paris, 1822.

————. *Monuments de l'Egypte et de la Nubie: Notices descriptives.* Paris, 1889.

————. *Pantéon égyptien.* Paris, 1923.

Chapman, Francis W. *The Great Pyramid of Gizeh.* London, 1931.

Charroux, Robert. *Phantastische Vergangenheit.* Berlin, 1966.

————. *Unbekannt, Geheimnisvoll, Phantastisch: Auf den Spuren des Unerklärlichen.* Munich and Zurich, 1973.

————. *Verratene Geheimnisse.* Berlin, 1967.

Chatzepetru, Lygere. *Relation Between Energy Production and Aerobic Growth.* Amsterdam, 1965.

Clarence, E. W. *Sympathie, Mumia, Amulette: Okkulte Kräfte der Edelsteine und Metalle.* Berlin, 1927.

Cottrell, Leonard. *Lost Pharaohs: The Romance of Egyptian Archaeology.* New York, 1951.

Curtius, Ludwig. *Deutsche und Antike Welt.* Stuttgart, 1950.

Däniken, Erich von. *Aussaat und Kosmos: Spuren und Pläne ausserirdischer Intelligenzen.* Düsseldorf and Vienna, 1972.

Dawson, Warren R. *Bibliography of Works Relating to Mummification in Egypt.* Cairo, 1929.

Desroches-Noblecourt, Christiane. *Tut-ankh-Amen: Life and Death of a Pharaoh.* Paris, 1971.

Diepgen, Paul. *Unvollendete: Vom Leben und Wirken früh verstorbener Forscher und Ärzte aus anderthalb Jahrhunderten.* Stuttgart, 1960.

Disher, Maurice W. *Pharaoh's Fool.* London, 1957.

Dogigli, Giovanni. *Strahlende Materie.* Stuttgart, 1947.

Duke, Mark. *Acupuncture.* New York, 1973.

Ebers, Georg. *Richard Lepsius: Lebensbild.* Leipzig, 1885.

Ebstein, Wilhelm. *Die Medizin im Alten Testament.* Stuttgart, 1901.

Eddington, Arthur. *The Nature of the Physical World.* New York, 1928.

————. *Philosophy of Physical Science.* New York, 1939.

Erman, Adolf. *Die ägyptische Religion.* Berlin, 1905.

————. *Die Hieroglyphen.* Berlin, 1912.

————. *Die Literatur der Ägypter.* Berlin and Leipzig, 1934.

————. *Die Religion der Ägypter.* Berlin and Leipzig, 1934.

————. *Hymnen an das Diadem.* Berlin, 1911.

————. *Mein Werden und Wirken.* Leipzig, 1929.

————. *Zaubersprüche für Mutter und Kind.* Berlin, 1901.

Esser, Alfred. *Geheimnisvolle Kräfte.* Cologne and Krefeld, 1949.

Ettinger, Robert C. W. *The Prospect of Immortality.* New York, 1964.

Felinau, Pelz von. *Titanic*. Frankfurt, 1954.

Freudenthal, Hans. *Wahrscheinlichkeit und Statistik*. Munich, 1968.

Friedell, Egon. *Kulturgeschichte Ägyptens und des Alten Orients*. Munich, 1951.

Gamow, George. *Thirty Years That Shook Physics*. New York, 1966.

Gardner, Martin. *The Ambidextrous Universe: Left, Right, and the Fall of Parity*. New York, 1964.

Garnier, C. J. *The Great Pyramid: Its Builder and Its Prophecy*. London, 1912.

Garry, Thomas G. *Egypt: The Home of the Occult Sciences*. London, 1931.

Gauquelin, Michel. *Die Uhren des Kosmos gehen anders*. Bern-Munich-Vienna, 1973.

Grapow, Hermann. *Ägyptisches Handwörterbuch*. Berlin, 1921.

————. *Die ägyptischen medizinischen Papyri*. Munich, 1935.

————. *Grundriss der Medizin der alten Ägypter*. Berlin, 1954.

————. *Todtenbuch*. Leipzig, 1915.

————. *Über die anatomischen Kenntnisse der altägyptischen Ärzte*. Leipzig, 1935.

————. *Untersuchungen über die ägyptischen Papyri*. Leipzig, 1935.

————. *Wie die alten Ägypter sich anredeten, wie sie sich grüssten und sprachen*. Berlin, 1960.

———— and Deines. *Wörterbuch der ägyptischen Drogennamen*. Berlin, 1959.

Gsell, A. *Eisen, Kupfer und Bronze bei den alten Ägyptern*. Karlsruhe, 1910.

Hahn, Herbert. *Der Lebenslauf als Kunstwerk: Rhythmen, Leitmotive, Gesetze in gegenübergestellten Biographien*. Stuttgart, 1966.

Harris, James E., and Kent R. Weeks. *X-Raying the Pharaohs*. New York, 1972.

Harris, John R. *Lexicographical Studies in Ancient Egyptian Minerals*. New York, 1962.

Hartel, Klaus D. *Rauschgift-Lexikon*. Munich, 1971.

Hartleben, Hermine. *Champollion*. Berlin, 1906.

Hedvall, Johan A. *Chemie im Dienste der Archäologie.* Göteborg, 1962.

Hein, Heinrich. *Das Geheimnis der grossen Pyramide.* Zeitz, 1921.

Hurry, Jamieson B. *Imhotep.* London, 1926.

Jaeckel, Karl-Heinz. *An den Grenzen menschlicher Fassungskraft.* Munich, 1955.

Jeans, James H. *The Mysterious Universe.* London, 1931.

Joachim, Heinrich. *Papyros Ebers: Das älteste Buch über Heilkunde.* Berlin, 1890.

Jung, Carl Gustav. *Structure and Dynamics of the Psyche* (originally published as "Die Dynamik des Unbewussten" in *Gesammelte Werke,* vol. 8. Freiburg im Breisgau, 1971.

———— and Wolfgang Pauli. *Naturerklärung und Psyche.* Zurich, 1952.

Kammerer, Paul. *Das Gesetz der Serie: Eine Lehre von den Wiederholungen im Lebens- und im Weltgeschehen.* Stuttgart and Berlin, 1919.

Karger-Decker, Bernt. *Gifte, Hexensalben, Liebestränke.* Leipzig, 1967.

Kingsland, William. *The Great Pyramid in Fact and in Theory.* London, 1932.

Kissener, Hermann. *Die Logik der Grossen Pyramide.* Munich, 1965.

Koestler, Arthur. *The Roots of Coincidence.* New York, 1972.

Krasilnikov, N. *Diagnostik der Bakterien und Aktinomyceten.* Jena, 1959.

Kubitschek, Wilhelm. *Grundriss der antiken Zeitrechnung.* Munich, 1928.

Lakhovsky, Georges. *L'Origine de la vie.* Paris, 1925.

Landone, Brown. *Die mystischen Meister.* Munich, 1958.

Langelaan, George. *Die unheimlichen Wirklichkeiten: Signale aus dem Unerforschten.* Bern-Munich-Vienna, 1969.

Lauer, Jean-Philippe. *Le Problème des Pyramides.* Paris, 1948.

————. *Observations sur les Pyramides.* Cairo, 1960.

Lepsius, Richard. *Auswahl der wichtigsten Urkunden des ägyptischen Altertums.* Leipzig, 1842.

————. *"Die ägyptischen Längenmasse"* von Dörpfeld, beleuchtet von R. Lepsius. Berlin, 1883.

————. *Die altägyptische Elle und ihre Einteilung.* Berlin, 1865.

————. *Folgerungen aus Mariette's Mittheilungen für die Chronologie der 26 manethonischen Dynastie und die Eroberung Ägyptens durch Cambyses.* Berlin, 1854.

————. *Über die manethonische Bestimmung des Umfangs der ägyptischen Geschichte.* Berlin, 1857.

Lewin, Louis. *Die Gifte in der Weltgeschichte.* Berlin, 1920.

————. *Die Pfeilgifte.* Berlin, 1923.

————. *Gottesurteile durch Gifte und andere Verfahren.* Berlin, 1929.

Lüddeckens, Erich. *Untersuchungen der ägyptischen Totenklagen.* Berlin, 1943.

Lüring, H. L. E. *Die über die medicinischen Kenntnisse der alten Ägypter berichtenden Papyri. . . .* Leipzig, 1888.

Macnaughton, Duncan. *A Scheme of Egyptian Chronology.* London, 1932.

Mally, Ernst. *Wahrscheinlichkeit und Gesetz.* Berlin, 1938.

Marbe, Karl. *Die Gleichförmigkeit in der Welt.* Munich, 1916.

Martensen-Larsen, Hans. *An der Pforte des Todes.* Hamburg, 1955.

Martiny, M. *Schlangen- und Insektengifte.* Berlin, 1939.

Maspero, Gaston. *The Tombs of Harmhabi and Touatankhamanou.* London, 1912.

Meissner, Gertrud. *Mykobakterien.* Jena, 1967.

Montgomery, Ruth. *A Gift of Prophecy: The Phenomenal Jeane Dixon.* New York, 1965.

Moodie, R. L. *Roentgenologic Studies.* Chicago, 1931.

Moreux, Abbé. *La Science Mysterieuse.* Paris, 1917.

Morton, H. V. *Through Lands of the Bible.* New York, 1956.

Moufang, Wilhelm. *Magier, Mächte und Mysterien: Handbuch übersinnlicher Vorgänge und deren Deutung.* Heidelberg, 1954.

Näbauer, Martin. *Terrestrische Strahlenbrechung.* Munich, 1929.

Naville, Henri Edouard. *Das ägyptische Todtenbuch der XVIII bis XX Dynastie.* Berlin, 1886.

Neubert, Otto. *Tut-ench-Amun: Gott in goldenen Särgen.* Vienna, 1956.

Noltenius, Friedrich. *Raum, Strahlung, Materie.* Leipzig, 1935.

Ostrander, Sheila, and Lynn Schroeder. *Psychic Discoveries Behind the Iron Curtain.* New York, 1970.

Paul, Carl. *Die geheimnisvollen Kräfte im Menschen.* Nuremberg, 1930.

Pauwels, Louis, and Jacques Bergier. *Aufbruch ins dritte Jahrtausend: Von der Zukunft der phantastischen Vernunft.* Bern-Munich-Vienna, 1962.

Peet, Thomas E. *Egypt and the Old Testament.* Liverpool, 1923.

————. *The Rhind Mathematical Papyrus.* London, 1923.

Petrie, W. M. Flinders. *A History of Egypt.* London, 1922.

————. *Medum.* London, 1892.

————. *Methods and Aims in Archaeology.* London, 1904.

————. *Ten Years' Digging in Egypt, 1881–1891.* London, 1892.

Prechtl, Robert. *Untergang der Titanic.* Munich, 1953.

Proctor, Richard A. *The Great Pyramid.* London, n.d.

Ranke, Hermann. *Ägypten und ägyptisches Leben im Altertum.* Tübingen, 1923.

Rhine, J. B. *The Reach of the Mind.* New York, 1947.

———— and J. G. Pratt. *Parapsychology: Frontier Science of the Mind.* Springfield, Ill., 1957.

Rutherford, Adam. *Pyramidology.* Dunstable, 1961.

Schäfer, Heinrich. *Von ägyptischer Kunst.* Wiesbaden, 1963.

Schmid, Frenzolf. *Die Ur-Strahlen.* Munich, 1928.

Schopenhauer, Arthur. *Über die anscheinende Absichtlichkeit im Schicksale des Einzelnen.* Leipzig, n.d.

Schulze, Rudolf. *Strahlenklima der Erde.* Darmstadt, 1970.

Schweinfurth, Georg. *Afrikanisches Skizzenbuch: Verschollene Merkwürdigkeiten.* Berlin, 1925.

Sethe, Kurt. *Amun und die acht Urgötter von Hermopolis.* Berlin, 1929.

————. *Übersetzung und Kommentar zu den altägyptischen Pyramidentexten.* Glückstadt, 1935–1939.

————. *Urgeschichte und älteste Religion der Ägypter.* Leipzig, 1930.

————. *Von Zahlen und Zahlworten bei den alten Ägyptern.* Strasbourg, 1916.

Settgast, Jürgen. *Bestattungsdarstellungen Ägyptens.* Glück-stadt, 1963.

Sinnett, A. P. *The Mahatma Letters.* Paris, n.d.

Spiegel, Joachim. *Das Auferstehungsritual der Unas-Pyramide.* Wiesbaden, 1971.

Spiegelberg, Wilhelm. *Der ägyptische Mythos vom Sonnen-auge.* Strasbourg, 1917.

Steindorff, Georg. *Ägypten vor Tut-ench-Amun.* Leipzig, 1927.

―――. *Die ägyptischen Gaue und ihre politische Entwick-lung.* Leipzig, 1909.

―――. *Die Blütezeit des Pharaonenreiches.* Leipzig, 1926.

―――. *Die thebanische Gräberwelt.* Glückstadt, 1936.

Steuer, R. O. *Myrrhe und Stakte.* Vienna, 1933.

Tristram, Henry B. *A Natural History of the Bible.* London, 1867.

Van Der Waerden, B. L. *Die Anfänge der Astronomie.* Gron-ingen, 1966.

Weaver, Warren. *Lady Luck: The Theory of Probability.* New York, 1963.

Weigall, Arthur. *A History of the Pharaohs.* London, 1925.

White, Stewart E. *Uneingeschränktes Weltall.* With a foreword by C. G. Jung. Zurich, 1948.

Wiedemann, Alfred. *Der Tierkult der alten Ägypter.* Leipzig, 1912.

Wildung, Dietrich. *Die Rolle ägyptischer Könige.* Munich, 1967.

Wittenzellner, Rudolf. *Strahlenbelastung des Menschen.* Mu-nich, 1960.

Wolf, Walther. "Vorläufer der Reformation Echnatons," in *Zeitschrift für ägyptische Sprache und Altertumskunde,* vol. 59. Leipzig, 1924.

Wood, Frederic H. *This Egyptian Miracle.* London, 1955.

――― and A. J. H. *Ancient Egypt Speaks.* London, 1937.

Wreszynski, Walter. *Der Grosse Medizinische Papyrus.* Leip-zig, 1909.

―――. *Der Londoner Medizinische Papyrus.* Leipzig, 1912.

―――. *Der Papyrus Ebers.* Leipzig, 1913.

Wüst, Joseph. "Beobachtungen über Schwankungen des magnetischen Feldstärkeunterschiedes bei einem Reizstreifen," in *Zeitschrift für Wünschelrutenforschung*, no. 11/12, 1941.

——. "Einige Bemerkungen zur Abhandlung von Volker Fritsch: Zur Frage neuartiger geophysikalischer Strahlungen," in *Zeitschrift für Wünschelrutenforschung*, no. 9/10, 1940.

——. "Einige physikalische und chemische Gesichtspunkte zur Frage der Häufung von Blitzeinschlägen, Staubexplosionen und Selbstentzündungen über Reizstreifenkreuzungen," in *Zeitschrift für Wünschelrutenforschung*, no. 10/11, 1939.

——. "Neue Untersuchungen über biologische Wirkungen der sog 'Erdstrahlen,'" in *Grenzebebiete der Medizin*, book 5, 1949.

——. "Pulsierende elektrische Ströme im biologischen Geschehen und ihre Beziehung zum Wünschelrutenproblem," in *Zeitschrift für Wünschelrutenforschung*, no. 7, 1939.

—— and Joseph Wimmer. "Über neuartige Schwingungen der Welscher Substanzen sowie biologischer Objekte," in *Wilhelm Roux' Archiv für Entwicklungsmechanik der Organismen*, Berlin, 1934.

Zinzius, Josef. *Die Antibiotika und ihre Schattenseiten.* Stuttgart, 1954.

Index

249